WINGS

GUIDE TO
BRITISH
BIRDS

HarperCollins*Publishers*
77–85 Fulham Palace Road
London W6 8JB

First published 1997

2 4 6 8 10 9 7 5 3

97 99 00 98

Artwork Norman Arlott
Additional artwork © Frank Jarvis
Text © HarperCollins*Publishers*

This book was the idea of Peter Ryley, and of Simon and Philippa Normanton of Lighthouse Films, to whom my thanks are due.

Thanks to Myles Archibald and Katie Piper of HarperCollins for all their hard work on the project. Thanks also to Rob Hume of RSPB for reading through the text and making corrections, and to Janet Beever for general advice and for helping with the final read-through.

Voice descriptions taken from the text of the cassette series *Teach Yourself Birdsounds*, reproduced by kind permission of Waxwing Associates, Tring, Hertfordshire

The copyright in the photographs belongs to: From RSPB: Tony Allen 209; Frank Blackburn 179; Dusan Boucny 179; Will Bown 27; Colin Carver 217; S. Craig 110; P. Doherty 33, 40; Gerald Downey 36, 37, 87, 111, 213; Raymond Franklin 41; R. Glover 111, 183; C.H. Gomersall 68, 72, 166, 167, 192; Dennis Green 193, 216; Jan Halady 124, 159; Mark Hamblin 166, 178, 183; E.A. Janes 40; David Kjaer 33; Chris Knights 87; George McCarthy 145; Philip J. Newman 82, 182 (both photographs); W.S. Paton 32, 86, 144, 217, 231; S.C. Porter 178, 209; M.W. Richards 36; J.L. Roberts 26, 212; D. Sewell 125; Roger Wilmshurst 26, 102, 125, 193, 213, 224, 230. From Natural Science Photos: Richard Revels 171; Ian West 171; AP Barnes 187. Dominic Couzens 213

Front cover photograph: David Hosking, FLPA
Back cover photographs: Paul Sterry, Nature Photographers Ltd.

ISBN 0 00 220069 4

Designed by White Rabbit Editions, Kingston, Surrey
Colour reproduction by Saxon Photolitho Ltd, Norwich
Printed and bound by Rotolito Lombarda SpA, Milan, Italy

COLLINS

WINGS

GUIDE TO BRITISH BIRDS

A CHANNEL FOUR BOOK

RSPB

DOMINIC COUZENS

Foreword

There has never been a more important time to stimulate interest in British birds, and by doing so to mobilise support for them, as they face an increasingly hostile natural environment. The Channel 4 series *Wings* and this companion volume, represent a valuable contribution to this vital task, and are wholeheartedly backed by the RSPB.

There are a number of guides available but none quite like this one, and unlike some other "handbooks", this volume really does fit into the hand, and the knapsack. It is concise and yet it contains a great deal of information. As well as superb identification illustrations, there is a wealth of interesting data on habitat, distribution (with maps showing breeding and wintering areas for each species), flight, voice, plumage and behavioural patterns. The author and the RSPB have ensured that although the language is not dauntingly scientific, the information is scrupulously accurate. It is the ideal handbook for the birdwatcher who is just starting out. The *Wings Guide to British Birds* is also a joy to use because it is cleverly laid out with artwork and photographs of outstanding quality.

At a time when even our "common" birds are in decline, it is crucial that as many of us as possible are looking out for their welfare in an informed manner. This guide will be of help in the task of monitoring the countryside and our back gardens to determine exactly what is happening out there to account for these worrying declines. It will also add greatly to the sheer joy of birdwatching.

Julian Pettifer
President of the RSPB

Contents

Introduction

About this book

This book serves as a complement to the Channel 4 series *Wings*, which sets out to excite people about British birds. Whereas *Wings* the series focuses as much on people as on the birds themselves, this guide presents the birds on their own. The aim of the book is twofold: to help readers identify the birds they see; and then to give extra information to show the reader how each bird species is different from the next, how they behave, and what is especially interesting about them.

It is here that the satisfaction in making an identification can lead to a fascination with the bird seen, and a passion to find out more about it – that same passion that stirs all the interviewees of the *Wings* series. So while plumage differences are not neglected and are shown on the "Identification guide" spreads, this emphasis on extra information, as given in the many "Notebook" spreads, aims to make this guide different from the many other field guides that are available.

How to use this book

If you leaf through this book, you will soon notice that there are two kinds of double-page "spreads", labelled "Identification guide" and "Notebook" respectively. As described above, Identification guide spreads are mainly concerned with what the birds look like (their various plumage patterns), whereas Notebook spreads are more focus more on what the birds do. These two different styles are arranged alternately, so that, as far as possible, the Notebook information follows closely on from the main illustrations of the bird, just by the turn of a page or two. For easy reference, the index at the back of the book indicates what extra information is given, and where.

"Identification guide" spreads are arranged as follows:

The far left column gives the name of the bird, its scientific name, size and various notes about structure. Miscellaneous identification tips are given where appropriate, especially if the bird can easily be confused with other species. Size is given as a measurement in centimetres from the tip of the bill to the end of the tail; beware of species with long bills and tails – the figure can be misleading. For many species a range of sizes is given, to cover individual extremes.

The "Map/Where Found" column includes a map for most species showing the bird's distribution in the British Isles (the Shetland Islands are not shown due to space restrictions). Where coloured yellow, the bird is a summer visitor only; where blue, it is a winter visitor only; where green, the bird is a resident, ie. it can be seen at any time of year. The maps are intended as a rough guide only, and give no indication of the bird's abundance. Under each map there is a paragraph that accompanies (and sometimes replaces) the map; this gives more detailed distribution information, including where the bird is found at certain times of year, how common it is, etc.

The middle columns show illustrations of each bird in various plumages and highlight identification features. It is important when reading these to know what the various parts of the bird are called, since a number of technical terms are necessarily used. Please consult the "Bird topography" diagram (see p.14), or consult the glossary (see p.248). The main plumage types shown in the illustrations are as follows:

Adult or adult male/female: in some species the sexes look much alike, in other species they look different.

Summer/winter: many birds (but not all) have different summer and winter appearance.

Breeding/non-breeding: same as above, but the breeding plumage is so short-lived as to be gone long before "summer" is over.

Juvenile: the first set of feathers acquired by a young bird, seen after it has left the nest. Most juvenile plumages are lost by early autumn.

Immature: an umbrella term for any discernible non-adult plumage, not just juvenile plumage but any that may follow before the bird is fully mature. A common term often used is First-Winter plumage, which follows on from juvenile plumage to cover the bird for its first winter of life. For a more detailed explanation see pp.128–129.

Eclipse: a specialised plumage adopted for camouflage purposes in the summer months, mostly by ducks (see pp.50–51).

The right-hand column gives information on flight and voice. The flight description includes both the style or manner of flight, and any special field-marks that the bird may show. Voice is normally divided into two sections: the call of the bird, as may be heard when it is flying, alarmed or responding to some situation; and the song, as may be heard when the bird is deliberately proclaiming its ownership of a territory, with a view to attracting or keeping a mate. Songs are usually much more complicated than simple call-notes.

"Notebook" spreads:

These vary greatly, but are designed to provide the kind of information that a birdwatcher might ask after identifying a bird. For example: what does it do differently from other, similar species? What is unusual about it? What interesting breeding/feeding habits does it have? As far as possible, the information given will also be of use in identification, but there is no strict rule to this. The Notebook spreads feature many illustrations that are of a different, freer style to the Identification guide illustrations, showing birds in action or giving a different perspective. Additional information also appears on Identification guide pages that feature three species only.

How to begin birdwatching

Be warned – if you like to watch the birds in your back garden, and you occasionally notice them elsewhere, and if you confess to a mild interest in them to family and friends in unguarded moments – you're on the edge of an addiction. It affects nearly one million people in this country. It will soon have you dashing out at weekends to visit anywhere from a bleak moorland to an urban sewage-farm, in all weathers, at all times of the year, including the middle of winter. Your agenda will be set by tiny, often unassuming bundles of feathers. Your days could be made by seeing a bird whose only difference from the others is a bar on a wing or a stripe over the eye. Every walk you take in the country will take on a special degree of interest and spice, as you notice things that you never noticed before. You'll meet people with the same happy addiction, and discuss topics of common interest.

And you'll be collecting memories all along the way. So how do you start?

Equipment

Strictly speaking, you do not actually need any equipment to watch birds – you just watch them with your eyes. But it won't be long before you wish to identify what species you're looking at, for which you need a book (like this one) and, sooner or later, a pair of binoculars. Other useful books are listed in the Further Reading section. A cheap but adequate pair of binoculars currently costs in the region of £100. The best policy is to buy your binoculars from a specialist who understands birdwatchers' needs. Binoculars come with a specification that reads, for example 8 x 40; the 8 is the magnification, the 40 is the diameter of the objective (bigger) lens in millimetres. The magnification should be between 7 and 10 (too little and you will not be able to see the bird well enough, too big and you can't hold the binoculars still) The second figure should be big enough to give a generous answer when you divide it by the magnification, for example 4 or 5 (40 ÷ 8 = 5). The binoculars should also be able to focus when the bird is a few feet away (be careful, many makes do not). After that, it's all down to personal choice – weight, comfort, expense, needing a better pair than your friend etc. Excellent reviews of binoculars (and telescopes) appear regularly in the monthly birdwatching magazines (see Further reading p.13).

The clothing you wear is important. Being regularly outdoors, you are at the mercy of the weather. Birdwatching also involves much standing around (it is very different from rambling, for example), which means that it's essential to be warm and dry at all times (and you may need a shooting-stick). Always wear suitable clothing and footwear, and put on at least one more layer than you think you will need. Ideally, the clothes you wear should be modestly coloured, since bright, garish colours frighten the birds away.

Fieldcraft

There are certain ways to behave when you are looking for birds, which help in finding them. The first rule is to be quiet and unobtrusive – you will see more if you are. A second rule is to find places and times when the birds are least disturbed by people – early morning is best, of course. When you go birdwatching, walk slowly – do not treat it like a hike; let the birds come to you, not the other way around. Take time in each place, and keep your eyes open and your ears tuned. If at all possible, try to keep yourself reasonably hidden: sit or stand under trees, in valleys, or in shade, for example. When you do find a bird, try to orient yourself so that the light is behind you, otherwise you will only get a silhouette. Keep concentrating on the bird, and do not allow yourself to be distracted by other movements. Good luck!

Identifying birds

Now that you have the equipment to go birdwatching, and you know how to approach birds, how do you identify them? It does not take beginners long to realise that this is not as straightforward as it may first appear. Lots of birds look very similar to one another, and even a single species can adopt a variety of plumages: the Herring Gull, for example, has at least nine separate ones, and much individual variation within these. The key to bird identification is to look at each bird thoroughly, and note as many features as you can, preferably writing it all down in a notebook. This may sound laborious, but if you learn your common birds thoroughly, you will become a much better birdwatcher, soon overtaking those who adopt a lazier approach. But, once you have a bird in view, what do you look for?

Try concentrating on the size and shape first. In regard to the former, try to compare it to another bird nearby. If you cannot, your estimate of size won't be of much help. Remember, too, that birds often look larger when they are backlit, fully silhouetted, or flying. Regarding the latter, look not just for overall shape, but also for the shape of the bill (beak), head, tail and wings. The shape of the bill is especially important, because it gives a clue to what the bird eats. Among small birds, insect-eaters have thin bills, and seed-eaters have thick bills. In wader identification, determining bill shape is the single most important criterion.

Next, be really thorough about the plumage. When identifying difficult species, almost any streak or speckle, bar or stripe, on any part of the body, could clinch an identification. In commoner species, such attention to detail can determine the sex or age. Try to rehearse a method whereby you cover everything, from head to tail. It's important to know what the various parts of the bird are called, too, because "primary coverts white" is easier to remember than "the bit behind the big feathers on the wing, above the breast: white". Most birds have "field marks" that help identify them: colourful rumps, wing-bars, outer tail feathers etc. It's often these apparently obscure plumage features that enable a snap identification to be made.

Never overlook behaviour. When all field marks fail, behaviour can make things ridiculously easy. Take the Snipe and Jack Snipe (pp.114–115). It will take you half an hour to note the differing plumage features, but when you realise than the Jack Snipe bobs up and down, as if on springs, when feeding, while the Common Snipe does not, it all becomes straightforward. Certain birds move in a way that is peculiar to themselves, which experienced birdwatchers latch on to straight away. A useful word is often used to describe the combination of a bird's shape and behaviour – "jizz".

If you have ever been woken up by the dawn chorus, you will know that birds make sounds. You will also probably know that certain species have certain songs and calls that identify them. The difficult bit is then learning which birds make which sounds. You need a good ear, a lot of persistence and a friendly expert to teach you if you are going to crack the problem fully, but there are a number of excellent bird tapes and CDs on the market which will help greatly when an expert is not available (see Further reading p.13). Hopefully, the voice descriptions and mnemonics (memory aids) given in this book will also help. Progress in song-learning is always very slow, but don't lose heart, because it is incredibly satisfying to be able to recognise bird songs and calls, and you'll detect twice as many birds as you did before.

Regardless of the bird's appearance, behaviour and vocalisations, there are still other ways to hunt down its identity. Bird species are often very specific in their choice of habitat (that is, the place where they live: marshes, farmland, woods etc.), and this is always a vital clue. So too is the region in which they live – their distribution. You just won't see a Crested Tit in Hertfordshire, for example, because they are only found in north-central Scotland. A third handy clue is the time of year. You won't find a Nightingale anywhere in Britain in the wintertime (they are in Africa). It should be said that birds are prone to break the above rules, quite regularly appearing in the wrong place, at the wrong time of year, in the wrong habitat. But these are the exceptions, and anyway, the element of surprise is part of the charm of birdwatching.

How birds live – some background

A great deal of information is given in this book about the way in which birds live – how they feed, where they sleep, their breeding strategies and their migration. This section gives a short summary of some of these subjects.

Migration

Just about every British bird migrates, in some form or another. Although we tend to think of the Swallow's journey, from Britain to Africa, as typical, a quick hop across the Channel, or even a movement from the higher reaches of a mountain to the lower slopes, is just as much a migration. The strategies for migrating are almost as varied as the birds themselves: Arctic Terns travel all the way to Antarctica (their round-trip

may be 30,000km), migrating by day, Chiffchaffs go only to Spain, migrating at night. In some species, such as the Stonechat, some of the population migrates away from Britain, the rest remains behind. While the most famous migrating birds – Swallows, Cuckoos, most Warblers – leave our shores for warmer climes in the autumn and go south, at least as many others arrive from the north, to spend their off-season with us in our comparatively mild climate. Among these winter visitors are huge numbers of wildfowl (ducks, geese and swans), vast flocks of thrushes, and many species that you wouldn't expect to be migrants: Chaffinches, Starlings, Robins and Goldcrests. Migration of some kind or another occurs in every month of the year – and that is why so many species are highly seasonal in their appearance in this country.

Migrating birds use many methods to find their way, and any individual migrant will use several on the same journey. They navigate using the sun, the stars, and the earth's magnetic field. They can also use landmarks and their sense of smell.

Roosting and resting

When the sun goes down, most birds go to roost, and it is one of the most important activities of their lives. Most birds sleep alone, so a good roosting site has to be found near where the bird lives and, if necessary, defended from intruders. Roost sites vary greatly: many birds sleep in holes or cavities, others on the ground, many on branches of trees, and some roost on water. A very few species, including Swifts and some seabirds, catch the odd nap when actually flying, or just don't seem to sleep at all. A minority of birds gather together to roost in groups – this has the disadvantage of attracting predators. Blackbirds and finches, wagtails and gulls, ducks, crows and waders are all examples of communal roosting species. Even better known is the Starling, which many congregate in enormous numbers – up to 500,000 has been recorded. A considerable din is caused by the chattering and the comings and goings of these birds, and it has been suggested that the roost may not only serve as a sleeping place, but also as a centre for information exchange.

Singing and territory

Birds sing in order to proclaim ownership of a territory, which keeps other male birds out. At the same time they are advertising their presence, and availability, to females. To be effective, a bird's song needs to be species-specific, otherwise the wrong kind of mate will be attracted! There is often variation in repertoire between individual birds, as well as between species. This fact is not lost on the females, who will tend to choose the best and most energetic singers for mates.

In most species, a male bird must acquire a territory if it is to obtain, or keep a mate. Not all birds sing, but instead rely on a series of ritualised gestures which are given as a display. To males competing for territories, these displays are often called "Threat Displays", and imply aggression. They are often accompanied by noisy vocalisations. Fighting is avoided as far as possible, because of the toll it is likely to take on both combatants.

Territories vary in size between species. The Golden Eagle has a huge territory, tens of square miles or even more; it is used year-round for all the eagle's needs. The Chaffinch has a small territory of a few tens of square metres; it is defended mostly in the spring and summer, since the owners tend to join flocks of other Chaffinches in the winter months. Many colonial birds have tiny territories, less than a metre square. They are used for the nest only, while the owners join all their neighbours on daily foraging trips to feeding grounds some distance away.

Pair-bonds, courtship and nests

Birds have a variety of pair-bonding systems. Monogamy (one male with one female) is the norm, as it is in people, although the length of the pair-bond ranges from one brood within a season (eg. some Blackbirds) to life (Swans, Magpies). Polygamy is also quite common: polygyny (one male has several partners eg. Marsh Harrier, Pheasant, Cetti's Warbler, Pied Flycatcher) is rather more frequent than polyandry (one female has several partners eg. Dotterel, Dunnock). A few species are just promiscuous – both males and females have many different partners (Ruff, probably Cuckoo, probably Quail). Recent work has shown that, even within monogamous species, extra-pair copulations are a common event, since males and females are both striving to maximise their reproductive capacity.

Pair-bonds are created and cemented by a series of courtship displays, characteristic of the species. Some of these are intricate and elegant, as if they were works of art – that of the Great Crested Grebe is a good example. In many birds, similar gestures are used to those which convey threat to males, but are subtly different, or performed in a different order. A good number involve use of nests or nest-building material, since this is the natural next step to take towards breeding.

Eggs and young

Some birds produce only one egg in a season (eg. Guillemot), and invest all their time in its protection and nurture. Others lay more eggs, to allow for losses. They may lay them in one go, to make one brood (as in tits), or they may lay several different clutches within a season. The strategy depends on many factors, notably food supply and the length of season available. In tits, the single, large brood is fed during the early summer glut of caterpillars, which quickly passes. Thrushes have several broods, which are fed on invertebrates, notably earthworms. Warblers are often double-brooded, feeding their young on small invertebrates, but all their activities must be condensed into the time between their arrival on migration and their departure.

Most species complete the laying of their clutch before incubation begins; this means that, despite the fact that only one egg is laid per day (often the interval is longer), all the eggs hatch at roughly the same time. If the brood is of mobile chicks, this means that they can be kept together when the family is on the move; in helpless, nest-bound broods, it gives a measure of equality when the young are fed. The other strategy is to begin incubation with the first egg, which leads to an age-difference of several days between young ("asymmetric hatching"). This allows for the oldest nestling to dominate feeding time, so much that the others cannot obtain food until it is satisfied. This inequality ensures that, in species with an unpredictable food supply, at least one youngster will survive, even if the others do not.

Young birds may leave the nest soon after hatching (in which case they are fluffy and highly mobile), or they may remain in the nest (naked and helpless). The former, "nidifugous" group, are able to feed themselves very early on, and might only receive a few hints from their parent(s). The latter, "nidicolous" group are completely dependent on their parent(s) for everything. Most small birds, such as tits, thrushes and inches, belong to the nidicolous group.

After they leave the nest, most young birds are still looked after by their parent(s) for some time. Young owls may remain dependent for several months, but for the majority of species, independence comes much more quickly.

The birds in this book

This book covers all our regular breeding species, all our common wintering birds, and a few passage migrants. Most rarer birds, even some quite regular ones, have been excluded. The aim of the book is to give as much information as possible about the most "relevant" species to the British or Irish birdwatcher.

A number of well known introduced species have also been omitted. These include the ornamental pheasants Golden Pheasant and Lady Amherst's Pheasant, which are both rare and secretive. Several ornamental ducks and geese also live in the wild in Britain. Some of these are discussed on pp.58–59, and three species that are becoming common and widespread are illustrated on p.15.

Further reading
The following titles have been particularly useful in research for this book, or are otherwise recommended reading. Some are field guides, others are about a subject or group.

Berthold, *Bird Migration – A General Survey.* 1993. OUP.
Bruun, Delin, Svensson, *The Hamlyn Guide to Birds of Britain and Europe.* 1992. Hamlyn.
Catchpole, Slater, *Bird Song – Biological Themes and Variations.* 1995. Cambridge University Press.
Cramp, Perrins *et al. Handbook of the Birds of Europe, the Middle East and North Africa – The Birds of the Western Palearctic.* (BWP) 1977–94 (9 vols). OUP.
Del Hoyo, Elliott, Sargatal, *Handbook of the Birds of the World.* 1992. Lynx Ediciones.
Ehrlich, Dobkin, Wheye, Pimm, *The Birdwatcher's Handbook.* 1994. OUP.
Ferguson Lees, Willis, Sharrock, *The Shell Guide to the Birds of Britain and Ireland.* 1983. Michael Joseph.
Gibbons, Reid, Chapman, *The New Atlas of Breeding Birds in Britain and Ireland: 1988–91.* 1993. Poyser.
Grant, *Gulls – A Guide to Identification.* 1982. Poyser.
Hammond, Pearson *Hamlyn Bird Behaviour Guides – Waders.* 1994. Hamlyn.
Harris, Tucker, Vinicombe, *The MacMillan Field Guide to Bird Identification.* 1989. MacMillan.
Harrison, *Seabirds – An Identification Guide.* 1983. Helm.
Hayman, Marchant, Prater, *Shorebirds – An Identification Guide to the Waders of the World.* 1986. Helm.
Heinzel, Fitter, Parslow, *Collins Pocket Guide Birds of Britain and Europe, with North Africa and the Middle East.* 1995. HarperCollins.
Hollom, *The Popular Handbook of British Birds.* 1971. Witherby.
Hume, Pearson, *Hamlyn Bird Behaviour Guides – Seabirds.* 1993. Hamlyn.
Jonsson, *Birds of Europe, with North Africa and the Middle East.* 1992. Helm.
Lack, *The Atlas of Wintering Birds in Britain and Ireland.* 1986. Poyser.
Ogilvie, Pearson, *Hamlyn Bird Behaviour Guides – Wildfowl.* 1994. Hamlyn.
Perrins, *British Tits* (New Naturalist Series). 1979. HarperCollins.
Perrins, *Collins New Generation Guide Birds of Britain and Europe.* 1987. HarperCollins.
Sharrock, *The Atlas of Breeding Birds in Britain and Ireland.* 1976. Poyser.
Turner, *The Swallow.* Hamlyn Species Guides. 1994. Hamlyn.

Magazines
*These are available from newsagents monthly (*Birdwatch, Birdwatching*) or by subscription (all four).*
Birding World, Stonerunner, Coast Road, Cley-next-the-Sea, Holt, Norfolk NR25 7RZ
Birdwatch, Solo Publishing Ltd, Bow House, 153–159 Bow Road, London E3 2SE
Bird Watching EMAP Pursuit Publishing Ltd, Bretton Court, Peterborough PE3 8DZ
British Birds, Fountains, Park Lane, Blunham, Bedfordshire MK44 3NJ

Bird recordings and cassettes
Couzens and Wyatt, *Teach Yourself Bird Sounds.* 1992–. Waxwing Associates.
Sample, *Collins Field Guide Bird Songs and Calls.* 1996. HarperCollins.

Bird topography

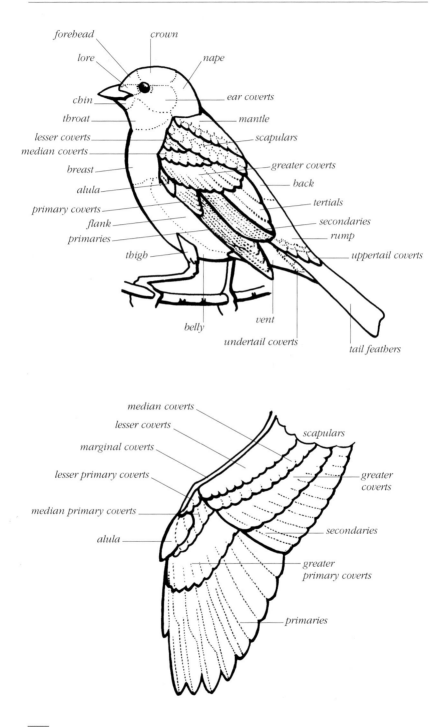

Introduced wildfowl

See also pp.58–59. Please note these birds are not to scale.

Egyptian Goose, *Alopochen aegyptiacus*
Adult: A distinctive bird with brownish-grey plumage, spot on the breast and shades around the eyes.
Juvenile (not illustrated): Similar to the adult but duller. Fewer head markings and no spot on breast.
Flight: The broad forewing is reminiscent of Shelduck, and flight action similar although heavier.
Voice: A grating honk.

Mandarin, *Aix galericulata*
Male: Unmistakable. Bright orange neck-plumes and wing-sails.
Female: Very different. Best identified by the white eyering which runs behind the eye to make a streak.
Male eclipse (not illustrated): Seen May–September. Similar to female but shows pink bill of the male.
Flight: Wings are dark in both sexes, with an obscure green speculum.
Voice: Females have a distinctive croaking quack; males call excitedly with a breathless whistle.

Ruddy Duck, *Oxyura jamaicensis*
Male summer: Distinctly ruddy-coloured. Bright red cheeks bordered with black and a large blue bill.
Female: Duller brown in colour still with a dark cap bordering the paler cheeks but also with a horizontal dark line along the face.
Male eclipse (not illustrated): Seen August–March. A brown version of male summer.
Flight: Not an enthusiastic flier.
Voice: Both sexes make non-vocal sounds in display: one like the sound produced by running a finger along the teeth of a comb; the other like rustling a paper bag.

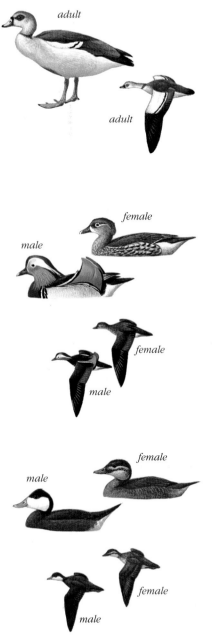

adult

adult

female

male

female

male

female

male

female

male

RED-THROATED DIVER
Gavia stellata

50–60cm. The smallest diver, and usually the commonest. On water, the head looks up at a slight (30°) angle to the thin, straight neck, the uptilt being accentuated by a small upcurve to the bill.

Where found: Breeds in north and north-west Scotland, including Orkney and Shetland Islands. Winters around our coasts. See also below.

adult winter

BLACK-THROATED DIVER
Gavia arctica

60–70cm. The "middle-of-the-road" diver in terms of size and overall bulk. On water, the head is not held up at an angle like Red-throated, but level – appropriately enough for a heavier bill. The neck is often held in an elegant, reptilian S-curve.

Where found: Breeds in north and north-west Scotland, but not Orkney or Shetland Islands; rare. Winters around our coasts, but in smaller numbers than the other two species. See also below.

adult winter

GREAT NORTHERN DIVER
Gavia immer

70–80cm. A large, stout, impressive bird, looking angular or "lumpy" about the head and neck, especially if there is a bump on the forehead (this does not occur on all birds). As in the smaller Black-throated, the head and bill are held level.

Where found: Does not breed in Britain, but is quite numerous on Atlantic-facing coasts in winter. Scarcer elsewhere. See also below.

adult winter

Feeding and breeding behaviour

Of the three British species of diver, only the Red-throated and Black-throated breed in this country. All species winter off our coasts in reasonable numbers. Divers must nest within 1m (3ft) of the water, since their legs are set well back on the body, and are almost useless on land. In the water, however, the legs are extremely efficient at providing forward propulsion at high speed – very necessary when catching fish.

Feeding
Red-throated Diver prefers shallow inshore waters and sandy bays; it will fish within 1–2km (0.6–1.2 miles) of the shore. Feeds mostly on fish, but some crab and shrimp.

Black-throated Diver feeds in similar locations. Diet consists almost exclusively of fish, but will also take some molluscs and crustaceans. Of these three species, the Black-throated is the least sociable, rarely occurring in groups of more than 2–3.

Great Northern Divers are happy with rocky coastlines and deeper and more agitated waters, and will fish much further out. Food once again is mostly fish, with some molluscs, crab and shrimp.

Breeding
Red-throated Divers select a variety of bodies of water, varying in size from small to huge. They are a familiar sight

Adult summer: Distinctive, living up to its name, with a gory red-brown throat (although in poor light this will just appear dark).

Adult winter: Compared to other divers, the face looks whiter, with the eye noticeable. The paler-grey back is powdered with white spots.

Flight: Shows faster and deeper wingbeats than other divers, and the neck seems to sag lower. The legs hardly project beyond the tail.

Voice: A goose-like cackle is heard in flight, and a gull-like wail during display. Only heard in breeding season.

adult summer

adult winter

Adult summer: The grey head contrasts with the smart black throat.

Adult winter: This black-and-white diver shows the greatest contrast, with a sharp border between white and dark plumage, especially on the head and neck. The grey on the crown and hindneck is paler than that on the back, the opposite to Great Northern. Identifiable by a white patch on the flanks, visible above water-line.

Flight: Has shallower, slower wing-beats than Red-throated, but deeper, faster wing-beats than Great Northern.

Voice: Mechanical double-croak, and a rising, almost wolf-like wail, mostly heard at night. Does not call in flight. Breeding grounds only.

adult summer

adult winter

Adult summer: Bottle-green head and neck is unique among divers.

Adult winter: The dark/pale contrast around the head and neck is ill-defined, with a definite pale "nick" behind the cheeks, and sometimes pale feathering around the eye. The crown and hindneck are a slightly darker grey than the back.

Flight: Shows the longest wings of the divers, and also the longest feet, which project well beyond the tail. The wing-beats are comparatively shallow.

Voice: Unlikely to be heard in our area.

adult summer

adult winter

in the mosaic of lochs and moorland characteristic of northern Scotland. They do not rely on their breeding lochs to supply all their food, so must commute regularly to feed in larger lochs or the sea during the breeding season. From late May they will lay 1–2 eggs in their nest which is made from a pad of vegetation. Incubation lasts around one month with the bulk of the duty being carried out by the female. The young swim soon after hatching and fly after about six weeks.

Black-throated Divers prefer large bodies of deep water for breeding. They obtain all their food from their "home" loch or lochs, so do not make regular commuting trips out of the territory. The loch is vigorously defended from rivals. The nest

of the Black-throated Diver varies in size according to the amount of vegetation available. From early May 1–2 eggs are laid and these are incubated by both sexes for a period of approximately one month. Once hatched chicks are tended by both parents and will fly after about eight weeks.

Identifying divers

Is it a diver?

Most birdwatchers do not see many divers, and then only in their drab winter plumage, so identifying the family in the first place can be difficult. They show marked similarities to grebes and cormorants, and at a distance can even resemble ducks, but they do have enough distinctive features to be placed in their own family.

On the sea

• *Cormorants* and *Shags* have longer tails than divers and are generally larger (althought the Great Northern Diver is larger than the Shag). Adult Cormorants and Shags are dark below, but beware of youngsters which often have white or pale breasts. Cormorants and Shags swim with their heads held up at an angle, quite unlike the larger divers and even more obviously than the Red-throated Diver.

• *Cormorants, Shags, grebes* and *seaducks* often "spring" from the water surface to dive; divers do so much less often.

• *Grebes* are all smaller, with thinner necks and usually smaller bills. Divers usually look much longer. Grebes do not hold their heads up at an angle, unlike the smallest diver, the Red-throated. Their dives usually last for no more than 40seconds, whereas divers often remain below for a minute or more.

• Divers and grebes, unlike Cormorants, "roll-over" to preen their suddenly white bellies, often with their feet in the air.

In flight

• *Divers* tend to show a sagging neck held below the line of the body, giving a "hump-backed" effect. The wing-beats are rapid, the flight powerful. No diver shows any white on the upperwings.

• *Grebes* also hold their necks below the line of the body, but their necks are proportionally longer. They have no discernible tail, and steer in flight with their feet. They seem reluctant to fly, preferring to escape by diving. Once airborne, the flight is weak. All species of comparable size to divers have white bars on their upperwings.

• *Cormorants* and *Shags* have slower wingbeats than divers, and show a longer tail. Most individuals are dark below.

Display

The *Red-throated Diver* defends the immediate vicinity of the nest as its territory although some pairs nest in loose colonies. Territorial encounters include the remarkable "Plesiosaur Race", in which the birds rear up on the water in the so-called "Penguin Posture" and rush forward silently with their bills lifted. In the "Snake Ceremony" the birds once again assume the "Penguin Posture" and rush forward calling loudly.

In the *Black-throated Diver's* less ritualised territorial displays, competing birds engage in a somewhat menacing "Circle Dance", with each individual showing off its black throat-patch.

Black-throated Diver

Red-throated Diver

Great Northern Diver

Red-throated Diver
performing the
"Plesiosaur Race"

GREAT CRESTED GREBE
Podiceps cristatus

48cm. The largest grebe, common and easy to see. It has an upright carriage, with a long, straight neck and a long, straight bill.

Where found: Common on freshwater lakes and large rivers year-round, and on the sea in winter. Less common in Scotland.

adult winter

RED-NECKED GREBE
Podiceps grisegena

43cm. Looks much shorter- and thicker-necked than the Great Crested Grebe, and is stockier overall. In winter plumage it looks more like a Black-necked or Slavonian Grebe than the similar-sized Great Crested.

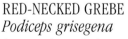

Where found: Uncommon winter visitor, mainly to east coast, and a few larger reservoirs. Small numbers are involved.

adult winter

SLAVONIAN GREBE
Podiceps auritus

33cm. This is the largest of the three smaller grebes, often looking the most elegant and long-necked (although all grebes may hold their necks down when danger threatens). It is distinguished from Black-necked Grebe by its flat crown and straight bill.

Where found: Rare breeding bird on lochs in central Scotland. Widespread off our coasts in winter.

adult winter

BLACK-NECKED GREBE
Podiceps nigricollis

30cm. Marginally smaller than the Slavonian Grebe, this species has a triangular, peaked head and a distinctly uptilted bill. It has a permanent surprised expression.

Where found: Rare breeding bird on well-vegetated lakes at a few sites in Scotland and England. Uncommon winter visitor offshore, mostly on southern coasts.

adult winter

LITTLE GREBE
Tachybaptus ruficollis

27cm. The smallest grebe, with the stubbiest bill and a ridiculous "fluffy bottom". This disappears when bird becomes alarmed and makes its body sleeker. It floats like a cork, but dives with maddening frequency.

Where found: Widespread and common breeding bird in all kinds of well-vegetated freshwater habitats. Some are found in estuaries in winter.

adult winter

Adult summer: Very distinctive, with white foreneck, black double-crest and chestnut-and-black "tippets".

Chick: As in all grebes, has the stripy-pyjama look, as if it has just escaped from jail. Often seen on adult's back.

Adult winter: Has the longest, whitest neck and cheeks of all the grebes, but perhaps the most important feature is the white stripe between the eye and crown. All other grebes' caps descend to the level of the eye. The bill is long and pink.

Flight: Very slim shape, with white on leading and trailing edges of the wings. Like all grebes, flies reluctantly, with weak, flappy action.

Voice: A variety of hoarse, braying sounds – the last thing you would expect to hear from a grebe. Young make an incessant peeping.

Adult summer: No tippets, only a white cheek bordered by black above and chestnut-red below.

Adult winter: Has a distinctly dusky neck, contrasting with its whiter (but not white) cheeks. The black cap comes down to cover the eye. A distinctive feature is the yellow bill with a black tip, shorter than the pink bill of the Great Crested Grebe.

Flight: Less long-looking than Great Crested Grebe. Has more white on the wings than the smaller grebes.

Voice: Quite similar to Great Crested Grebe but more croaking, almost frog-like. Silent in winter.

Adult summer: Black head has golden plumes running right through to nape, and the neck is reddish-chestnut in colour.

Adult winter: Looks very black-and-white, unlike Little Grebe. The black "cloth-cap" contrasts sharply with the white cheeks. The border between black and white runs through the eye. There is a pale spot in front of the eye, and the black bill has a pink tip.

Flight: The wings have a broad white trailing edge, and each has a mere speck of white on the front, by the shoulder.

Voice: Nasal trill – more trilling than Great Crested Grebe, more nasal than Little Grebe (quite like a Guillemot).

Adult summer: The black head has a fan of golden plumes spreading out behind the cheeks, barely reaching the nape. Unsurprisingly, the neck is black.

Adult winter: Looks very black-and-white, but is much less clean-looking than Slavonian Grebe, especially on head and neck. The black crown drops well down below the eye, offering less contrast with the duskier cheeks.

Flight: The wings have a longer white trailing edge than in Slavonian Grebe, but lack any white on the shoulder.

Voice: A shrill, squealing chatter, not unlike the Water Rail (see pp.88–89).

Adult summer: It shows rich chestnut coloration on the throat, cheeks and foreneck, bordered with black. At the base of the bill is a yellow-green patch.

Adult winter: The only grebe that does not look black-and-white; instead it looks black and brown. The capped effect is accentuated by the loss of chestnut colour, replaced by pale buff. The yellow-green patch becomes much less obvious.

Flight: A very hurried pattering over the water. Alone among grebes, the Little has no white on the wings.

Voice: A marvellous giggling whinny, often performed in duet.

Feeding and display behaviour

Feeding and habitat

In the breeding season, all our grebes occupy subtly different habitats, each geared to their separate feeding requirements. Of the common species, the *Great Crested Grebe* is the only specialist fish-eater (it has a typical dagger-like fish-eater's bill), so it is quite at home on large bodies of water with a limited amount of vegetation around the banks – although it must have enough to build and anchor its nest. The *Little Grebe*, which feeds mainly on insects and molluscs, needs far more sheltered water, with a great deal of dense vegetation.

The rarer grebes also occupy slightly different habitats. The *Slavonian Grebe*, which eats fish and insects, can breed in quite open, unproductive lakes, for example those which are surrounded by acidic moorland. The *Black-necked Grebe* needs much more fertile, productive lakes, with a considerable growth of vegetation where it can seek out its diet which is based more on invertebrates than fish.

In winter, many of our grebes can be found on the sea where they all feed mainly on fish. *Great Crested, Red-necked* and *Slavonian Grebes* appear to need less sheltered water than the two smaller species, *Little* and *Black-necked*, which are mainly found in estuaries and harbours. Of all the five species, the *Slavonian Grebe* is the most marine in winter, quite at home in rough seas, and usually staying away from inland sites.

Uniquely among birds, grebes eat large quantities of their own feathers, probably to provide a "padding" against the sharp bones of the fish that they eat. Not surprisingly, the *Great Crested Grebe*, our true fish specialist, eats the most feathers.

Display

The grebes are famous for their courtship displays. For most people, these are easiest to observe in the *Great Crested Grebe*, which performs from February onwards.

- *Head-shaking* – The commonest display. When intense, the birds raise and lower their necks at the same time as head-shaking. For grebes, a shake of the head means "yes".

- *Habit-preening* – Takes place during a bout of Head-Shaking. It is merely a posture, nothing to do with plumage care.

- *Cat-display* – Adopted by one bird during the "Discovery Ceremony", while the other dives.

- *Weed-ceremony* – Both birds dive at the same time to collect weed, then swim towards each other rapidly. When they meet, they rear up on the water, breast to breast, and shake their heads from side to side, holding the weed.

Each of these ceremonies serves to cement the pair-bond between grebes, and each can be seen performed over and over again in early spring, and sometimes for longer.

The *Slavonian Grebe* has somewhat similar ceremonies to the Great Crested Grebe, but during the Weed Ceremony, the pair turn away as one, and rush along the surface of the water for up to 10m (30ft), side-by-side. This is called the "Weed-Rush".

The *Black-necked Grebe* has a less conspicuous set of displays, none of which involve the use of weed, although many of the postures are similar. The *Little Grebe's* displays are so subtle as to be easily missed.

Great Crested Grebe in flight (above and below) and as seen from behind (left)

Great Crested Grebe performing the Cat-display (below)

Black-necked grebe

Red-necked Grebe

Slavonian Grebe

leaps before diving

CORY'S SHEARWATER
Calonectris diomedea

46cm. The largest, palest shearwater with
a lazy, gull-like flight action. Somewhat
featureless, it could be confused with a gull
or a young gannet as well as with another
shearwater. It looks distinctively broad-
and pale-headed, so gives a front-heavy
appearance. The bill is yellow; all other
shearwaters have dark bills.

Where found: A rare but
regular visitor offshore, mostly in
early autumn, and mostly to
south-west England.

adult

GREAT SHEARWATER
Puffinus gravis

46cm. Another large shearwater which flies
with a much quicker and stiffer wing
action than the Cory's – in fact, more like a
smaller shearwater.

Where found: A rare but
regular visitor offshore, at similar
times and locations to Cory's.

adult

SOOTY SHEARWATER
Puffinus griseus

41cm. A quite large, cigar-shaped
shearwater with long, slightly backswept
wings and a powerful, direct flight. The
wings are longer and more pointed than
those of the Manx Shearwater.

Where found: An uncommon
but regular autumn visitor to
mostly northern and eastern
coasts.

adult

MANX SHEARWATER
Puffinus puffinus

35cm. The smallest and most common
shearwater, often appearing black then
white as it "shears" over the waves, tilting
from side to side. The wings are held
stiffly, accurately centred in the middle of
the body to make a cross shape.

Where found: Large colonies
are concentrated at a limited
number of sites, mostly on
Atlantic coasts. Birds are present
from February–October.

adult

Upperside: Greyish-brown above, paler about the head and body. There is no sign of a collar. Some birds show a small white patch at the base of the tail.

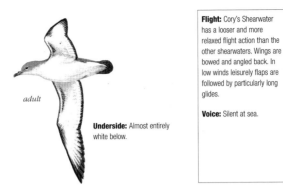

adult

Underside: Almost entirely white below.

Flight: Cory's Shearwater has a looser and more relaxed flight action than the other shearwaters. Wings are bowed and angled back. In low winds leisurely flaps are followed by particularly long glides.

Voice: Silent at sea.

Upperside: Soon becomes easy to recognise with its obvious black cap and clear white patch at the base of the tail. The black cap is terminated at the nape by a white collar. Otherwise, this species is largely dark brown above.

adult

Underside: In side-view the black cap is still obvious. Black markings on the wings and belly distinguish this species from Cory's and Manx Shearwaters.

Flight: Powerful flight action holding its wings straighter than the Sooty Shearwater. "Towers" in high winds.

Voice: Silent at sea.

Upperside: All dark – sooty, in fact – with no contrast; unlike the two larger shearwaters.

adult

Underside: Sooty except for paler centres to the wings.

Flight: Similar action to the Manx Shearwater, but is powerful and direct, and is less affected by high winds. It still looks stiff-winged, and alternates flaps with glides, but wings are clearly backswept. "Towers" in high winds (see above).

Voice: Silent at sea.

Upperside: All dark above, it shows no "capped" effect like the Great Shearwater, and no white at the base of the tail.

adult

Underside: Can appear capped from below, in view of the strong contrast between white throat and dark cheeks. The underparts, however, are dazzling white, unspoiled by any dark on the belly.

Flight: In low winds it shears the water tilting from side-to-side, shallow flaps alternating with glides. In higher winds it has a rising and falling action. Groups of Manx Shearwaters can be seen flying in single file.

Voice: Croons, cackles and hiccoughs with occasional breathless pauses.

Breeding behaviour

Only four members of this group breed in Britain and Ireland – the Fulmar, Manx Shearwater, Storm Petrel and Leach's Petrel. The other three species are ocean wanderers that breed far away, the Cory's Shearwater in the Mediterranean and Atlantic, and the Great and Sooty Shearwaters off the southern tip of South America.

Since they are adapted to a life at sea, shearwaters and petrels never need to do much walking, and consequently have become feeble and vulnerable when they are on land. So, when they come to land to breed, they face predation from land mammals and other birds. Our species have tried two different methods to solve this problem.

The *Fulmar*, our largest and bulkiest member of the group, is also the most powerful flier, and has taken to breeding on sheer cliffs, usually at the top. This gives it the edge over any ground predators, and the Fulmar's size helps it against bird predators. It also has the capacity, like all our species, to spit foul-smelling stomach oil at a potential trouble-maker. Fulmars attend their home cliffs all year round, although they may commute hundreds of miles each day to feed.

While the Fulmar attends its nest in an exposed position by day and by night, the other species only visit their colonies at night, and they each nest in burrows. The burrows are secluded, but still vulnerable to ground predators, so these species tend to be confined to isolated, offshore, rat-free islands. Amazingly,

A Storm Petrel at its nest

A Fulmar colony nesting on a cliff

The Storm Petrel nests in natural crevices or may dig its own burrow

they use their excellent sense of smell to find the individual nesting-burrow.

Manx Shearwaters arrive at their colonies after dark, and nest in burrows, either excavated by themselves or by rabbits, in soft ground. The *Storm Petrel* also arrives after dark, but it prefers a natural crevice, such as a rock fissure or under a stone. It will dig its own burrow where necessary, and also uses artificial sites such as stone walls and buildings. The *Leach's Petrel* arrives later in the night than the Storm Petrel, and digs a burrow in soft ground such as soil or peat, only occasionally using crevices.

For a birdwatcher lucky enough to witness the extraordinary nocturnal comings and goings of petrels and shearwaters around their breeding colonies, it is not the sight that makes it memorable, but the sound. In the dark, visual signals are no good, so these seabirds have compensated by the development of loud vocal signals

Manx Shearwater emerging from its burrow

– wild, maniacal wails and cackles.

The *Manx Shearwater* croons, cackles and hiccoughs, with occasional breathless pauses. A colony sounds like an overcrowded chicken-run. The *Storm* and *Leach's Petrels* make loud, purring noises interspersed with high notes.

The *Fulmar*, not needing to make such memorable sound, utters a few cackles, like a duck fighting over bread.

FULMAR
Fulmarus glacialis

47cm. The Fulmar is most people's
introduction to the mysterious family of
shearwaters and their allies, being by far
the easiest member to see. A common cliff-
top dweller, it is superficially like a gull,
but look for the tubular ridge along the top
of the bill that gives its family the
alternative name of "Tube-noses".

adult

Where found: Common
breeding bird on cliffs all around
our coasts, present all year.

Adult: Gull-like, but with a very
thick head and neck and, of
course, a different bill. Note the
dark smudge by the eye. On the
water, floats buoyantly.

STORM PETREL
Hydrobates pelagicus

15cm. Storm Petrels are tiny, dark seabirds
which fly daintily on long, fluttering wings.
They more closely resemble a House
Martin or Swallow than any of their true
"Tube-nosed" relatives. The Storm Petrel
has a direct, fast, fluttering flight on fairly
stiff wings. It alternates flutters with glides,
and often patters on the water surface. It
recalls a bat.

adult

juvenile

Where found: Large colonies
are found on a few isolated
islands, mostly to the north and
west, present from April–October.
Britain and Ireland hold over two-
thirds of the world population.

Here the adult and juvenile Storm
Petrel are shown in proportion to
the larger Fulmar. On the facing
page they have been enlarged so
that the identification features
can be seen more clearly.

LEACH'S PETREL
Oceanodroma leucorhoa

20cm. This species is slightly larger than
the Storm Petrel, with longer wings and a
generally more attenuated look. It has a
much more buoyant flight than Storm
Petrel with more glides and with sudden,
jerky changes of direction. The wings are
held characteristically angled at the joints,
making a flat "M"-shape. It seldom patters
on the water surface.

adult

juvenile

Where found: There are less
than ten colonies, all in north
and north-west Scotland. Some
appear inshore after strong
north-westerly gales in late
autumn.

Here the Leach's Petrel is shown
in proportion to the larger Fulmar.
On the facing page it has been
enlarged so that the identification
features can be seen more
clearly.

Life on the seas

Members of both the Shearwater and Storm Petrel families
are superbly adapted to a life spent on the open oceans –
they only come to land to breed. All species are able to fly for
long periods of time, covering vast distances; they obtain
most of their moisture from their food, expelling excess salt
from their bodies through salt glands; and they detect food
by sight (either by spotting the food itself or by seeing other
birds feeding), and by smell.

The "Tube-nose", or tubular nostrils that are characteristic
of shearwaters and petrels, are a clue to their enhanced
sense of smell. There is evidence that they are able to detect
the smell of food that has been carried on the wind from
many miles away.

Obtaining food on the oceans
Most of these birds obtain a wide variety of animal food,
including squid, plankton, small fish and crustaceans. They
may catch this food by plunging from the air into the water,
by picking it directly from the surface, or even by diving
underwater while swimming on the surface (mainly Manx
Shearwater and Sooty Shearwater).

Most of these species benefit from attending trawlers and
collecting thrown-out offal (all except Leach's Petrel), so it is
well worth fixing a trip with some fishermen, or hoping a
trawler sails past the sea-watching point.

A smaller number of species habitually follow ships,
including ferries, presumably attracted by the way in which

chick

adult blue

Adult (blue phase): Blue Fulmars replace any white plumage with ashy-grey. Rare, but more common in the north.

Chick: Fluffy, white and ready to spit stomach-oil at any intruder.

adult

Flight: The wings are held very stiffly, in contrast to a gull's more relaxed flight. Rapid flaps are interspersed with glides; also soars around the cliffs. At a distance, may resemble closely-related shearwaters, but has a white head.

Voice: The Fulmar utters a few cackles, like a duck fighting over bread.

adult

Adult: All dark except for a broad white rump and a paler patch on the wing. The legs are quite long.

juvenile

adult

adult

Flight (upperside): The white of the rump leaks over onto the underside of the bird. The wing-bar is faint, the tail is blunt-ended.

Flight (underside): A bar on the underside of the wing makes this bird identifiable. The amount of white or pale colour varies between birds.

Voice: Loud purring noises interspersed with high notes.

Adult: Shows a larger pale band on the wing than Storm Petrel.

adult

adult

Flight (upperside): Smaller white rump than Storm Petrel, and does not leak over onto the underside. There is sometimes an indistinct dark bar splitting it in two. Tail is forked and the forewings are noticeably paler than Storm Petrel, giving more contrast.

Flight (underside): All dark.

Voice: Similar to Storm Petrel, but with longer purrs.

they stir up the water. Other species ignore or avoid ships. The main ship-followers are: Fulmar, Cory's Shearwater and Storm Petrel.

Watching shearwaters and petrels

To see the shearwaters or petrels, a visit to a breeding colony, or a trip by ferry over the open sea, is necessary. These birds do not give themselves up easily; even on a long ferry crossing, just a few may be seen, if any at all. The more hardened, fanatic "sea-watchers" look out for them from well-known sites on land, usually high, rocky coastal outcrops, that jut out some distance from the land. When favourable winds prevail, "flocks" of sea-watchers adorn these sites, telescopes trained on the vast expanse of water, ready to pick out a distant, heart-stopping shape. As shearwaters and petrels are usually seen on the move, make sure you use a telescope or binoculars to help you distinguish between the flight profiles of the different species.

GANNET
Sula bassana
90cm. A huge seabird, unmistakable when
seen well. Adults are obvious even at a
great distance, showing blazing "whiter-
than-white" plumage with black wing-tips.
The younger immature stages are more
easily picked out by their size, cigar-
shaped bodies and leisurely, slow-flapping
flight. The deep flaps are often interspersed
with glides.

adult summer

Where found: There are a few
widely-scattered colonies, mostly
on offshore islands, which hold
between them 70 per cent of the
world population. Frequent off
any coast in winter.

Adult: White with black wing-
tips; head stained butterscotch
yellow.

chick

Chick: Already shows
the beginnings of the
powerful dagger-bill.

CORMORANT
Phalacrocorax carbo
90cm. The closely-related Cormorant and
Shag are very large, mostly black birds with
long necks, thick bodies and powerful,
back-set feet. The Cormorant is the larger,
bulkier species with a thicker bill and neck
than its smaller relative.

adult summer

Where found: Common coastal
breeder; inland mainly in winter.

Adult summer: Black plumage
with bluish sheen is relieved by a
white throat and white patch on
thigh.

SHAG
Phalacrocorax aristotelis
76cm. The Shag is much smaller than the
Cormorant, but this is only obvious when
the two are together. However, at all times
the bill looks much thinner, and next to the
steep forehead, it looks as though it could
be snapped off easily. The Cormorant's
thick bill sinks deeply into the flatter
crown.

adult summer

Where found: Common breeder
on the coast; outnumbers
Cormorant in Scotland. Rare
inland. We have a quarter of the
world population.

Adult summer: Black, glossed-
green plumage is undisturbed
by white, but below the pert,
forward-pointing crest, is a
bright yellow patch of skin.

Breeding behaviour

Gannet
Gannet nest-sites must be within easy reach of fish, and
must also be situated in places where there are plenty of
updraughts to help these large birds take off and land.
Spectacular windy sea-cliffs and rocky islands fit the bill
perfectly. Gannets nest in colonies which are often very
large. They nest so close together that there is not enough
room for a gull to land between them, with each bird situated
just outside pecking distance from the the next (see
photograph pp.32–33). Pairs of Gannets within a colony are
extremely territorial over their small nesting areas and may
attack chicks and other adult birds that stray into their
territory. Gannets begin nesting in April and eggs are laid
either at the end of April or in May. The nest is cone-shaped
and is made from seaweed and lined with softer material
such as grass or feathers. Only one egg is laid and it is
incubated by both parents. Unusually, the egg is kept warm
using the feet, with the attendant parent actually standing on
top of it. Fed by both parents, the young bird will leave the
colony after about 90 days. During its time in the nest the
young bird consumes about 30kg (65lb) of fish. When the
time comes to leave, the bird flop-glides from the cliff into
the water and is unable to fly until its fat reserves have been
used up – usually about a week. From there the young birds
fly south to the west African coast and may not return for
two years.

juvenile

2nd/3rd-year

Juvenile: Brown all over, quite a contrast to adult. Distinguished from a large shearwater by long bill and neck, and long, pointed tail. Becomes whiter with age.

Second-/third-year: Some white coloration invades the dark, giving a mottled effect.

4th-year

Fourth-year: Shows the adult's pattern but for a few black streaks on the secondaries. Some third-years look like this.

adult winter

Adult: Plumage acquired at 4–6 years.

Flight: The body is often angled above the horizontal. It appears cigar-shaped with characteristic black-tipped wings.

Voice: A rumbling honking. Only uttered at the colony.

adult winter

immature

immature

Adult winter: The white thigh-patch disappears, and the white on the throat becomes more dusky.

Immature: First-year birds are brown, often with much more white on the belly than is shown here. They become darker as they mature.

Flight: Flies high and straight, with slow wing-beats, sometimes gliding.

Voice: Guttural tummy-rumbling sounds, often with a gargling quality.

adult winter

immature

immature

Adult winter: The crest is lost. There is a small patch of dirty white on the chin.

Immature: Similar to Cormorant but darker on the breast and thighs.

Flight: Faster wing-beats than the Cormorant and holds its neck straighter when flying. The Shag can be seen flying low over the water; it rarely glides.

Voice: Similar to Cormorant but harsher still, with no gargling.

Cormorant

Another colonial bird, the Cormorant nests on coastal cliffs and sea-stacks, favouring broad ledges, or flat sections of stacks. Unlike the other two species featured here, it can also be found nesting inland among trees or reedbeds, along river valleys or near lakes. The nest is constructed from seaweed and twigs. In general between three and four eggs are laid from early April. They hatch at intervals and are incubated by both parents. The chicks are born blind and naked and look almost reptilian. Initially fed on liquid regurgitated by the parents, the young subsequently take solid food from their parents' throats. The young leave the nest after about 50 days.

Shag

The Shag nests in similar coastal locations to the Cormorant but prefers narrower ledges, crevices among bolders, or even sheltered ledges inside sea caves. From early March between two and six (but usually three) eggs are laid in a nest made from a pile of seaweed or other vegetation. The young leave the nest after around 53 days but will continue to be fed by the parents for another month.

Feeding and nesting behaviour

Gannet

Distant white objects flying way out over the sea sometimes perform a special trick that sets them apart as Gannets: rising high above the water surface, they stall for a moment, and then plunge-dive into the water with a tremendous splash. This spectacular performance is the Gannet's main fishing technique, and enables it to reach deeper fish than other birds.

Plunge-diving necessitates several adaptations for the Gannet: it has forward-set eyes which help it to judge the distance it has to dive; it has special nostrils in its mouth, to prevent water getting up its nose; and it has copious air-sacs to take some of the force of plunging. Some plunges take the bird 10m (30ft) below the surface; most fish are caught on the way back up.

Gannets live in large noisy colonies within easy reach of the feeding grounds

Cormorants and Shags

These two species are very similar to look at, but are in fact ecologically distinct.

Both species are fish-eaters, chasing their prey in the water during a dive from the surface. They are propelled by their powerful, back-set feet. Studies have shown that, while the Cormorant takes much of its food from the sea bed, the Shag takes

A Cormorant holds its wings out – to dry?

more free-swimming fish from nearer the surface. To do this, the Shag prefers deeper water, especially that found around rocky shores. The Cormorant prefers shallower water, in more sheltered places undisturbed by strong currents, and unlike the Shag it may venture inland to feed.

After fishing, both species can be seen "hanging their wings out to dry" in the well-known heraldic posture. The reason for this behaviour is not fully understood, since they continue to do it in the rain, when it could hardly make them dry. It may help them to lose heat or, alternatively, to obtain it from the sun's rays. Another theory suggests that it helps the birds digest their meal of fish. The fact is, no-one knows for sure. The posture is slightly different between the species: the Shag stretches out its wings a little further than the Cormorant.

The Cormorant is a fine flier. To reach its favoured feeding grounds it may need to travel up to 50km (30 miles) each way. Parties of Cormorants can be seen commuting to and fro in large groups, flying high and straight, sometimes gliding. The slow wing-beats are similar to those of a goose. The Cormorant uses its powerful flight to good effect; at the end of the breeding season, birds will disperse all around our coasts.

The Shag is a good, but less enthusiastic flier. Most of its fishing needs are fulfilled closer to the colony, so it rarely travels more than 15km to forage. Groups or individuals can be seen flying low over the water, never very high, and they seldom glide. The wing-beats are much quicker than those of the Cormorant; when flying, the Shag shows a straighter neck, without the Cormorant's kink, and a more rotund belly. Throughout the year, Shags stay in the vicinity of their breeding grounds, rarely dispersing far, so there is very little likelihood of finding them any distance from a coastline of seacliffs and rocky islands. They are rare in the north-west, south and south-east of England.

The Cormorant uses its powerful flight to good effect

BITTERN *Botaurus stellaris*

76cm. Like all species in this family, the Bittern has a dagger-like bill, a long neck, and long legs for wading. This secretive bird is, however, much less easy to see than its relatives, almost always remaining hidden away in dense reedbeds. It walks forward at a very slow, deliberate pace, its body rocking to and fro like a reed in the wind.

adult

Adult: Perfect camouflage is afforded by its patchwork of brown, buff and black.

Where found: Very rare resident in a few large reedbeds, mostly in East Anglia and one site in Lancashire. A few come to winter, mostly in south-east England.

LITTLE EGRET *Egretta garzetta*

56cm. This, the only regularly occurring "White Heron" in Britain is a small, dainty version of the usual heron type. This species can always be recognised by its black bill, and by its black legs with incongruous yellow feet. The main identification pitfall is most likely to be a nearby gull!

adult summer

Where found: A rare but increasing resident, yet to breed. Commonest in autumn and winter on estuaries, mostly in the south.

Adult summer: There are two crest-plumes, and more plumes adorning the back and breast.

GREY HERON *Ardea cinerea*

90cm. A large, tall, stately bird which moves slowly and deliberately when searching for fish. By far the commonest heron in Britain, and unlikely to be confused with anything else.

adult summer

Where found: Common, widespread resident in all kinds of freshwater habitats; also estuaries.

Adult: Mostly grey, but fading to white on the neck and breast. The long black eyebrows develop into a crest, and a series of dotted lines cascade down the throat and breast. There is a black patch at the shoulder.

Social and breeding behaviour

Bittern

Male and female Bitterns probably do not form real pair bonds, and associate mainly for breeding. Males may take between one and five mates. From winter onwards the male will defend his territory aggressively. The female will nest within the male's territory often near his calling place. She builds the nest herself using reeds and other vegetation. The female usually tends the young on her own. She lays 3–7 olive-green eggs which are incubated for 25–26 days. once the young have hatched, she will continue to add material to the nest until the chicks are well grown (14–21 days), and the nest may reach up to 90cm (3ft) in diameter. She will also care for them for a further 5–6 weeks after leaving.

Little Egret

Although the Little Egret is yet to breed in this country it is still interesting to compare its breeding behaviour with the other herons featured on these pages. Pair-bonds are probably formed for one breeding season only and both parents tend the young until after fledging. Nests in reedbeds, bushes and various kinds of trees. The Little Egret is colonial. Usually nests with other herons. The male and female build the nest together using sticks or reeds. The eggs are green-blue in colour and are incubated by both sexes for about 21 days. Both parents continue to feed and care for the young after hatching. The fledglings begin to leave the nest after about 30 days.

adult

Flight: Once airborne, the neck of the Bittern is retracted in the normal heron way. The wings are rounded and beaten more quickly than the Grey Heron's, thus immediately recalling an owl. The legs only just project beyond the tail.

Voice: Unmistakable and unforgettable. The "booming" of the Bittern is similar to the sound made by blowing over the rim of a bottle. This sound, which carries a long way, is best heard at dawn and dusk in the early spring. Recent research has shown that each individual male has its own special "boom", which helps greatly in determining the numbers present in any particular reedbed.

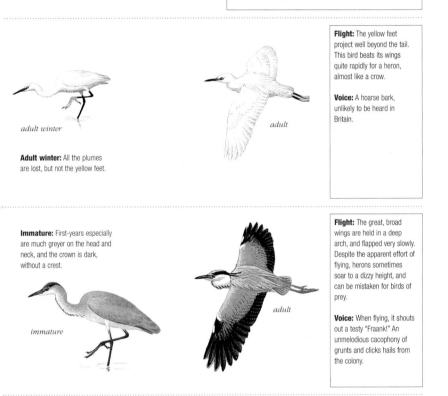

adult winter

Adult winter: All the plumes are lost, but not the yellow feet.

adult

Flight: The yellow feet project well beyond the tail. This bird beats its wings quite rapidly for a heron, almost like a crow.

Voice: A hoarse bark, unlikely to be heard in Britain.

Immature: First-years especially are much greyer on the head and neck, and the crown is dark, without a crest.

immature

adult

Flight: The great, broad wings are held in a deep arch, and flapped very slowly. Despite the apparent effort of flying, herons sometimes soar to a dizzy height, and can be mistaken for birds of prey.

Voice: When flying, it shouts out a testy "Fraank!" An unmelodious cacophony of grunts and clicks hails from the colony.

Grey Heron

Forms pair-bonds for the duration of a breeding season, although if attempts to mate have been unsuccessful, the bond may end earlier. There is some promiscuity among males that already have a mate, and some males may raise young with more than one mate. Grey herons usually nest in colonies but may sometimes do so as solitary pairs. Within a colony the male defends a territory that is used for pair-formation, nesting and raising the young.

Nests are usually built in trees up to 25m (75ft) above the ground, but are sometimes found low down in trees and bushes, and occasionally on the ground. The female constructs the nest from twigs brought to her by the male.

During the breeding season males and females perform a 'Greeting Ceremony' when bringing twigs or simply alighting on the nest. As one mate flies in to the nest the other usually responds in one of two ways. First, by stretching its neck upright with its head and bill pointing downwards, or second by pointing head and neck upwards, bending the legs, and then leaning the neck back.

In Britain, the first eggs appear in February, and the last and the end of April. The pale blue eggs (4–5) are incubated by both parents for about 25–26 days and continue to be fed and tended by them for 20–30 until they leave to climb on branches near the nest.

Feeding and breeding behaviour

The Grey Heron in its familiar stalking pose ready to stab its prey just under the surface

Feeding techniques

Fishermen have to be patient, and our members of the heron family are no exception. Each species, however, uses slightly different methods, or fishes in a slightly different habitat.

Our most familiar species, the *Grey Heron*, can often be seen standing in an upright posture, motionless, beside a pond or river, or in the water. It is watching and waiting. Once prey is sighted it will edge its bill down towards the water, assuming a crouched position, until the quarry is within range of a strike. By patience and stealth, therefore, it earns itself an opportunity. The strike, when it comes, is aimed at grabbing the fish, not spearing it – any wriggly prey can be speared to death later, once it is under control. The whole technique requires an element of surprise to be successful. Although mostly employed against fish, the method also works for catching mammals, amphibians and even birds.

To be efficient, herons must hunt alone; fish are very easily spooked by any careless movements, so disturbance is unwelcome. For most of the year, Grey Herons defend their own feeding territories from other individuals, sometimes very aggressively, and even occasionally with fatal results.

The *Bittern* employs a similar strategy in obtaining its food. It hunts alone, mostly by stealth, and takes a wide range of items that include fish, amphibians, worms, insects, small mammals and birds, although medium-sized eels are a particular

A Little Egret employs one of the several fishing techniques it can call upon

favourite. Its technique differs from the Grey Heron's in that the prey is normally taken "on the run", so to speak, without long periods of standing still.

Although employing the same slow wading technique of the Grey Heron and Bittern to obtain some of its food, the *Little Egret* also uses other methods. In shallow water, the sighting of a fish will sometimes elicit an excited dash and rapid plunge as the quarry is chased, perhaps even with a leap as well, as if the bird were enacting some kind of paddling, shoreline ballet. Capture, therefore, is more of a chase than a dignified wait. In other situations, the Little Egret has been seen to place one foot in the shallow water, and vibrate it rapidly; this "Foot Stirring" apparently flushes prey into striking range. The process is evidently aided by the brightly coloured yellow feet – well, they had to be of some use, didn't they? Despite this inventiveness, the Little Egret eats much the same kind of food as its larger relatives.

Breeding strategies

Where is the last place you would expect a large, long-legged, broad-winged, fish-eating bird to make its nest? Perhaps the top of a tree? Well, that, of course, is precisely what the *Grey Heron* does. It builds large constructions out of sticks and places them in robust branches of such trees as elm, oak and pine, far out of reach of all but the most persistent predators. Most birds nest in colonies, known as "heronries", which make a spectacular sight when seen against a late winter background of bare, leafless branches. Nest refurbishment often begins in January, a prelude to a very early start to breeding. Eggs are usually laid in March, giving the eventual youngsters plenty of time to practise fishing before the hard times come the following winter.

The *Bittern* builds a nest deep in the reedbeds, where its best protection comes from concealment. Bitterns are not colonial, because all the activity which resonates from a colony would make their nests too easy to find. All their movements are geared to camouflage: mostly silent, they sway like a reed when moving about, and, when threatened, look to the skies in the "Bitterning" posture and sway still more. The camouflage is truly extraordinary, they just melt into the reedbeds.

Camouflage and inaccessibility are the Bittern's main line of defence

The Bittern's camouflage is so effective that they would have great difficulty finding each other were it not for the male's extraordinary "booming" call. Each male has a slightly different boom, which helps those who study Bitterns to estimate the population in a particular reedbed. At present, the Bittern's status as a breeding bird here is parlous, although stringent conservation efforts are now in place to try and reverse recent declines in this charismatic bird's fortunes.

MUTE SWAN
Cygnus olor

152cm. Unmistakably a swan, this is Britain's largest bird. When swimming, it normally holds its neck in an elegant S-curve, with the bill pointing downwards, in contrast to the other swans. It also has a longer tail, which is often cocked upwards, giving a high rear end. When angry, the Mute Swan arches its wings over its back, which the other swans do not do.

Where found: A resident over most of lowland Britain, wherever there is water.

Adult male/female: In both adults, the bill is orange and black, with a large knob, making the head look square, especially in flight. Male has a larger knob, especially in spring.

Juvenile/immature: Cygnets have brown plumage, which gradually whitens as they mature, but some still have darker feathering when a year old. The brown plumage is uneven and mottled, in contrast to the young of other swan species.

WHOOPER SWAN
Cygnus cygnus

152cm. This winter visitor is Mute Swan-sized, but can be distinguished at a distance by shape. The neck is held straight, not curved, and the tail is shorter and less upward-pointing.

Where found: A winter visitor September–April, northerly, found in a range of habitats, from lakes to estuaries.

Adult: The bill is black and yellow, set well into the head to give a "long-nosed" effect. The pattern of the bill is characteristic: the yellow cuts sharply into the black bill tip to make a wedge shape.

adult

BEWICK'S SWAN
Cygnus columbianus

122cm. Similar in many ways to the Whooper Swan, but much smaller, with a shorter neck and a gentler expression. It holds its neck erect like a Whooper Swan, but in size and proportions resembles a goose.

Where found: A winter visitor October–March, patchily distributed in England, Wales and Ireland. Rare in Scotland.

Adult: If anything, there is more black than yellow on the bill; the border between the colours varies greatly, but is always blunter than on Whooper Swan.

adult

Swan watching

Most swans seen in Britain all year round will be Mute Swans – certainly all those on park lakes, in cities or on flooded gravel pits. In fact, any swan seen in summer, from May until September, will be a Mute Swan, because this is the only species that breeds here.

The other two species featured here are winter visitors from the north, occurring only in certain selected places in Britain. The Bewick's Swan is a High Arctic bird, which arrives from Russia in October at the earliest and concludes its short stay in March. It is found mostly in England and Ireland, on shallow freshwater lakes and floodlands.

The Whooper Swan has less far to come, since most of our birds breed in Iceland. It arrives earlier (often

September), leaves later (often April), and generally tends to inhabit more northerly sites than the Bewick's, including Scotland, where Bewick's is practically absent. It uses a wider range of habitats, including deep, unproductive lakes, and intertidal mudflats. In winter, Bewick's tend to stick to certain localities in large groups; Whoopers spread out more, and into smaller groups.

Swan lakes

In a few places in Britain, swans of all three species can be seen together. Two of the best known sites are managed by the Wildfowl & Wetlands Trust: the Ouse Washes in Cambridgeshire (parts of which are also an RSPB reserve)

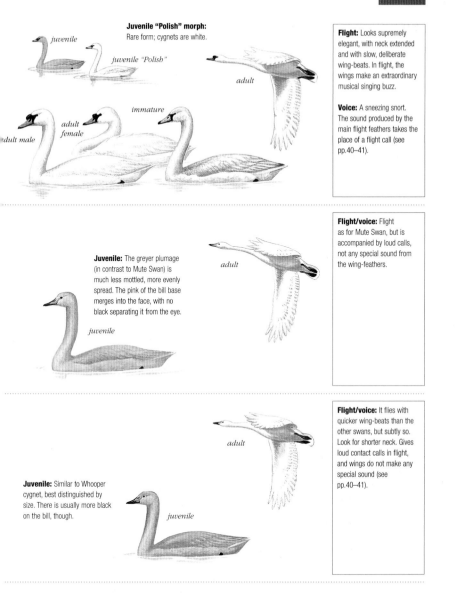

Juvenile "Polish" morph:
Rare form; cygnets are white.

juvenile

juvenile "Polish"

adult

immature

adult female

adult male

Flight: Looks supremely elegant, with neck extended and with slow, deliberate wing-beats. In flight, the wings make an extraordinary musical singing buzz.

Voice: A sneezing snort. The sound produced by the main flight feathers takes the place of a flight call (see pp.40–41).

Juvenile: The greyer plumage (in contrast to Mute Swan) is much less mottled, more evenly spread. The pink of the bill base merges into the face, with no black separating it from the eye.

juvenile

adult

Flight/voice: Flight as for Mute Swan, but is accompanied by loud calls, not any special sound from the wing-feathers.

Juvenile: Similar to Whooper cygnet, best distinguished by size. There is usually more black on the bill, though.

juvenile

adult

Flight/voice: It flies with quicker wing-beats than the other swans, but subtly so. Look for shorter neck. Gives loud contact calls in flight, and wings do not make any special sound (see pp.40–41).

and Slimbridge in Gloucestershire. At the latter site especially, close study of the Bewick's Swans has revealed important information on their family life, migration and survival. Much of this has been helped by the fact that the families of these swans – adults and young – migrate and spend the winter together.

Bill patterns
One of the most interesting discoveries has been that every individual Bewick's Swan is recognisable by the unique pattern of its bill, so that it can be identified in the field, given a good view. Over the years, a swan's family history can be worked out: the age of the swan, the identity of its partner,

how many offspring they have had, and to whom their offspring are paired. There are very few opportunities in the bird world to obtain such an intimate understanding of a species' lifestyle and fortunes.

Flight and breeding behaviour

The unmistakable profile of the Mute Swan in flight

Flight sounds

In flight, the main flight feathers (primaries) of the *Mute Swan* produce an unmissable rhythmic sighing sound, which can be heard from a mile or more away. Most people are familiar with this majestic sound, which takes the place of a flight call-note, serving to keep the birds in contact.

Whooper and *Bewick's Swans*, in contrast, fly on virtually silent wings. They keep in contact by calling, making a range of crooning and trumpeting sounds. The two species are difficult to distinguish, but the Bewick's Swan makes a more yelping flight-call, and the Whooper Swan makes deeper, more nasal flight calls – often in bugle-like triple blasts. Both species are likely to be seen flying at higher altitudes than Mute Swans. The Bewick's Swan can be picked out with practice by its shorter neck and slightly faster wing-beats.

Swans create huge nests on which the female does most of the incubation

Swan family life

The population of the *Mute Swan* is divided into two groups: breeding pairs, which hold a territory for the whole year; and non-breeding flocks, which gather on substantial bodies of water and seem to spend most of the year loafing and engaging in bouts of courtship. One courtship display you might observe is "Head-turning", which takes place when a courting pair are facing each other with their breasts almost touching. This is also used as a greeting between mates.

Cygnets join a non-breeding flock when they are forced out of the family territory by their parents. For the next two or three years they will consort with other youngsters in an apparently idyllic adolescence, during which they find and "become engaged to" a mate. First breeding can be at age three (females) or four (males), although of course this varies. As suggested by popular lore, most pairs remain together for life.

The nest is a huge structure built by both sexes from various segments of vegetation, such as reeds and rushes, and takes about ten days to build. The male picks up pieces of vegetation and drops them over his shoulder into the nest. The female then presses them down using her breast, bill and feet. Once the eggs have been laid, the female does most of the incubation which lasts over a month, although the male will watch over her and defend his family with considerable aggression during this time. When the chicks hatch, they are carried on the back of an adult (usually the female) for extra protection until they are a week to ten days old. The cygnets climb aboard where the tail meets the folded wings. The cygnet is not actively helped by the parent, although it may be allowed to use the parent's heel as a step. Neither Whooper nor Bewick's Swans offer this special "piggyback" service to their cygnets. When isolated, cold or hungry, cygnets emit a distress call, sitting erect with their neck stretched out and beak open.

The week old cygnets of the Mute Swans have the added protection of a piggyback service

GREYLAG GOOSE
Anser anser

80cm. This is the largest and heaviest of the so-called "Grey geese" (greyish-brown at best). It has a comparatively big head and thick neck. It has a heavier walking step than its relatives.

Where found: Uncommon breeding bird in western and northern Scotland where truly wild, but much more widely as an escapee from captivity. See also pp.44–45.

Adult: Key features are the large, orange bill; the pink legs; and the comparatively pale head and neck, without the neck/breast contrast shown in Pink-foot and Bean. Most adults have a few dark spots on the breast, but nothing like the patterning seen in White-front.

BEAN GOOSE
Anser fabalis

75cm. This species rivals Greylag in size, but is less bulky, with an easier gait and a more long-necked, upright stance.

Where found: See also pp.44–45.

Adult: The long, thin bill is black and orange-yellow; the legs are orange. The head and neck are very dark, contrasting strongly with the breast and back. Bean Geese are close to Greylags in size, and their plumage resembles the Pink-foot – the best distinction, therefore, is in shape and bill-colour.

PINK-FOOTED GOOSE
Anser brachyrhynchus

70cm. Although similar in plumage to Bean Goose, it is smaller, with a much shorter, thicker neck and a small, compact head and bill. Overall, this is the daintiest and smoothest in movement of all the Grey geese.

Where found: See also pp.44–45.

Adult: The short bill is two-toned, pink and black; the legs are pink, of course! It shares with the Bean Goose a sharp contrast between dark head and neck/paler breast. The back has a distinctly frosty wash to it, more so than the Bean Goose, on which the thigh and back are much the same colour.

WHITE-FRONTED GOOSE
Anser albifrons

70cm. A small, long-winged, brownish goose, with several distinctive features that readily identify it.

Where found: See also pp.44–45.

Adult: The white "front" refers to the white forehead, seen especially well when a flock of birds flies towards the observer. Beware that all other Grey geese can show small amounts of white at the base of the bill, but never as much as this species. In addition, the White-front shows a considerable amount of dark feathering on the belly, quite unlike the other species. The legs are orange.

Eurasian race: Birds wintering in the southern half of Britain have a pink, unpatterned bill.

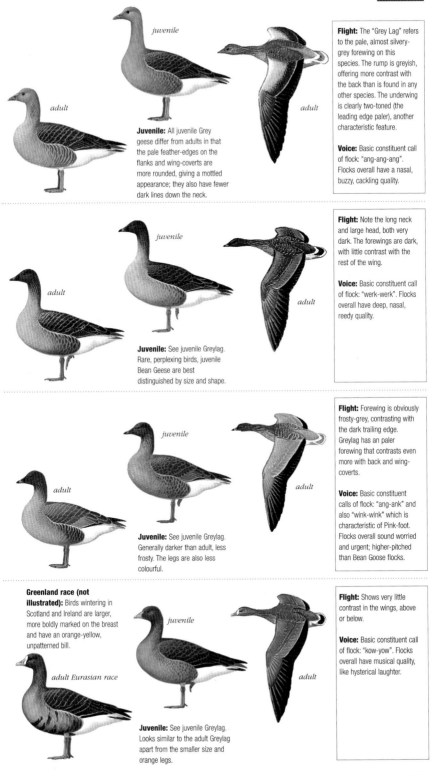

Flight: The "Grey Lag" refers to the pale, almost silvery-grey forewing on this species. The rump is greyish, offering more contrast with the back than is found in any other species. The underwing is clearly two-toned (the leading edge paler), another characteristic feature.

Voice: Basic constituent call of flock: "ang-ang-ang". Flocks overall have a nasal, buzzy, cackling quality.

juvenile

adult

adult

Juvenile: All juvenile Grey geese differ from adults in that the pale feather-edges on the flanks and wing-coverts are more rounded, giving a mottled appearance; they also have fewer dark lines down the neck.

Flight: Note the long neck and large head, both very dark. The forewings are dark, with little contrast with the rest of the wing.

Voice: Basic constituent call of flock: "werk-werk". Flocks overall have deep, nasal, reedy quality.

juvenile

adult

adult

Juvenile: See juvenile Greylag. Rare, perplexing birds, juvenile Bean Geese are best distinguished by size and shape.

Flight: Forewing is obviously frosty-grey, contrasting with the dark trailing edge. Greylag has an paler forewing that contrasts even more with back and wing-coverts.

Voice: Basic constituent calls of flock: "ang-ank" and also "wink-wink" which is characteristic of Pink-foot. Flocks overall sound worried and urgent; higher-pitched than Bean Goose flocks.

juvenile

adult

adult

Juvenile: See juvenile Greylag. Generally darker than adult, less frosty. The legs are also less colourful.

Greenland race (not illustrated): Birds wintering in Scotland and Ireland are larger, more boldly marked on the breast and have an orange-yellow, unpatterned bill.

Flight: Shows very little contrast in the wings, above or below.

Voice: Basic constituent call of flock: "kow-yow". Flocks overall have musical quality, like hysterical laughter.

juvenile

adult Eurasian race

adult

Juvenile: See juvenile Greylag. Looks similar to the adult Greylag apart from the smaller size and orange legs.

Where to find wild geese

The colloquial term "Wild Goose Chase" implies a fruitless, frantic search for something unattainable. The search for true wild geese in Britain is not unattainable, but it requires effort, and a trip to one of these birds' favourite winter haunts, often to a place that is cold, windswept and inhospitable. Moreover, the birds, wild to the core, will seldom make things easy for you due to their wariness. But the observation of a large group of these birds, perhaps rising at dawn and flying against a pink sky on their way from their roost to a feeding area, all the while calling in a musical babble, is one of the great thrills of British birdwatching and is definitely worth the effort.

Most breeding geese in Britain are here artificially. All our Canada Geese arise from introductions from North America; most of our Greylags arise from escapes from captivity. Except for a few precious Greylags in western and northern Scotland, the summering geese are poor relations to their relatives, which visit us from the far north to spend the winter.

This map shows the areas in which different species of wintering geese are most likely to be found in Britain. Geese are extremely difficult to identify, so exactly where they are seen is an important clue.

Good Sites for Wild Geese

1. South Uist, Outer Hebrides: Greylags (breeding and wintering), a few Greenland White-fronts.
2. Inner Hebrides, especially Islay: Barnacles from Greenland, Greenland White-fronts, Greylags, also rare geese.
3. Loch Leven, Tayside: Mostly Pinkfeet, also some Greylags.
4. Loch Ken, Dumfries and Galloway: Greylags, Greenland White-fronts, a few Bean Geese.
5. Caerlaverock, Dumfries and Galloway: Pinkfeet, Barnacles from Spitzbergen, Greylags, rare geese.
6. Donegal, Eire: Greenland White-fronts, Greylags, Light-bellied Brents, Barnacles from Greenland.
7. Wexford Slobs, Rep. Ireland: Greenland White-fronts, Light-bellied Brents.
8. Northumberland: Pinkfeet, Greylags and both Light and Dark-bellied Brents.
9. Lancashire: Mostly Pinkfeet.
10. North Norfolk: Pinkfeet, Dark-bellied Brents and smaller numbers of Russian White-fronts and Greylags.
11. Yare Valley, Norfolk: Home to the only substantial regular flock of Bean Geese in Britain.
12. North Kent/Essex: Russian White-fronts and Dark-bellied Brents.
13. Slimbridge, Gloucestershire: Mostly Russian White-fronts, with a few oddities.

South Uist ①

Loch Leven ③

Inner Hebrides ②

⑧ Northumberland

Loch Ken
④ ⑤
Caerlaverock

⑥ Donegal

⑨ Lancashire

North Norfolk
⑩
⑪ Yare Valle

Wexford Slobs ⑦

⑬ Slimbridge

⑫
North Kent,
Essex

BARNACLE GOOSE
Branta leucopsis

63cm. This and all Britain's so-called "Black geese" have a black head and neck, relieved somewhere by white. The Barnacle Goose is similar in shape and general behaviour to one of the smaller Grey geese.

Where found: See also pp.44–45.

juvenile

adult

BRENT GOOSE
Branta bernicla

58cm. The smallest goose in Britain (not much bigger than a Mallard), and the one most confined to the coast.

Where found: See also pp.44–45.

Adult: In this Black goose there is a small white mark on the side of the neck, less than half way down to the breast. Because of its generally dark plumage, the blazing white bottom of the Brent Goose is distinctive.

Juvenile: Differs in either race by lacking white neck-patch (gained in late autumn). The lower back and wings look barred; there are often four obvious white bars visible, contrasting with the black primaries.

CANADA GOOSE
Branta canadensis

95cm. The largest, or at least the tallest goose in Britain, and the one most familiar to most people. Its great long neck makes it almost swan-like. It is quite unafraid of people, in profound contrast to most of its relatives.

Where found: A common freshwater breeding bird mostly in England, but spreading in all directions. Introduced from North America in the 18thC, but only became common after c.1945.

adult

Adult: In this Black goose (hardly deserving of the name, since it is mostly brown), the snaky neck is all black, but the chin is white, looking like a bandage over a cut.

SHELDUCK
Tadorna tadorna

61cm. This is a mixture between a duck and a goose, seemingly undecided where its affinities lie. It looks more like a duck in the water, but more like a goose on land and in flight. The sexes are similar, unlike the ducks. It is larger than most ducks, and does not dive.

Where found: A common resident species, found all around our coasts; uncommon inland. A bird of estuaries and muddy shores.

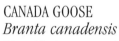

adult male

Adult: Looks mostly bold black-and-white. Dark, glossy-green head and neck, chestnut breast-band. The male Shoveler has the same main colours, but it has a short neck, huge bill, and a chestnut side, not breast band.

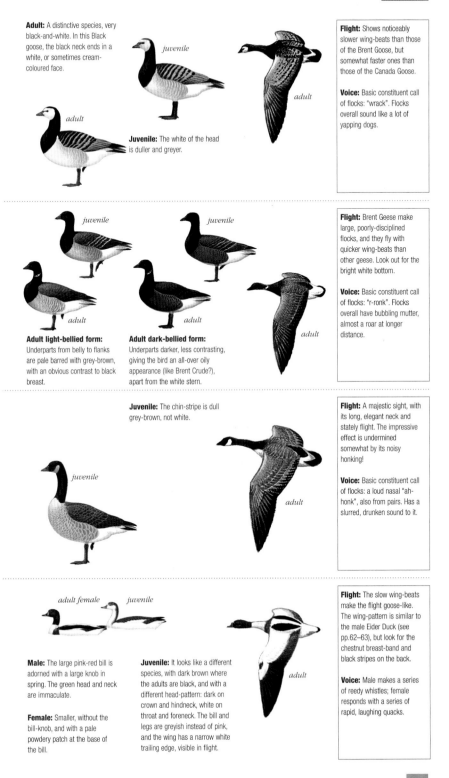

Adult: A distinctive species, very black-and-white. In this Black goose, the black neck ends in a white, or sometimes cream-coloured face.

juvenile

adult

adult

Juvenile: The white of the head is duller and greyer.

Flight: Shows noticeably slower wing-beats than those of the Brent Goose, but somewhat faster ones than those of the Canada Goose.

Voice: Basic constituent call of flocks: "wrack". Flocks overall sound like a lot of yapping dogs.

juvenile

juvenile

adult

adult

adult

Adult light-bellied form: Underparts from belly to flanks are pale barred with grey-brown, with an obvious contrast to black breast.

Adult dark-bellied form: Underparts darker, less contrasting, giving the bird an all-over oily appearance (like Brent Crude?), apart from the white stern.

Flight: Brent Geese make large, poorly-disciplined flocks, and they fly with quicker wing-beats than other geese. Look out for the bright white bottom.

Voice: Basic constituent call of flocks: "r-ronk". Flocks overall have bubbling mutter, almost a roar at longer distance.

Juvenile: The chin-stripe is dull grey-brown, not white.

juvenile

adult

Flight: A majestic sight, with its long, elegant neck and stately flight. The impressive effect is undermined somewhat by its noisy honking!

Voice: Basic constituent call of flocks: a loud nasal "ah-honk", also from pairs. Has a slurred, drunken sound to it.

adult female   *juvenile*

adult

Male: The large pink-red bill is adorned with a large knob in spring. The green head and neck are immaculate.

Female: Smaller, without the bill-knob, and with a pale powdery patch at the base of the bill.

Juvenile: It looks like a different species, with dark brown where the adults are black, and with a different head-pattern: dark on crown and hindneck, white on throat and foreneck. The bill and legs are greyish instead of pink, and the wing has a narrow white trailing edge, visible in flight.

Flight: The slow wing-beats make the flight goose-like. The wing-pattern is similar to the male Eider Duck (see pp.62–63), but look for the chestnut breast-band and black stripes on the back.

Voice: Male makes a series of reedy whistles; female responds with a series of rapid, laughing quacks.

Identifying geese

This section illustrates all seven species of geese featured both standing and in flight to help you identify the species in front of you quickly and easily.

BEAN *(Ground)*: Larger than Pink-foot; wedge-shaped head because of longer bill; long neck; much darker back. Same size, but less heavy-looking, than Greylag. Quite upright and regal. Easier walk than similarly-sized Greylag. Feeds at slower rate than similarly-plumaged Pink-foot. Usually isolated individuals, except in Yare Valley in Norfolk.

(Flight): Like a Greylag without the pale forewing. Neck looks longer.

Bean

PINK-FOOT *(Ground)*: Quite small. Frosty-grey on back. Short neck and bill. Walks more quickly than Greylag or Bean, and feeds faster. Often in huge groups.

(Flight): Grey forewing obvious. Flight buoyant, with quicker wing-beats and with more tumbling than, for example, Greylag or Bean. Sometimes moves some distance between roost (on lakes or estuaries) and feeding sites (fields).

Pink-footed

WHITE-FRONT *(Ground)*: Brownish goose. White forehead and black markings on breast are distinctive. Easy walk. Often in huge flocks, which are shier than the flocks of other species.

(Flight): Characterised by fast wing-beats. The most expert goose in the air, with a particularly fast take-off. Flocks tend to bunch.

White-fronted

GREYLAG (*Ground*): Heavy goose with slow, waddling walk. Large orange bill; neck not very dark. Less gregarious than Pink-foot. Birds of captive origin on park lakes and other habitats in southern England. Tamer than any other Grey geese.

(*Flight*): Grey forewing obvious, contrasts with back and wing-coverts. Rump paler than back. Underwing two-toned. Take-off not easy, requires run-up. Flocks feed near to roosting areas.

BARNACLE (*Ground*): Black neck, white face. Less wary than many other geese. Often feeds further inland than Brent Goose. Often in huge flocks.

(*Flight*): Slower wing-beats than Brent.

BRENT (*Ground*): Small and dark, oily, except for white bottom. Black neck and head except for "neck nick". Essentially coastal, often seen feeding on the sea itself, unlike other geese (feeds on the marine plant Eel-grass). Two races separated by colour of bellies.

(*Flight*): Short neck, quick wing-beats – often do not look like geese. Undisciplined flocks.

CANADA (*Ground*): Big and very brown, but for the long, black neck. White blob on chin. Elegant. Not shy, often found in close proximity to people, unlike all other geese except feral Greylags. Sometimes in large groups. Fairly quiet on ground.

(*Flight*): Slow wing-beats, very long neck. Does not normally fly higher than treetop height, in contrast especially to Grey geese.

MALLARD
Anas platyrhynchos

58cm. This is the largest member of the surface-feeding, or dabbling duck group; they do not dive for their food (ducklings do). The Mallard is a large, long-bodied bird with a bold temperament, making it the commonest and most familiar of all our ducks. Besides those species illustrated here, there are domestic breeds showing many different shapes and plumages.

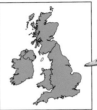

adult male

Where found: Abundant wherever there is water, throughout the year.

Male: Very distinctive; there is a white collar between the green head and purple-brown breast. The black tail curls up. The bill is yellow.

GADWALL
Anas strepera

51cm. Slightly smaller, and definitely more elegant than a Mallard, with a steep forehead offset by the smaller, shorter bill. The Gadwall holds its head up high when swimming, in superior fashion.

adult male

Where found: Scarce but increasing breeding bird, mostly in south-east England, on freshwater. Commoner and more widespread in winter.

Male: Although more soberly-dressed than most drakes, it shows intricate brushwork worthy of an Impressionist painter. The "stern" is black, offset by grey flanks instead of white flanks as in the Wigeon. Bill is dark grey.

WIGEON
Anas penelope

46cm. Another elegant, high crowned duck with a small, light-grey bill; the tail is noticeably pointed.

adult male

Where found: Uncommon breeding bird on upland freshwater, mostly northern. Common and widespread in winter.

Male: A mostly pale grey body is divided by a very conspicuous white mid-line (actually the forewing). The black rear is bordered with white, and the breast is the colour of strawberry ice-cream. A buffy-pink head and neck are crowned by a peach-coloured forehead. The superficially similar male Pochard has a black breast, and dives.

Moults, movements and migration

January–February
During this period adult male and female ducks are in full plumage. In many species pairing takes place at this time – you may see them taking part in courtship displays, but it may have already occurred the previous autumn.

March–May
Most ducks are migratory, with different summer and winter haunts, and during this period they return to their breeding areas. For many this may involve a long journey, for instance from Britain to Iceland or even further. Many species now look at their very best, such as the Long-tailed Duck that has a special spring plumage.

June–September
Males do not take part in incubation or chick-rearing because their colourful plumage would be a liability. Instead they leave the breeding area to go on MOULT MIGRATIONS gathering together in favoured areas. As early as late May they lose their colourful breeding plumage and change into ECLIPSE PLUMAGE. This unobtrusive coloration is necessary as the birds shed all their flight feathers simultaneously and lose the power of flight. Different species show eclipse plumage for different lengths of time, and different individuals of the same species may enter or leave eclipse at slightly different times. Although there are exceptions, in general, by the end of September or October most male

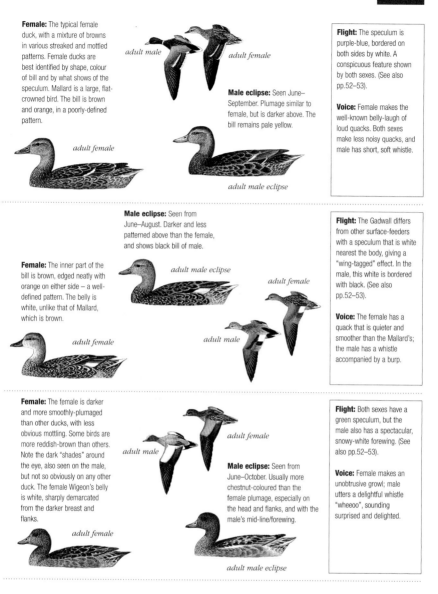

Female: The typical female duck, with a mixture of browns in various streaked and mottled patterns. Female ducks are best identified by shape, colour of bill and by what shows of the speculum. Mallard is a large, flat-crowned bird. The bill is brown and orange, in a poorly-defined pattern.

adult male

adult female

Male eclipse: Seen June–September. Plumage similar to female, but is darker above. The bill remains pale yellow.

adult female

adult male eclipse

Flight: The speculum is purple-blue, bordered on both sides by white. A conspicuous feature shown by both sexes. (See also pp.52–53).

Voice: Female makes the well-known belly-laugh of loud quacks. Both sexes make less noisy quacks, and male has short, soft whistle.

Male eclipse: Seen from June–August. Darker and less patterned above than the female, and shows black bill of male.

Female: The inner part of the bill is brown, edged neatly with orange on either side – a well-defined pattern. The belly is white, unlike that of Mallard, which is brown.

adult male eclipse

adult female

adult female

adult male

Flight: The Gadwall differs from other surface-feeders with a speculum that is white nearest the body, giving a "wing-tagged" effect. In the male, this white is bordered with black. (See also pp.52–53).

Voice: The female has a quack that is quieter and smoother than the Mallard's; the male has a whistle accompanied by a burp.

Female: The female is darker and more smoothly-plumaged than other ducks, with less obvious mottling. Some birds are more reddish-brown than others. Note the dark "shades" around the eye, also seen on the male, but not so obviously on any other duck. The female Wigeon's belly is white, sharply demarcated from the darker breast and flanks.

adult male

adult female

Male eclipse: Seen from June–October. Usually more chestnut-coloured than the female plumage, especially on the head and flanks, and with the male's mid-line/forewing.

adult female

adult male eclipse

Flight: Both sexes have a green speculum, but the male also has a spectacular, snowy-white forewing. (See also pp.52–53).

Voice: Female makes an unobtrusive growl; male utters a delightful whistle "wheeoo", sounding surprised and delighted.

---

ducks are back to their old colourful selves. The females remain in their breeding area to look after the young and do not undergo moult migrations (apart from the Shelduck). They enter into eclipse later than the males, but it looks little different to their usual plumage.

October–December

This is the time when the migrant birds return to their wintering grounds (usually different from their breeding and moulting grounds). Male birds tend to arrive first and may so dominate a suitable location that the females have to fly further on to find one for themselves. In some species of waterfowl, such as the Smew, the sexes are segregated by

different migrations. The males winter near home, while the females must move further south and west. That is one reason why we see more females than males in Britain.

Birds which hatched in the summer soon face their first winter. They are called FIRST-WINTERS and sport first-winter plumage. In most species (eg. Mallard) first-winter plumage resembles that of the adult, but there are exceptions, such as the Shoveler, whose young males do not look like adults until at least the end of the year. The process is even more complicated for the Eider and Long-tailed Ducks who seem to have a wardrobe for every occasion!

Identifying ducks in flight

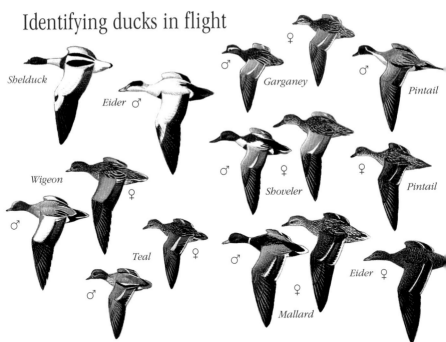

This spread shows all our featured ducks in flight, giving information particularly on their method and style of flight. Pay attention too to the SPECULUM (the often colourful bar made by the secondaries), and to the colour of the forewings.

White forewing contrasting with dark hindwing

Shelduck (both sexes): Takes off with run. Goose-like, slow wing-beats.
Eider (male): Laboured take-off from water. Very fast, powerful flight low over the sea, often in lines. Stocky, short-winged. Head held low.
Wigeon (male): Springing take-off. Long, narrow wings and short neck; obviously pointed tail. Often in tight flocks, high overhead.

Green speculum

Wigeon (both sexes): Often seen together, when male's forewing obvious.
Teal (both sexes): Quickfire, springing take-off, almost vertical. Distinctive: flies in tight groups on rapid wing-beats, twisting and turning like a group of waders, erratically.
Garganey (both sexes): Springing take-off, but not as agile as Teal, and not subject to such erratic flight. Looks longer-bodied.
Pintail (male): Springy take-off. Rapid wing-beats, often in tight flocks, sometimes high up. In many ways similar to Wigeon, but is, of course, longer tailed.
Shoveler (both sexes): Springing take-off, to accompaniment of distinctive wing-rattle. Wings set far back, beats rapid. Small flocks often fly high.

Brown speculum bordered by white

Pintail (female): Actually bronzy, bordered by white (beware of Mallard).
Eider (female): Big, dumpy duck, usually low over sea.

Purplish-blue speculum

Mallard (both sexes): Happily, this common duck has a unique purplish speculum bordered by white. Rises

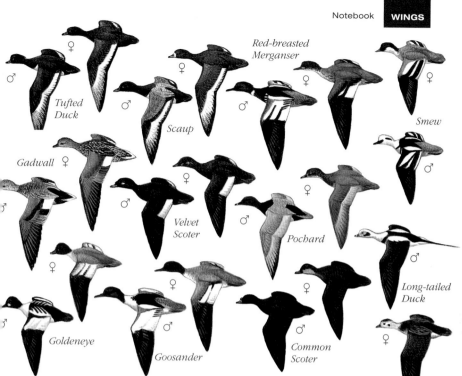

spring-like. Steady but still fast, distinctively shallow wing-beats on quite broad wings. Often, of course, in large groups.

Trailing half of wing mostly white

Tufted Duck (both sexes): Rises with greater ease than Pochard or Scaup, but less than surface-feeders. Rapid wing-beats, much faster than Mallard.
Scaup (both sexes): Rises with difficulty, but similar to Tufted Duck.

Inner half of wing has white trailing edge

Gadwall (both sexes): Rises with spring. Pointed wings with rapid wing-beat. In small groups only. Looks "wing-tagged".
Velvet Scoter (both sexes): Rises from surface of water with some difficulty. Usually seen flying low over sea.
Goldeneye (both sexes): Springs from water, flies easily and often, usually low. Quick wing-beats make unique singing note, like miniature Mute Swan.
Goosander (both sexes): Rises with difficulty. Flight powerful, straight and

rigid. Very cigar-shaped. Very long neck is noticeable. Wings make hum.
Red-breasted Merganser (both sexes): As Goosander, but wings are quieter. Also bird is smaller.
Smew (both sexes): Trailing edge of white is very thin, wings have complex black-and-white pattern. Easy take-off and fast, agile flight.

Wings somewhat featureless

Pochard (both sexes): Trailing half appears significantly paler. Rises with difficulty. Short wings, large body, but fast, powerful flight on rapid wing-beats.
Common Scoter: Rises fairly easily, more so than Velvet. Flies in long lines over sea, sometimes high (more so than Eiders of same habitat).
Long-tailed Duck: Very distinctive. When flying, swings from side to side, one moment showing white underparts, the next showing dark upperparts, like a fat Shearwater. Wings do not rise much above body, and has deep downstroke. Usually seen over sea.

PINTAIL
Anas acuta

66cm. A large, very elegant, tapered duck; the eponymous long tail is rivalled by an equally long neck, which is held up in regal fashion. Both sexes have a lead-grey bill.

adult male

Where found: Rare breeding bird on freshwater in scattered localities; much commoner and more widespread in winter, but local.

Male: The grey body does not show a white mid-line. With its long tail, and chocolate-brown head split by a white "crack", this bird should present no problems.

SHOVELER
Anas clypeata

51cm. Quite small, but with a ridiculously outsized bill making it look front-heavy, and not at all elegant. When the bird is feeding, the shovel-shaped bill appears to be stuck to the water surface.

adult male

Where found: Uncommon breeding bird on a few scattered freshwater marshes. Common in winter, mostly southern and western.

Male: The white breast is a surprisingly useful feature at long distance but it is important to remember that the Pintail and Shelduck also have this feature. The chestnut-red belly and flanks are unique.

TEAL
Anas crecca

35cm. The smallest British duck, tiny and neckless. In its foraging behaviour and flight, it seems to think it is a wader, not a duck.

adult male

Where found: Fairly common breeding bird, mostly northern. Common in many habitats in winter.

Male: A black-and-white mid-line cuts the dark-grey body in two, a good field-mark from distance. The bottom is buttery yellow, like Pintail's. A swirl of green, bordered by gold, breaks into the red-chestnut head, like a modern-art painting.

GARGANEY
Anas querquedula

38cm. Our second smallest duck, shy, uncommon, and a summer visitor only. The shape is similar to Teal, but it is distinctly longer bodied and front-heavy.

adult male

Where found: Rare breeding bird in freshwater marshes. Summer visitor from March–September.

Male: The male has a unique crescent-like white eyebrow set against its bran-coloured head and neck; otherwise greyish.

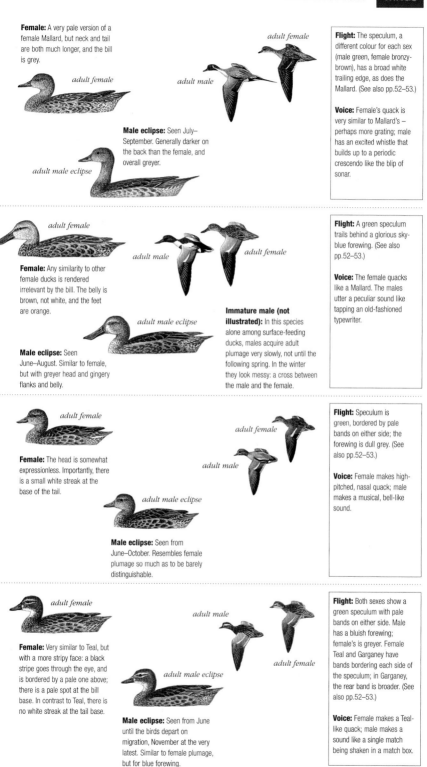

Female: A very pale version of a female Mallard, but neck and tail are both much longer, and the bill is grey.

adult female

adult male

adult female

Male eclipse: Seen July–September. Generally darker on the back than the female, and overall greyer.

adult male eclipse

Flight: The speculum, a different colour for each sex (male green, female bronzy-brown), has a broad white trailing edge, as does the Mallard. (See also pp.52–53.)

Voice: Female's quack is very similar to Mallard's – perhaps more grating; male has an excited whistle that builds up to a periodic crescendo like the blip of sonar.

adult female

Female: Any similarity to other female ducks is rendered irrelevant by the bill. The belly is brown, not white, and the feet are orange.

adult male

adult female

adult male eclipse

Male eclipse: Seen June–August. Similar to female, but with greyer head and gingery flanks and belly.

Immature male (not illustrated): In this species alone among surface-feeding ducks, males acquire adult plumage very slowly, not until the following spring. In the winter they look messy: a cross between the male and the female.

Flight: A green speculum trails behind a glorious sky-blue forewing. (See also pp.52–53.)

Voice: The female quacks like a Mallard. The males utter a peculiar sound like tapping an old-fashioned typewriter.

adult female

Female: The head is somewhat expressionless. Importantly, there is a small white streak at the base of the tail.

adult female

adult male

adult male eclipse

Male eclipse: Seen from June–October. Resembles female plumage so much as to be barely distinguishable.

Flight: Speculum is green, bordered by pale bands on either side; the forewing is dull grey. (See also pp.52–53.)

Voice: Female makes high-pitched, nasal quack; male makes a musical, bell-like sound.

adult female

Female: Very similar to Teal, but with a more stripy face: a black stripe goes through the eye, and is bordered by a pale one above; there is a pale spot at the bill base. In contrast to Teal, there is no white streak at the tail base.

adult male

adult female

adult male eclipse

Male eclipse: Seen from June until the birds depart on migration, November at the very latest. Similar to female plumage, but for blue forewing.

Flight: Both sexes show a green speculum with pale bands on either side. Male has a bluish forewing; female's is greyer. Female Teal and Garganey have bands bordering each side of the speculum; in Garganey, the rear band is broader. (See also pp.52–53.)

Voice: Female makes a Teal-like quack; male makes a sound like a single match being shaken in a match box.

The ecology of ducks: freshwater

Many species of ducks can be seen on freshwater or on the sea at various times in their lives, but most have a preference for one or the other. Within each habitat the different species take different types of food in different ways and in different conditions.

Surface-feeders
Surface-feeding ducks feed from the surface using the techniques of dabbling, head-dipping and upending.

The following three species feed almost exclusively in freshwater.

Gadwall – this duck is an exclusive vegetarian and feeds mostly by head-dipping. Unusually, its ducklings are vegetarians; other ducklings feed largely on flies and other insects. Gadwalls often feed with Coots who provide a useful service: Coots dive for the same type of vegetation as Gadwalls but must bring it to the surface to eat. The Gadwalls then repeatedly steal food from the Coots.

Garganey – secretive and marsh-loving. Plant and animal material is obtained mostly by head-dipping.

Shoveler – very much a specialist on animal food. The huge bill filters the water, which enters through the front of the bill, forced in by the forward movement of the bird, and it is expelled through the sides, forced out by the tongue. The sides of the mandibles have a special "mesh" which traps any edible particles caught in this current, which are then eaten. For most effective feeding, Shovelers need to forage in small groups. They follow one behind the other, in circles; mud kicked up by the bird in front is filtered by the bird behind, which kicks up mud for the bird behind it, and so on.

The remaining surface-feeders are less specialised, able to feed in brackish or salt-water as well as freshwater.

Mallard – mostly a freshwater species. Feeds using many techniques, from snapping for flies, to dabbling for seeds, to pleading for bread from visitors to city parks. Not surprisingly, it is our most successful duck.

Teal – this duck has a catholic diet, although it probably prefers plant material. Males mostly feed in the water, by head-dipping and upending; females feed more by filtering the mud at the water's edge, thus avoiding competition. Teals feed in freshwater and salt-marshes in winter, and are mostly found in acidic bogs, and nutrient-poor marshy tarns during the breeding season.

Pintail – breeds by freshwater but winters both on inland sites and on estuaries. It has an unspecialised bill, but its long neck makes it the professional upender among ducks, able to reach down deeper than any other. Inland, most birds feed on plant matter, but on estuaries they take more animal food.

Wigeon – has the same breeding and wintering habitats as the Pintail but is a specialist grazer, with a small bill served by a strong jawbone. Feeds mostly out of water, taking grass from inland locations, and seaweed and other estuarine plants from coasts.

Diving ducks
Tufted Duck – is almost exclusively confined to freshwater where it dives down to about 3m (9ft) to obtain mostly animal material, often gleaning from the vegetation. In Britain, many individuals take large numbers of the Zebra Mussel, but they also take other molluscs, small fish, and some plant material.

Mallard upending

Pintail taking off (above) and upending (below)

Gadwall

Wigeon grazing

Tufted Duck diving

Goldeneye – has similar tastes, though it takes a higher proportion of more mobile prey, and often from deeper down. Unlike the Tufted Duck it regularly winters on the sea.

Pochard – is mostly a vegetarian. Its dives are relatively shallow, and it almost always shuns the sea. Unlike the diving ducks which feed mostly on animal prey, the Pochard is presumably able to hunt just as easily by night as by day, since many flocks seem to spend their daylight hours asleep.

The two following species of diving ducks, known as Sawbills, specialise on fish. The third species of Sawbill is the Red-breasted Merganser (see pp.60–61).

Smew – this small bird takes small fish (3–6cm, 1–3in). It feeds on freshwater although may inhabit offshore waters in winter.

Goosander – also a freshwater feeder but takes larger fish than the Smew, thus avoiding competition, and is restricted to large, deep lakes.

POCHARD
Aythya ferina

46cm. Diving ducks are more streamlined than surface-feeding ducks, and tend to hold their rear-ends down, not up. The Pochard has a distinctive head shape, with a flat forehead giving a neat slope from the tip of the bill to the top of the head. The male has red eyes, the female brown.

adult male

Where found: Widespread but not common breeding bird, common in winter.

Male: Tricoloured, with black front and rear, ashy grey in the middle, and a chestnut head and neck.

TUFTED DUCK
Aythya fuligula

43cm. A very common duck that fearlessly inhabits many freshwater habitats including park lakes. Often found in the company of Pochards, from which it can be distinguished by its rounded, not sloping forehead. At closer range, the yellow eye can be seen.

adult male

Where found: Widespread and common year-round, mostly on freshwater.

Male: Bold black-and-white, with a drooping crest and a purplish tinge to the head and neck. Young males are similar but for duskier flanks where the adults are dazzling white.

SCAUP
Aythya marila

48cm. Compared to the similar Tufted Duck, the Scaup is a larger, front-heavy bird, with a heavier bill and a rounded head which curves smoothly round the back in the absence of a crest. It looks broader-beamed in the water.

adult male

Where found: Very rare nesting duck on freshwater, mostly north-western; quite widespread, but seldom common, off coasts in winter.

Male: Differs from Tufted Duck by having a grey, not black back, and a greenish, not purplish, gloss to the head and neck. At a distance, the mid-body looks all-white behind the black neck and breast.

Breeds, introductions and hybrids

With over 30 species to choose from, each with their own male, female, eclipse and even immature plumages, wildfowl would appear to pose enough identification difficulties for the birdwatcher, but there are further confusions. Here we mention some additional pitfalls – breeds, introduced species and hybrids.

Breeds
The Mallard has been domesticated for many centuries, since both eggs and flesh are good to eat. Over the years, special breeds have been created, each with their own characteristics. They vary not only in colour from the ancestral Mallard, but also in size and shape. Breeds will not necessarily mate with others of the same breed if they escape from captivity (which they frequently do), and this results in further interbreeding and genetic mixing.

Introduced species
There are about 150 species of wildfowl in the world, many of which are kept in captivity in waterfowl collections around the country. The following four species of exotic wildfowl are commonly seen in Britain.
Egyptian Goose: (70cm) this species is a close relative of the Shelduck (see pp.46–47) but is slightly larger with longer legs. It can be distinguished by "sunglasses" or darker patches around its eyes and a spot on the breast. Its walking

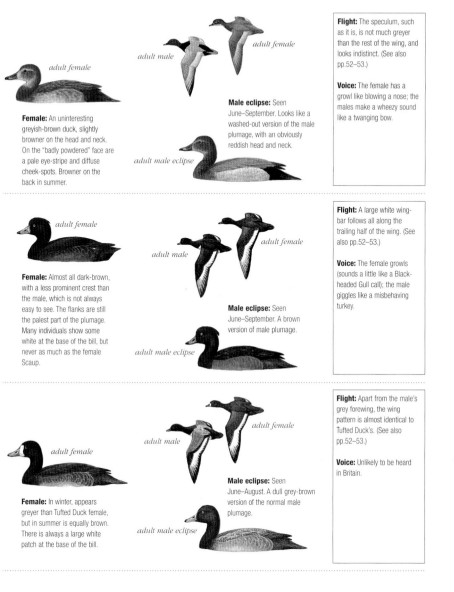

adult female

adult male

adult female

Flight: The speculum, such as it is, is not much greyer than the rest of the wing, and looks indistinct. (See also pp.52–53.)

Voice: The female has a growl like blowing a nose; the males make a wheezy sound like a twanging bow.

Male eclipse: Seen June–September. Looks like a washed-out version of the male plumage, with an obviously reddish head and neck.

adult male eclipse

adult female

Female: An uninteresting greyish-brown duck, slightly browner on the head and neck. On the "badly powdered" face are a pale eye-stripe and diffuse cheek-spots. Browner on the back in summer.

---

adult female

adult male

adult female

Flight: A large white wing-bar follows all along the trailing half of the wing. (See also pp.52–53.)

Voice: The female growls (sounds a little like a Black-headed Gull call); the male giggles like a misbehaving turkey.

Male eclipse: Seen June–September. A brown version of male plumage.

adult male eclipse

Female: Almost all dark-brown, with a less prominent crest than the male, which is not always easy to see. The flanks are still the palest part of the plumage. Many individuals show some white at the base of the bill, but never as much as the female Scaup.

---

adult female

adult male

adult female

Flight: Apart from the male's grey forewing, the wing pattern is almost identical to Tufted Duck's. (See also pp.52–53.)

Voice: Unlikely to be heard in Britain.

Male eclipse: Seen June–August. A dull grey-brown version of the normal male plumage.

adult male eclipse

Female: In winter, appears greyer than Tufted Duck female, but in summer is equally brown. There is always a large white patch at the base of the bill.

---

action is lighter than that of many other waterfowl, and its feeding action is brisk. It is well-established in Norfolk but is rare elsewhere. (See illustration on p.15.)

Mandarin: (43cm) a small surface-feeding duck with rather dainty movements. The male is unmistakable with neck-plumes and wing-sails the colour of mandarin oranges. The female is small and grey with streaked sides. Found on freshwater lakes surrounded by woodland, mainly in southern England but is expanding rapidly. (See illustration on p.15.)

Red-crested Pochard: (56cm) a large duck, it appears buoyant and long-bodied in the water. The male has a stunning chestnut-red head. The centre of the body is brown above, whitish below. Legs and bill are red. The female is

pale brown and is distinguished by head pattern: white cheeks bordered by a white crown and hindneck. Scarce resident; wild birds from Continental Europe also visit.

Ruddy Duck. (41cm) a tiny diving duck that cannot actually walk on land. It holds its tail up at an angle of 45°. The male is ruddy-coloured, with white cheeks bordered with black, and a bright blue bill. The female is a duller brown bird. The Ruddy Duck is a local resident mainly in central England. (See illustration on p.15.)

Hybrids

Closely-related species of wildfowl will hybridise, such as the Grey geese and the diving ducks of the genus *Aythya*.

The ecology of ducks: saltwater

Seven species of ducks commonly make use of salt and brackish water, in preference to freshwater. Of these, the Shelduck (see pp.46–47) is primarily an estuarine bird, except when moulting. It does not dive below the surface of the water, in contrast to all the other ducks described below.

Eider – the best known of our seaducks, breeding very commonly around our coasts, and inhabiting much the same places in winter. Flocks of Eiders usually stay within sight of land, feeding in the shallow water around estuaries and rocky shores. The large bill has powerful jaws, which can crack open the shells of their favourite food, molluscs, although Eiders also take a selection of other animal items, including crustaceans and starfish. When diving, this heavy duck puts its head into the water, half opens its wings, and slips under; there is no hint of a forward jump.

Common and *Velvet Scoter* – scoters are similar in many ways to the Eider, although both species nest by freshwater (only the Common Scoter breeds in Britain). In winter, both feed on a diet of molluscs and other animals, which are obtained by diving in reasonably shallow water. Usually, the Common Scoter prefers sheltered waters off the coast, but not necessarily close to land; the Velvet Scoter comes closer in, to feed among the more agitated water around rocky shores. Birdwatchers have noticed several subtle differences in the behaviour of the two scoters, which help in their identification. While feeding or loafing, Common Scoters are usually in large, tight flocks, which are organised, and often synchronise their dives; Velvet Scoters

occur in small, more scattered flocks which often swim in single file. When diving, Common Scoters tend to leap forward, submerging with their wings closed; Velvet Scoters dive like an Eider, without a leap and with their wings partly open. Finally, when flapping their wings and stretching (a form of "comfort behaviour", much as we might do after watching television), the Common Scoter thrusts its head and neck downwards, whereas the Velvet Scoter keeps its head and bill above the horizontal plane. When viewing scoters on the water, the first two hints are merely a useful pointer, whereas the differing characteristics of the "flap-stretch" are peculiar to each bird.

Scaup – another species that likes to feed around bays and estuaries in winter, although it also nests by freshwater. Quite at home in rough weather, it dives with expertise, often performing a high forward leap before entering the water. Large flocks of these birds dive for the usual molluscs and crustaceans, but they have a more varied diet than other seaducks, and are alone in taking a fair amount of plant material. Scaup flocks often feed at night, sometimes preferentially.

Red-breasted Merganser – like other sawbills this species feeds very largely on fish and therefore does not compete with the other seaducks we have met so far. It prefers shallow waters close to the shore, especially estuaries, where it dives with great expertise.

Long-tailed Duck – the best diver and the species best adapted to coping with the sea in all its moods. This multi-talented species is a superb diver

Eider

Common
Scoter

Red-breasted Merganser

Long-tailed
Duck

and flier, and in its breeding range in the tundra can nest by both fresh and saltwater. Flocks ride out the swells far out to sea, often out of sight of land, right through the winter. A few do come closer inshore, too. They can probably dive deeper than other seaducks: a depth of 10m (30ft) is regular, and up to 55m (180ft) has been claimed for birds trapped in nets. Not surprisingly, birds dive with a forward leap and, no doubt, a very deep breath! From the studies that have been made, it seems that the Long-tailed Duck takes much the same foods as the other seaducks, including those hard-pressed molluscs.

COMMON SCOTER
Melanitta nigra

48cm. A small, compact diving duck with a squarish head which is usually seen in rafts on the sea. The legs are blackish.

adult male

Male: This is the only duck with entirely black plumage. There is a yellow patch on the upper part of the bill.

Where found: Rare breeding species on freshwater in northern Scotland and Ireland. Common off many coasts in winter.

VELVET SCOTER
Melanitta fusca

56cm. A larger bird than the Common Scoter, almost as big as an Eider, with a more sloping forehead than Common Scoter, and a larger bill. The legs are red.

adult male

Where found: An uncommon winter visitor only, to a few selected coasts, mostly by North Sea.

Male: The black plumage is relieved by a small white tear-drop around the eye (hard to see), and by the white hindwing (also not always visible). The larger amount of yellow on the bill can be seen at long range.

EIDER
Somateria mollissima

58cm. A common seaduck with an overweight appearance and no sense of hurry. The large, powerful bill fits comfortably into the head, giving a long, straight forehead. The frontal lobes of the bill reach up towards the eye, to make a "nose".

adult male

Where found: Seen off many coasts in winter, and breeds commonly, mostly in Scotland and Northern Ireland.

Male: Several duck species are black above and light below, but the male Eider reverses this, adding an apricot-coloured breast and black crown. The nape is incongruously coloured marzipan-green, with a white streak separating the two "chunks".

LONG-TAILED DUCK
Clangula hyemalis

53cm/41cm. A small seaduck, which despite its many plumages is usually quite easy to identify. An alert species which is always diving or taking flight. This is the only British duck with very distinct summer and winter plumages; there is also eclipse plumage, and a variety of immature plumages.

adult male summer

Where found: A winter visitor off many coasts, but more common in the north.

Male summer: Seen in May and June, a distinctive but uncommon sight. It keeps the head and neck pattern for much of the summer, then whitens as autumn progresses.

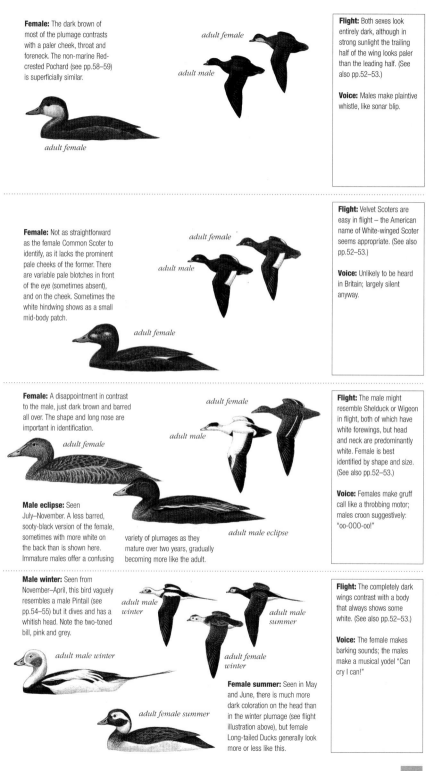

Female: The dark brown of most of the plumage contrasts with a paler cheek, throat and foreneck. The non-marine Red-crested Pochard (see pp.58–59) is superficially similar.

adult female

adult female

adult male

Flight: Both sexes look entirely dark, although in strong sunlight the trailing half of the wing looks paler than the leading half. (See also pp.52–53.)

Voice: Males make plaintive whistle, like sonar blip.

Female: Not as straightforward as the female Common Scoter to identify, as it lacks the prominent pale cheeks of the former. There are variable pale blotches in front of the eye (sometimes absent), and on the cheek. Sometimes the white hindwing shows as a small mid-body patch.

adult female

adult male

adult female

Flight: Velvet Scoters are easy in flight – the American name of White-winged Scoter seems appropriate. (See also pp.52–53.)

Voice: Unlikely to be heard in Britain; largely silent anyway.

Female: A disappointment in contrast to the male, just dark brown and barred all over. The shape and long nose are important in identification.

adult female

adult female

adult male

Male eclipse: Seen July–November. A less barred, sooty-black version of the female, sometimes with more white on the back than is shown here. Immature males offer a confusing variety of plumages as they mature over two years, gradually becoming more like the adult.

adult male eclipse

Flight: The male might resemble Shelduck or Wigeon in flight, both of which have white forewings, but head and neck are predominantly white. Female is best identified by shape and size. (See also pp.52–53.)

Voice: Females make gruff call like a throbbing motor; males croon suggestively: "oo-OOO-oo!"

Male winter: Seen from November–April, this bird vaguely resembles a male Pintail (see pp.54–55) but it dives and has a whitish head. Note the two-toned bill, pink and grey.

adult male winter

adult male winter

adult female winter

adult male summer

adult female summer

Female summer: Seen in May and June, there is much more dark coloration on the head than in the winter plumage (see flight illustration above), but female Long-tailed Ducks generally look more or less like this.

Flight: The completely dark wings contrast with a body that always shows some white. (See also pp.52–53.)

Voice: The female makes barking sounds; the males make a musical yodel "Can cry I can!"

GOLDENEYE
Bucephala clangula

46cm. A small duck with a readily recognisable shape: the head is peaked, almost triangular, as if the bird had received a bump on it. The head, moreover, seems too large for the neck.

adult male

Where found: Nests in tree-holes in forests in Scotland and northern England; rare. Widespread in many habitats in winter.

Male: Resembles the male Tufted Duck, which shares the same freshwater lakes in winter, but has a white breast, a green gloss on its head, and a round white "blob of paint" between the bill and the eye.

SMEW
Mergus albellus

41cm. Another small duck, not much larger than a Teal, but easy to recognise. One of three British "Sawbill" ducks, which have long bills with serrated edges for holding slippery fish.

adult male

Where found: Very scarce winter visitor, mostly to south-east England.

Male: Unmistakable, but so white that it can be difficult to see at a distance.

RED-BREASTED MERGANSER
Mergus serrator

55cm. Apart from Smew, the Sawbills are large, angular ducks with long necks and long bodies. They are generally shy. The Red-breasted Merganser is the smaller, more marine species. The conspicuous long red bill is slightly slimmer than that of the Goosander.

adult male

Where found: Breeds on rivers and sealochs in Scotland, Ireland, Wales and the Lake District; western. Common in winter off many coasts.

Male: The "punk duck", with its unkempt, spiky crest. When seen properly, this bird looks like no other.

GOOSANDER
Mergus merganser

62cm. This species is larger and longer than its close relative the Red-breasted Merganser, and its long, bushy "hair" flops down in a bob instead of sticking out crazily.

adult male

Where found: Breeds on rivers in upland areas throughout much of our area, but not Ireland. Winters on freshwater lakes in many areas, but again, not Ireland.

Male: The white body is fitted with too large a head. The breast is white, often tinged with cream.

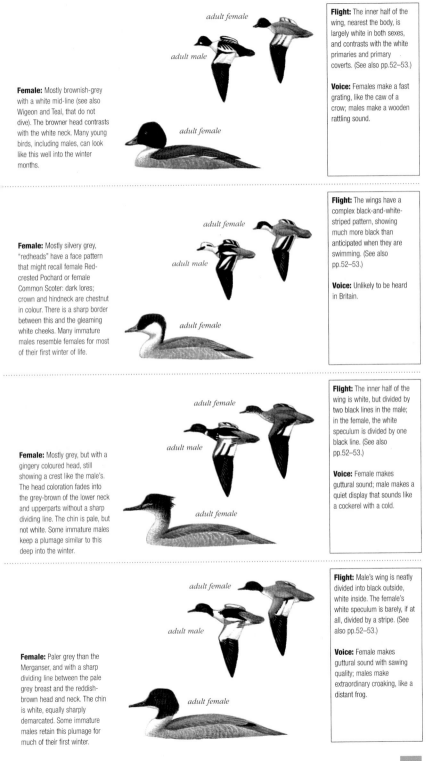

Flight: The inner half of the wing, nearest the body, is largely white in both sexes, and contrasts with the white primaries and primary coverts. (See also pp.52–53.)

Voice: Females make a fast grating, like the caw of a crow; males make a wooden rattling sound.

adult female

adult male

adult female

Female: Mostly brownish-grey with a white mid-line (see also Wigeon and Teal, that do not dive). The browner head contrasts with the white neck. Many young birds, including males, can look like this well into the winter months.

Flight: The wings have a complex black-and-white-striped pattern, showing much more black than anticipated when they are swimming. (See also pp.52–53.)

Voice: Unlikely to be heard in Britain.

adult female

adult male

adult female

Female: Mostly silvery grey, "redheads" have a face pattern that might recall female Red-crested Pochard or female Common Scoter: dark lores; crown and hindneck are chestnut in colour. There is a sharp border between this and the gleaming white cheeks. Many immature males resemble females for most of their first winter of life.

Flight: The inner half of the wing is white, but divided by two black lines in the male; in the female, the white speculum is divided by one black line. (See also pp.52–53.)

Voice: Female makes guttural sound; male makes a quiet display that sounds like a cockerel with a cold.

adult female

adult male

adult female

Female: Mostly grey, but with a gingery coloured head, still showing a crest like the male's. The head coloration fades into the grey-brown of the lower neck and upperparts without a sharp dividing line. The chin is pale, but not white. Some immature males keep a plumage similar to this deep into the winter.

Flight: Male's wing is neatly divided into black outside, white inside. The female's white speculum is barely, if at all, divided by a stripe. (See also pp.52–53.)

Voice: Female makes guttural sound with sawing quality; males make extraordinary croaking, like a distant frog.

adult female

adult male

adult female

Female: Paler grey than the Merganser, and with a sharp dividing line between the pale grey breast and the reddish-brown head and neck. The chin is white, equally sharply demarcated. Some immature males retain this plumage for much of their first winter.

OSPREY
Pandion haliaetus

55cm. A large, Buzzard-sized, long-winged raptor that specialises in eating fish. The Osprey is usually found near water, so beware of confusion with a large gull, which also has long, bowed wings.

Adult: The pale underparts and head make this species obvious; there is a dark breast band (more obvious in the female), and a broad black stripe through the eye. Slightly crested. The legs are blue.

adult

Where found: A rare summer visitor, March–October. Although passage birds are often seen in England, this species currently breeds only in Scotland, especially the central Highlands.

WHITE-TAILED EAGLE
Haliaeetus albicilla

70–90cm. This bird is simply enormous, imposingly so. The great, broad wings, straight-edged and clearly fingered, are offset by a rather short head and tail. The flight profile has been compared to both a vulture and a flying door!

adult

Where found: A very rare resident in the Inner Hebrides of Scotland; the population stems from deliberate reintroductions. Mostly found on the coast, nesting on cliffs.

Adult: All over dark brown, but the head can be much paler. The tail is, not surprisingly, white. The huge bill is yellow, and the legs are half feathered, like baggy shorts.

GOLDEN EAGLE
Aquila chrysaetos

80cm. Another huge bird, easily dwarfing the Buzzards that share its home. The Golden Eagle has a pleasing, even profile, with a much longer tail than the White-tailed Eagle's. The tail is slightly rounded, and certainly not wedge-shaped.

adult

Where found: A rare resident, virtually confined to Scotland but quite widespread there. Inhabits the more remote mountains and glens; hard to find.

Adult: Brown all over, the colour of well-polished antique furniture, with a paler, golden-brown head and nape. The bill is black-and-yellow, and the legs are completely feathered.

Hunting methods and diet of birds of prey

Our birds of prey adopt a variety of strategies for obtaining their prey. The degree to which a certain type of prey predominates in a species' diet varies, too, ranging from the true specialist (eg. Osprey) to the true generalist (eg. Buzzard). Here we aim to show which species take which type of prey and how, and in many cases, this will help to identify them.

Osprey
The Osprey is a specialist, plunge-diving into water for fish. The hunting bird at first circles high over a lake (or the sea), prospecting. When prey is sighted it hovers over the spot, often reducing its height stepwise and adjusting for

movements below. The final lunge, sometimes from 30m (100ft), is spectacular: the bird enters the water feet-first with a great splash, sometimes going a metre or more below the surface. If the dive has been successful, the fish will be carried away in both feet, torpedo-like, to a perch where it can be eaten.

White-tailed Eagle
The White-tailed Eagle also takes fish from the water, though usually with a quick snatch as it flies low and level. This great bird has quite a catholic diet: besides fish, it also takes birds and mammals, either alive after a short chase and snatch, or dead as carrion. White-tailed Eagles often take

juvenile

The adult Osprey's long, angled wings give it a silhouette reminiscent of a gull. It is also identifiable by its comparatively small head. Strong legs and feet, long claws, scales on the underside of toes, and a reversable outer toe help the Osprey when hunting for fish. You are most likely to see one near a lake or river, either perched in a tree or flying over the water.

Juvenile: Paler in colour, with creamy tips to the feathers on the upperparts making it look spotted at close range. There is more streaking on the crown.

Flight: Whitish from below, with black wing-tips, black carpal patches and a black line formed by the greater wing-coverts.

Voice: The alarm call is a whistled "pew-pew", fairly similar to a Green Woodpecker's call. The male also makes a mournful cheeping.

Juvenile: Young birds are darker than the adults, at first with brown tails and dark bills. Immature birds take about five years to acquire full adult plumage.

Flight (adult): The short, white, wedge-shaped tail makes them unmistakable.

Flight (juvenile): No white tail, darker head. Below there is a pale panel in mid-wing and pale "arm-pit" spots.

Voice: In display, both sexes make a raucous stuttering: that of the female recalls a Raven, that of the male recalls a Green Woodpecker's laugh.

Juvenile: Even when perched, young birds show the white at the tail-base that separates them from fully-grown birds. They acquire adult plumage at about six years.

Flight (adult): These birds look relatively unpatterned from below in comparison to most other birds of prey.

Flight (juvenile): White tail base, and very prominent white patch in the middle of the wing. There is still white, but less, on the upperwing.

Voice: Largely silent, but makes almost pathetic yelping sounds, mostly at the nest.

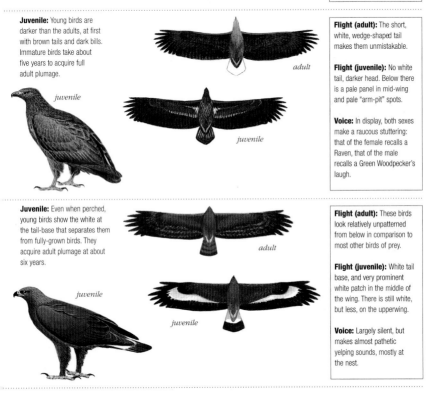

advantage of abattoirs, fisheries or anywhere there are dead and dying bodies, and may also rob smaller predators.

Golden Eagle
The Golden Eagle searches lonely, open mountains and moorland for an impressive range of prey. It flies at a moderate height and at slow speed ("quartering"), hoping to flush prey out of its hiding place so that it can finish it off with a quick pounce. Sometimes Golden Eagle pairs hunt co-operatively, one bird disturbing, while the other catches. Birds up to the size of grouse are taken, and mammals as large as deer. In the Scottish Highlands Mountain Hares are a particular favourite. Many eagles also take carrion.

Kestrel (see pp.78–79)
The Kestrel, our commonest bird of prey, is something of a generalist, but is famous for its hovering. Birds hang in the air, usually flying into the wind ("passive" hovering), holding their heads still as their wings beat rapidly. If prey is sighted, the bird will often move downwards in "steps" before a final, feet-first plunge. Small mammals are the main quarry. Kestrels also take birds in a more direct, Sparrowhawk-type approach. On occasions they will also dive down from a perch, or even walk along the ground to catch beetles and worms. It is not surprising, of course, that such a common bird can use so many hunting methods; adaptability means success.

Flight actions and profiles of birds of prey

The way a bird of prey flies, and the shape it assumes while doing it, will often determine an identification, even at great distance. These pages will help provide some clues.

Osprey – Soars with bowed wings: primaries down, inner wing up; gives impression of large gull. Glides with carpals projecting forward. Flaps slowly in normal flight. Often hovers and circles over water. Long wings are quite narrow.

White-tailed Eagle – Soars with flat or slightly raised wings, slightly arched. Often flies very high. Glides with horizontal but slightly arched wings, giving a very fingered look. In normal flight mostly flaps, with short glides in between. Huge, broad wings, short tail.

Golden Eagle – Soars with wings raised in shallow V. Glides with less of a V, or even with wings flat. In normal flight, 6–7 deep wing-beats are followed by a glide. An effortless, majestic flier, often hanging on the wind, or circling. Longish tail, longer than head.

Honey Buzzard – Soars with wings held flat, tail fanned. Glides with wings arched downwards, angled back, tail closed and steering. In normal flight, flaps without stiffness of Buzzard, more flexibility. Does not hover. Long tail, small head. Wings pinched in.

Buzzard – Soars with wings in shallow V upward, tail fanned. Glides with flat wings. In normal flight, alternates stiff, shallow flaps with glides. Hovers and hangs in wind. Thick neck, short tail, wings not pinched in.

Rough-legged Buzzard – Soars with wings raised in shallow V, tail fanned. Glides on wings slightly raised, mostly at carpals. Alternates glides with looser flaps than Buzzard. Hovers a great deal, hangs on wind. Typically looks longer-winged than Buzzard.

Red Kite – Soars with wings kinked, carpals up, primaries down. Glides with similar shape, but wings pressed back. In normal flight, makes heavy wing-beats, but highly manoeuvrable. Tends to droop head and tail down when flying. Very distinctive flight profile.

Immature White-tailed Eagle in flight

Common Buzzard
gliding

Golden Eagle
soaring

Honey Buzzard
gliding

Rough-legged
Buzzard

Osprey
fishing

HONEY BUZZARD
Pernis apivorus

55cm. This large bird of prey has a distinctive flight shape which readily distinguishes it from all other similar-sized relatives – long, narrow wings pinched in at the body; long tail with rounded corners; small, projecting head and neck, giving a "Pigeon-like" appearance. A yellow staring eye makes the Honey Buzzard look more dopey than fierce.

adult pale

Where found: Rare summer visitor May–September. The tiny breeding population is fragmented over a wide area, mostly in southern England where there are large forests.

Adult: Rarely seen perched, this species does walk and run on the ground. Basically plumage is grey-brown above (greyer in male), paler but mottled below. Has a small head and a weak bill.

BUZZARD
Buteo buteo

54cm. A common species in contrast to the others on this page, the Buzzard is characterised by broad, blunt wings, a thick neck, and by its short, frequently spread tail, angled at the corners. It is a stocky, rather "macho" species.

adult dark

Where found: A common resident, mostly in the north and west (particularly Wales and south-west England). Favours places where rolling hillsides are broken up by small woodlands.

Adult (dark individual): Almost all birds in Britain are dark, although there is still considerable variation in plumage between individuals. Basically this species is dark above and below.

ROUGH-LEGGED BUZZARD
Buteo lagopus

55cm. This rare bird is slightly larger than the Buzzard, with longer, narrower wings and a slightly longer tail. If seen perched, it looks as if it is wearing "long johns" rather than "baggy shorts", since the legs are feathered; this explains the name.

adult dark

Where found: A very rare winter visitor, October–March, mostly to the east coast. More numerous in some years than others. Hunts over fields but needs trees for roosting.

Adult (dark/pale individual): As in the Buzzard, there is a certain amount of variation in body colour between individuals, but most Rough-legs are paler than most Common Buzzards, especially around the head.

Hunting methods and diet of birds of prey

Honey Buzzard

Astonishingly for a bird of its size, the Honey Buzzard is an insect specialist, and is unique among European birds of prey in its preference for colonial insects, particularly wasps. When hunting a Honey Buzzard watches for workers commuting from their foraging areas to the nest. When the nest is located, the bird digs it out, mostly to harvest the nutritious grubs inside. The worker wasps become agitated and attack viciously, but to no avail – Honey Buzzards have special thick feathering on the face to protect them from stings and are probably immune to the venom. Blunt, chicken-like claws help them to dig. Honey Buzzards do not take honey, but they do eat part of the combs of the nest.

Buzzard

Buzzards often share the same habitat as Kites (see pp.74–75), but they are mostly hunters rather than scavengers. A variety of foods are on the menu, procured by various means. If there are good conditions for flying the Buzzard will soar, then hover or hang in the wind, and finally lunge down, feet first, to catch a small mammal – probably a small vole or rabbit. In bad weather, it will scour the ground from an elevated perch, watching below for any movement in the grass. On other occasions it will walk over the ground, especially on ploughed fields, searching for insects and worms. Birds are also taken by this adaptable and successful predator.

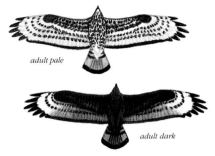

adult pale

adult dark

**Flight
(dark individual):** Individuals vary, and there are intermediates between light and dark. A feature peculiar to the Honey Buzzard, when seen from below, is the three-banded tail: two dark bars are close together at the base of the tail, and there is one at the end.

**Flight
(pale individual):** These individuals show mottled underparts, but they still exhibit the tail-bands. From below, the wings show three or four dark dotted lines, and dark carpal patches.

Voice: Sounds much less impressive than the Buzzard. Makes a musical, breathless whistle, "peee-lu"; sounds like someone whistling who is not very good at it.

adult pale

adult dark

The Buzzard often features a noticeable pale band across the breast. Buzzards are often seen perched on fences, poles and on the ground.

**Flight
(pale individual):** Most pale individuals seen in Britain are immigrants from the Continent, as this form is rare in the breeding population here. They show very dark but thin carpal patches set against a very pale underwing. Such birds can show extensive white on their upperparts.

**Flight
(dark individual):** From below, look for the typical Buzzard combination of dark wing-tips and carpal patches set against a mostly dark-brown underwing, but with a pale patch at the base of the primaries. The tail is barred, but only obscurely so, quite different from the other buzzards.

Voice: An atmospheric mewing, a familiar sound to those who live in "Buzzard" areas.

adult pale

adult dark

Juvenile (not illustrated): Many birds seen in Britain are juveniles, which have only one broad band at the tail-base, sometimes quite obscure.

**Flight
(dark/pale individual):** From above or below, the major identification pointer shown by Rough-legged Buzzards is the white base of the tail, contrasting with the large black band (there are often several smaller bands) at the end of the tail. Common Buzzard has obscure tail markings, and Honey Buzzard shows two black bars at the tail base. In most Rough-legged Buzzards, the black carpal patches are very obvious, set against a paler underwing than Buzzard's. When seen head-on, the Rough-legged Buzzard shows a pale leading edge to the wing.

Voice: Unlikely to be heard in Britain. Similar call to Buzzard with a more complaining tone.

Rough-legged Buzzard

The rare Rough-legged Buzzard eats mainly voles or lemmings, only taking birds if numbers of these small mammals are low. These birds only visit Britain in years when voles are scarce in Continental Europe, so it is possible that in this country they will eat a more varied diet. The Rough-legged Buzzard is an expert hoverer, often remaining in the same place for considerable lengths of time, showing much greater skill than the Common Buzzard.

Merlin (see pp.78–79)

A feature of many birds of prey is a discrepancy in the size of the male and female; usually the latter is larger. This is particularly pronounced in bird specialists such as the Merlin. The Merlin hunts in wild open spaces. When approaching its quarry it flies very low, often less than 1m (3ft) above the ground. Sometimes it will conceal its identity by imitating the flight of a potential prey species. One such disguise is in the form of an undulating, wing-flicking "Thrush-flight". Presumably some victims are fooled, recognising their assailant too late to escape.

Flight actions and profiles of birds of prey

A male and female Marsh Harrier perform a "Food Pass" (see pp.76–77)

Marsh Harrier – All harriers hold their wings in "V"-shape when soaring, in a more pronounced upward tilt than other birds of prey. All fly low over ground, quartering. Marsh glides on upwardly-tilted wings, alternating glides with heavy flaps on broad wings, moving more quickly than other harriers. Sometimes soars high.

Hen Harrier – Soars with wings in shallow "V". Glides with wings almost flat. Intersperses shorter glides than Marsh Harrier with quicker wing-flaps. Narrower wings than Marsh; broader, rounder wings than Montagu's.

Montagu's Harrier – Soars and glides with wings held in "V"-shape, probably deeper when soaring. Alternates these glides with 5–6 very bouncy, light wing-flaps, almost like a tern. Effect is underscored by the very long, narrow wings.

Goshawk – Soars in circles with wings held flat and slightly forward, and with the tail fanned. Soars are maintained by bouts of flapping. In normal flight, alternates deep, slow flaps with very long glides. Note the short, blunt wings and long, slightly rounded tail.

Sparrowhawk – Soars in tight circles with wings held flat and slightly forward, usually not with the tail fanned, except momentarily. In normal flight, alternates quick, busy flaps with short glides. The wings are shorter and blunter than those of Kestrel, the tail is more square-ended, and the Sparrowhawk never hovers.

Kestrel – Soars on flat wings which do not look as pointed as they really are, and with the tail spread. In normal flight, alternates fast, shallow wing-beats with glides; can look like Sparrowhawk, but the latter flaps more deeply on much blunter wings. Hovers effortlessly, with great regularity.

Merlin – Does not soar much. In purposeful flight, shows flickering, clipped wing-beats alternated with short glides, in which the wings are held especially close to the body. Often the flight path is undulating, or unpredictable. A dashing species. The short but broad-based wings give a distinctive flight profile.

Hobby – Soars on flat wings, slightly angled back, with tail fanned. Makes short glides between deep but stiff wing-beats. Constantly switches direction and accelerates. Swift-like profile is very characteristic.

Peregrine – Soars on flat wings, fully extended. In normal flight, flaps with shallow beats, interspersed with short glides; everything intensifies when bird begins to hunt. Always looks powerful, with thick body and broad-based, but very pointed wings.

Hen Harrier

Montagu's Harrier

Goshawk

Kestrel hovering

Marsh Harrier

Sparrowhawk

Hobby

Peregrine

RED KITE
Milvus milvus

61cm. There is no mistaking this large bird of prey with its long, deeply-forked tail. The wings are also long and angled, giving supreme elegance in the air.

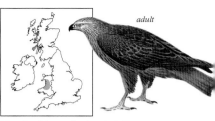

adult

Where found: A rare resident in Wales, recently reintroduced into England and Scotland, and increasing everywhere. Mostly found in hill country with broad valleys and some woodland.

Adult: The rusty-red colour is palest on the head (which can be almost white), and most intense on the belly and upper tail. Juveniles have darker heads than adults.

GOSHAWK
Accipiter gentilis

50–60cm. This species and the Sparrowhawk have relatively short wings and long tail in comparison with most birds of prey. Much the larger of the two, the Goshawk is a big, bulky, heavy-chested bird, with a shorter tail, more rounded at the tip. The wings are longer and more pointed. Both sexes have a more pronounced white eyebrow.

adult male

Where found: A scarce resident, patchily distributed over much of Britain but not Ireland. Needs extensive woodland for nesting, but also hunts over open country.

Male: 50cm. Concentrate on the bulk and body shape. The bird appears hooded due to dark ear coverts contrasting with a white throat. The breast is pale, with no warmer coloration.

SPARROWHAWK
Accipiter nisus

30–38cm. A small version of the Goshawk, the Sparrowhawk is much more common. The edge of the hindwing looks straighter in flight, not bulging at the secondaries; flight action is much lighter and quicker with a characteristic "flap-flap-glide" flight action. Both sexes sometimes have white spots on their shoulders. The similar-sized Kestrel, equally common, has narrower, more pointed wings, and hovers.

adult male

Where found: Widespread and common resident. Nests in woodland, but will hunt over fields and marshlands, and even terrorise the birds of suburban gardens.

Male: 30cm. Male Sparrowhawks have an orange wash to their underparts and cheeks, although this varies between individuals.

Hunting methods and diet of birds of prey

Red Kite
The Red Kite is a food robber and carrion eater. It spends much of its time circling and soaring over the countryside in search of recently dead or dying mammals and birds. Kites are particularly fond of visiting rubbish-dumps for such items. They can also be predators: a quick lunge downwards onto unsuspecting prey will often result in the capture of a small mammal or even a bird.

Sparrowhawk
A bird specialist, the Sparrowhawk sits concealed on a perch, planning its attack; its quarry will be a flock of birds. Eventually it slips down and flies low over the ground, typically using an obstacle such as a hedge to keep out of sight until the last moment when it will come out of hiding to round on its quarry. Having built up speed, it will hope to attack by surprise, selecting a victim as it comes into view. The chase can be relentless, the predator following the victim's escape path into vegetation or onto the ground if necessary. In bird specialists such as the Sparrowhawk and Goshawk, there is a considerable discrepancy between the size of males and females, almost certainly to reduce competition between the sexes outside the breeding season. The smaller male Sparrowhawk hunts mainly in woodland, taking sparrows and tits; the female, almost twice as heavy, hunts mainly in open country taking thrushes and starlings.

The Red Kite used to be a common scavenging bird in Britain but a combination of man-made and natural hazards combined to reduce the population to just a few pairs at the turn of the century. Persecution, illegal poison traps (used to trap animals such as foxes), a fall in the amount of available carrion, and bad weather during the breeding season, all contributed to the fall in the Red Kite population. Now, however, careful protection and reintroduction programmes have led to increasing numbers.

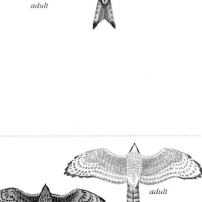

adult

Flight: The tail is always obviously forked, even when fanned. A strong white patch at the base of the primaries is offset with black wing-tips. From above the secondary coverts are clearly paler than the hindwing. On juvenile birds, a small pale bar shows the line of the greater wing-coverts, above and below.

Voice: Mews like a Buzzard, but in series: "Whee-ooo, wheoo-wheoo-wheoo".

Female: 60cm. A powerful, Buzzard-sized bird which always looks far more impressive than Sparrowhawk. Female is paler than male, with less strong markings on head.

adult female

juvenile

adult

juvenile

Juvenile: Looks quite different from parents: brown above, and with streaks, not bars, on the breast. These streaks are large, almost like spots, and set against the straw-coloured breast.

Flight (adult): Mainly barred below. Best distinguished by conspicuous white undertail coverts (not so easily noticeable in Sparrowhawk).

Flight (juvenile): The unusually coloured underparts are distinctive.

Voice: Makes a chattering, panicky "kek-kek-kek" call. Also makes a squeal, "peee-oo", intense and hoarse.

---

adult female

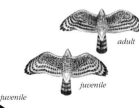

adult

juvenile

juvenile

Female: 38cm. The upperparts are brownish-grey, and there is little or no orange on the underparts. Both sexes may have white spots on their shoulders.

Juvenile: Tends to be much browner above than the female, almost warm brown. The bars on the breast are irregular and broken, in contrast to adult birds.

Flight: Shorter- and blunter-winged than Goshawk. Adults always have warmer-coloured underparts, from orange-brown to very pale sandy-brown.

Voice: Makes a series of "kek" sounds like Goshawk, but faster, higher pitched and more staccato; squeals also higher pitched.

Goshawk
Although the Goshawk is also a bird specialist, it will also regularly take mammals. It is less relentless in its pursuits than the Sparrowhawk, possibly because it is larger and less agile.

Hobby (see pp.78–79)
Hobbies are aerial hunters, spending much of their time airborne. They are supremely adapted for speed and manoeuvrability and are able to catch those most aerial of birds – swifts and swallows. Hobbies rely on some degree of surprise when they chase after such difficult prey, but there are places where prey congregates and opportunities

proliferate. It is probably just as well, however, that Hobbies have another major food-source: insects. These too are caught in flight, in a more leisurely way than swifts and swallows; the birds swoop and glide, catching the insects in their talons and transferring them to the bill in mid-air. Dragonflies are a particular favourite.

MARSH HARRIER
Circus aeruginosus

52cm. The harriers are characterised by their long, narrow wings, long tail and long legs. This is the largest, heaviest species, with broader wings than the others. The plumage patterns of both sexes are distinctive.

adult male

Where found: A very rare summer visitor (April–September) and passage migrant; just a handful of birds winter. Most breeding birds are found in large reedbeds in East Anglia.

Male: The only male harrier that is at all dark: largely brown above and almost chestnut-coloured on the belly. The head is streaked.

HEN HARRIER
Circus cyaneus

47cm. Hen Harriers fit in the middle between Marsh and Montagu's Harriers in size, bulk and buoyancy. The Montagu's Harrier has very similar plumage, but it has a very different flight action (see pp.72–73). Also, pay attention to the wing-tips: Hen Harriers have blunt wing-tips, with four or five obvious "fingers", Montagu's Harriers have more pointed wing-tips, with only three or four prominent "fingers".

adult male

Where found: Breeds in areas with extensive moorland, mostly in the north and west of Britain, including Ireland. More widespread in winter, on farmland, moorland and coastal marshes.

Male: A beautiful, smoky-grey bird that is almost gull-like at a distance. Wing-tips are black, rump and underparts white. The contrast between the grey throat and white breast is sharp.

MONTAGU'S HARRIER
Circus pygargus

44cm. The smallest harrier, and the most buoyant and elegant in flight. It has the longest tail and wings of the three, and the wings are the most pointed (see above).

adult male

Where found: A very rare summer visitor, May–September. The scattered, south-eastern breeding population utilises open arable farmland.

Male: This bird is readily identified by the red-brown streaking on its underparts, and by the black bar across its wing.

Hunting methods and birds of prey

Harriers
The harriers are all adapted for quartering; their long, narrow wings give them buoyancy and manoeuvrability when gliding slowly forward just above ground level. Each of the three following species feeds on mammals and birds, which they catch using a surprise lunge, dropping feet first onto the prey.

Marsh Harrier
The Marsh Harrier hunts mostly over marshes taking waterbirds on the ground, in the water or in the nest; also a few mammals and frogs. It does not actively pursue prey which has been flushed. During the aptly named "Food Pass"

the male Marsh Harrier will pass food to the female (see pp.72–73). The female turns on her back with her claws out to receive the food.

Hen Harrier
The Hen Harrier hunts mostly over moorland, taking mammals such as rodents and young rabbits, and small birds, sometimes pursuing the latter when they have been flushed. The Hen Harrier also performs a food pass.

Montagu's Harrier
Agricultural fields with sparse vegetation are the favoured hunting ground for the Montagu's Harrier. It takes birds,

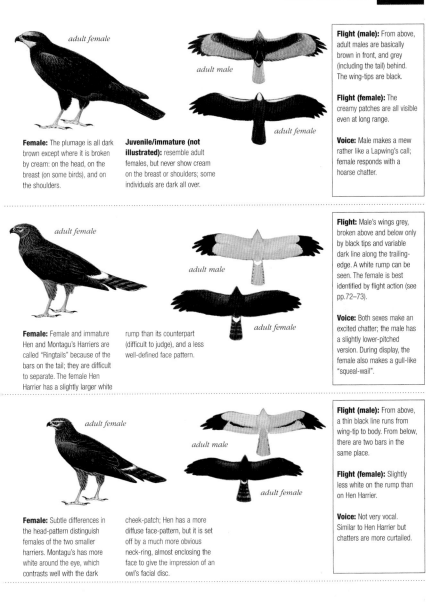

adult female

adult male

adult female

Flight (male): From above, adult males are basically brown in front, and grey (including the tail) behind. The wing-tips are black.

Flight (female): The creamy patches are all visible even at long range.

Voice: Male makes a mew rather like a Lapwing's call; female responds with a hoarse chatter.

Female: The plumage is all dark brown except where it is broken by cream: on the head, on the breast (on some birds), and on the shoulders.

Juvenile/immature (not illustrated): resemble adult females, but never show cream on the breast or shoulders; some individuals are dark all over.

---

adult female

adult male

adult female

Flight: Male's wings grey, broken above and below only by black tips and variable dark line along the trailing-edge. A white rump can be seen. The female is best identified by flight action (see pp.72–73).

Voice: Both sexes make an excited chatter; the male has a slightly lower-pitched version. During display, the female also makes a gull-like "squeal-wail".

Female: Female and immature Hen and Montagu's Harriers are called "Ringtails" because of the bars on the tail; they are difficult to separate. The female Hen Harrier has a slightly larger white rump than its counterpart (difficult to judge), and a less well-defined face pattern.

---

adult female

adult male

adult female

Flight (male): From above, a thin black line runs from wing-tip to body. From below, there are two bars in the same place.

Flight (female): Slightly less white on the rump than on Hen Harrier.

Voice: Not very vocal. Similar to Hen Harrier but chatters are more curtailed.

Female: Subtle differences in the head-pattern distinguish females of the two smaller harriers. Montagu's has more white around the eye, which contrasts well with the dark cheek-patch; Hen has a more diffuse face-pattern, but it is set off by a much more obvious neck-ring, almost enclosing the face to give the impression of an owl's facial disc.

---

especially Skylarks, and mammals. Sometimes it will engage flushed prey in active pursuit.

Peregrine (see pp.78–79)
The largest of the falcons, the Peregrine relies on muscular power, rather than the cunning of the Merlin (see pp.70–71), to catch its bird prey. Although this species uses several hunting methods, the most famous is the aerial plunge or stoop. After a prospecting soar, the Peregrine rises above its prey, then hurtles down towards it with wings that are almost fully closed, gathering astonishing speed, perhaps more than 180k.p.h. (100m.p.h.), and momentum. There is a mid-air collision, feathers fly and the prey is killed or incapacitated.

The most common victims of this type of attack are pigeons. Peregrines also take other medium-sized birds such as crows, seabirds, grouse and occasionally mammals.

KESTREL
Falco tinnunculus

34cm. All falcons have conspicuously pointed wings, and fly with rapid, busy wing-beats. Most are rather small in comparison to other birds of prey. The Kestrel is famous for its hovering, often seen over motorway verges and other open ground; no other small bird of prey regularly hovers. This species has a longer tail than other falcons. Beware of confusion with similarly-sized Sparrowhawk.

adult male

Where found: A very common resident found in a wide variety of open country habitats, even waste ground in large cities.

Male: Head and tail are grey. Both adults are brown or red-brown above. Both have a small black moustache. Male is slightly more reddish above, with uncluttered spotting on the back,

MERLIN
Falco columbarius

30cm. This is Britain's smallest bird of prey, but only just; confusion is possible with other falcons, and with the similarly-coloured Sparrowhawk. The sharply pointed wings should eliminate the latter, as should the streaks, not bars, down the breast. The other falcons are all more boldly marked, especially on the face. The Merlin is characteristically short-winged and short-tailed.

adult male

Where found: Mostly breeds on upland moorland in the north and west; uncommon. In winter, much more widely distributed, in various kinds of open country, including coastal marshes.

Male: About the size of a large thrush. Predominantly grey above and light rufous below, with strong streaks down the breast and more subtle ones above. On the head is an obscure moustache. A wide black

HOBBY
Falco subbuteo

34cm. A highly aerial species that makes flying look effortless. The long, scythe-like wings and short tail give a startling resemblance to a huge Swift (see pp. 168–169) – a very useful pointer in the field.

adult

Where found: An uncommon summer visitor, April–October, breeding on heathland and well wooded farmland; southern.

Adult: A jet-black hood seems to be fitted over its very white cheeks. The upperparts are uniformly dark, although the female is slightly browner above. Underneath, heavy streaking on

PEREGRINE
Falco peregrinus

40–46cm. Peregrines are powerful, muscular birds with cigar-shaped bodies and long, broad-based, very tapered wings. They look plumper than other falcons. The Peregrine is uncommon but is gradually increasing in numbers.

adult

Where found: Nests on crags in mountainous or hilly areas, also on cliffs. In winter its travels (or "peregrinations" – hence the name) take it to other habitats, including estuaries.

Adult: Both sexes have a black hood and moustache like a Hobby, but they have bars, not streaks down the breast. The barring reaches down to the under tail coverts, always against wings and breast. Back of head and tail are grey. Tail also has a broad black subterminal band.

Female: Slightly larger than the male, and much more heavily spotted and streaked above. The breast has streaks, not spots. Tail is brown, and features bands other than the broad subterminal band. No grey on the head.

Juvenile/immature (not illustrated): show female-like plumage; males acquiring more grey as they get older (mature at three years).

adult male

adult female

adult female

Flight (male/female): No other falcons show warm reddish-brown coloration on the back. Note how the outer half of the wing is darker than the inner half. Best distinguished by its shape and flight pattern.

Voice: All falcons make hoarse, accelerating series of "kay" or "kek" notes, the Kestrel making a particularly rasping version, becoming more quavering at the nest.

---

subterminal band is set at the end of the sparingly barred grey tail.

Female: Larger than the male, and dark brown wherever the male is grey. The brownish breast streaks are set against a white, not rufous ground colour, and the tail also is dark brown, with several well defined pale bands making a ladder down its length.

Juvenile/immature (not illustrated): Very similar to adult females.

adult male

adult female

adult female

Flight (male/female): Both sexes are much darker on the back than any Kestrel. Look for the short, very pointed wings and shortish tail.

Voice: Similar to the Kestrel, but huskier and petulant.

---

the white breast gives way to richly coloured thighs and undertail coverts: the chestnut coloration catches unexpectedly in good light. Male is smaller than the female.

adult

juvenile

juvenile

Juvenile (see left): Juvenile Hobbies are a dull version of their parents, lacking the smartness of the upperparts and completely lacking any chestnut on the underparts. Instead, the breast is pale buffy brown.

Flight: Hobbies look very dark. Even the paler underparts are only visible at reasonably close range.

Voice: More distinctive than other falcons; with the same basic pattern, but the notes are upslurred and ringing.

---

a white background, never with any chestnut coloration. Females are larger than males, slightly darker above, and with heavier barring below.

adult

juvenile

juvenile

Juvenile: Juveniles are brown above, not grey. They have a hood like their parents, but often show a white forehead and a pale supercilium. The bill base and legs, yellow in the adults, are blue-grey.

Flight: On adults, the rump and tail look paler grey than the rest of the upperparts. Look always for the powerful, compact build, with short tail and tapered wings.

Voice: A raucous version of the falcon theme, developing into loud swearing or even hysterical quacking.

RED GROUSE
Lagopus lagopus

40cm. This is the dark-coloured gamebird that is so characteristic of upland heather moors. In its small-headed, rotund shape it resembles a Partridge, but is larger, darker and quite specific to its habitat.

adult female

adult male

Where found: Heather moorlands are occupied year-round, and the populations are often managed for shooting.

Male: Males are all-over sherry-red, with whitish feathered legs. There is a red comb above the eye.

PTARMIGAN
Lagopus mutus

35cm. A high-altitude version of the Red Grouse, sometimes sporting all-white plumage to match the snowy mountain-tops. The Ptarmigan moults three times a year to make sure its camouflage keeps up with the changing seasons. The legs are feathered right to the toes.

Where found: Most Ptarmigans are found above 600m (1970ft), inhabiting rocky slopes and mountaintops year-round. Only found in Scotland.

Male winter: Seen at its best from December–April, the fine white plumage is unique in British landbirds. Note, however, that there is a red wattle above the eye, a black line between the bill and the eyes, and that the sides of the tail are also black.

Male summer: Summer plumage (May–June) makes this bird look like a small, slim version of a Red Grouse, but look for white on the belly, not just the legs, and for white on the wings. It also gives an overall greyer impression than its relative.

BLACK GROUSE
Tetrao tetrix

30–41cm. Mostly a woodland grouse, which always looks longer-necked and longer-tailed than the Red Grouse. The Capercaillie can look very similar, but is much larger.

adult male

Where found: Found in a mosaic of habitats – coniferous forests, young plantations, meadows, bogs, moorland with birch trees – throughout the year. Commonest in Scotland.

Male: Distinctive lyre-shaped tail. White on vent, shoulder, and wings contrasts black plumage. In summer (June–July), males acquire a female-like "eclipse" plumage, but still show red combs and some black blotches.

CAPERCAILLIE
Tetrao urogallus

62–86cm. A huge grouse of the forest; the turkey-sized males can become so aggressive in spring that they attack deer, people, even bicycles! The sheer bulk usually identifies this species.

Where found: Confined to coniferous forests (especially of Scots Pine) with plenty of undergrowth.

Male: Very large, but might resemble the Black Grouse male at a distance. However, it is mostly dark blue-grey all over, showing very little white, and the tail is very broad, not lyre-shaped. The bill is pale yellow, not grey.

Female: The plumage pattern resembles the females of other grouse, but the breast has a rich chestnut wash, and the flanks are noticeably white. This bird is comparatively large, dwarfing even the male Black Grouse.

Female: Similar, but less richly red than the males. The ground colour is browner, allowing more plumage patterning to be apparent. Some have red above the eye, but this is usually barely visible. Both sexes turn darker in winter.

adult male

adult female

Flight: Flight is strong and fast with rapid wing-beats. While flying away the Red Grouse is noisy, making protesting sounds. Long glides follow, often with the birds rocking from side to side before they land. From above, they look very plain, lacking any wing-bars or other markings. From below, some white on the wing-coverts is usually visible.

Voice: In spring the Red Grouse makes a variety of throaty sounds: barks, accelerating rattles, and an unmistakable "Go back! Go back!" call.

Female winter: In winter, females are distinguishable from males by a lack of markings on the head, no red comb, no black stripe. Some individuals have a few black smudges on the head.

Female summer: Warm in colour, sometimes almost yellowish-brown, and sporting attractive barring patterns. Differ from Red Grouse in showing white on the belly and wings.

adult male, winter

adult male, summer

adult autumn

adult female, summer

adult female, summer

adult male, winter

adult female, winter

Adult autumn: From July until December, adult Ptarmigans take on a much greyer appearance above, and there are usually white blotches on the back. Both sexes have a red comb. Females moult into their white plumage faster than the males.

Flight: Flies off in the manner of a Red Grouse, but it has narrower wings and slightly faster flight. It can make impressive bursts both up and down steep hills. The startling white wings should always make identification straightforward.

Voice: When flushed, gives a rhythmic series of dry croaks, almost retching, drier than the notes of Red Grouse, and quieter. Some have rendered the rhythm as "Here comes the bride".

Female: Smaller than males, these can look similar to Red Grouse but are greyer and darker, and lack the white leg-feathering of Red Grouse. The tail is conspicuously long, and forked. Lack of rich rufous coloration on the breast rules out Capercaillie.

Juvenile: Similar to the female, but often slightly paler coloured and with less well-defined barring.

adult female

adult male

adult female

juvenile

Flight (male): Fast wing-beats interspersed with glides, often quite high, (unlike Red Grouse). Shows white wing-bar and white on underside of the wings.

Flight (female): Look out for the long, forked tail, and white wing-bar (sometimes two) on upperside of wing.

Voice: At lek males make bubbling, cooing sounds and hisses. Females bark.

Juvenile: Smaller and less well-marked than females, but still show a chestnut breast-band. First year males are a mixture of male and female plumage.

adult male

juvenile

adult male

adult female

adult female

adult female

Flight (male): All dark except for some white under the wings (less than Black Grouse). Broad wings and tail.

Flight (female): Longer tail than Black Grouse, rounded, not forked end. Tail is chestnut. No wing-bars, less white under the wings.

Voice: At the male's lek, slow taps accelerate into a sound like popping a cork, followed by a grinding gurgle.

Habitat, feeding and display behaviour

Habitat
Each of our four grouse species is found in a habitat of its own, different from the others.

Ptarmigan – a hardy bird, drawn to bare, drafty mountaintops; it is rarely found below 600m (2000ft), even in the midst of winter. It eats the vegetation of the high tops, including a variety of berries. At night, it often selects a snowfield on which to roost, so that the white plumage can melt safely into its background.

Red Grouse – this species rarely overlaps with the Ptarmigan, instead occurring on the lower slopes below 600m (2000ft). It is almost exclusively confined to heather moorland, where it feeds on the young shoots of heather plants, and chooses the older, denser patches for a roosting site. Red Grouse also take a few berries in winter.

The other species of grouse are found in woodland.

Black Grouse – needs a mosaic of habitats in order to do well, including open ground, woodland, heathland and bogland. Among a variety of vegetable foods taken are the shoots and buds of birch, hazel and pine, and the berries and stems of bilberry.

Capercaillie – a bird of coniferous forests, especially those with an undergrowth of herbs and low bushes. In summer they feed on the ground, in the field layer, taking berries, shoots and leaves; in winter they "migrate" up to the treetops, and feed entirely on the shoots, buds and needles of Scots Pine and other conifers. The needle-sharp winter diet of Capercaillies produces a very distinctive dropping: cylindrical, bent, and as thick as a little finger.

Display
Both *Ptarmigan* and *Red Grouse* advertise their presence by brief song-flights accompanied by rhythmic calling. They take off, rise steeply for a few moments, sail, then drop down with the wings beating, the tail fanned and the head and neck extended. On landing, the tail remains fanned, the wings are drooped, and the birds stand erect and proud.

Black Grouse males at lek

The Ptarmigan can be seen only in Scotland, where it inhabits rocky slopes and mountaintops all year-round. It is rarely found below 600m (2000ft)

Black Grouse mostly remain on the ground to display. A number of males occupy a special arena where Black Grouse of many generations have displayed. The arena is divided into territories, over which the males fight, posturing and leaping into the air in fits of aggression. The best territories, in the middle of the displaying ground or "lek", are obtained by the fittest, strongest combatants, and the females make a bee-line for central males. Usually the dominant and therefore central male will virtually monopolise the copulations that take place at the lek. Once mated, the female leaves the arena for the day; she might return, but will be solely responsible for all subsequent breeding and nesting duties, without the male. A Black Grouse lek is easiest to see in the early morning in springtime.

Capercaillies also perform at leks, but the males have larger, more spaced out territories. In the early morning they will often begin their songs and posturing in the trees, retreating to the ground later, where fights sometimes occur. The sounds accompanying the displays are extraordinary: a tapping sound accelerates into a "drum-roll", a cork-pop, a grinding sound and a belch.

PHEASANT
Phasianus colchicus
60–90cm. The Pheasant is the most familiar of our gamebirds, often seen in the open on fields by roadsides. The spectacular male is better known than the brown, camouflaged female. Both have longer tails than any other ground-living British birds.

Where found: Widespread and common in agricultural areas where there are fields and woods.

Male: Generally unmistakable, but individuals vary considerably in their colour and pattern. Consistent features are the green head and red face wattle. Only birds which originate from China have the white neck collar.

Female: Females also vary in their ground colour, some being much darker brown than others. The characteristically spiky tail is still a giveaway.

RED-LEGGED PARTRIDGE
Alectoris rufa
34cm. Partridges crouch low in fields, looking like clods of earth until they fly away! It is astonishing how similar the two species look at a distance, given the great differences in plumage between them. The Red-legged is a marginally larger, more upright bird. Red-legs perch on fences, roofs and even trees, which Grey Partridges never do.

adult male

Where found: Most common in agricultural areas with arable crops, especially sugar-beet. The distribution is restricted to drier parts of Britain. Introduced into Britain from France in the 18thC.

Here the Red-legged Partridge is shown in proportion to the larger Pheasant. On the facing page it has been enlarged so that the identification features can be seen more clearly.

GREY PARTRIDGE
Perdix perdix
30cm. More of a ground-dweller than the Red-leg, the Grey Partridge is hard to flush, much preferring to run away and never perching on fences or trees – so much for the Partridge in a Pear-tree! (this was probably derived from "Per-drix", the French name).

adult male

Where found: A farmland species, prefers cereal growing areas. Not restricted to areas with low rainfall, so has a wider distribution than the Red-leg. Has declined almost catastrophically.

Here the Grey Partridge is shown in proportion to the larger Pheasant. On the facing page it has been enlarged so that the identification features can be seen more clearly.

QUAIL
Coturnix coturnix
18cm. The chances of seeing a Quail are slim, since it prefers to remain hidden among stands of various crops in fields. This gamebird is so tiny, it is more likely to be mistaken for a wader or rail than one of its closer relatives.

adult male

Here the Quail is shown in proportion to the larger Pheasant. On the facing page it has been enlarged.

Where found: Mostly a summer visitor, May–September, but occasionally winters. Prefers agricultural fields of corn or pasture. Always very scarce. Widespread, but rare in Ireland.

Male: Sandy-coloured below; brown above with white streaks. Some are redder than others.

Flight: Explodes like a rocket from concealed vegetation, calling noisily, and making the observer jump. These birds, typically among their family, have a fast, low, whirring flight with long glides.

Voice: Both sexes make the familiar staccato, coughing crow, to which the male adds a loud wing-flapping for effect when displaying. Flushed birds burst away with a hysterical cackling.

adult male *adult female* *juvenile*

adult female

adult male

Juvenile: The young of this species are quite tricky, in that they are smaller than the adults, and might resemble partridges. Even so, the pointed tail lacks both partridges' obvious chestnut edging, and young Pheasants are larger, taller and longer-necked.

Adult: The throat and upper breast are white, ringed by a black eyestripe above and a black breast-stripe and spotted "necklace". White supercilium.

 adult male

juvenile *adult*

 adult

The back is a plain, unstreaked grey-brown colour, and the belly and vent are orange. The bill (and legs of course) are crimson-red.

Juvenile: Juveniles are pale, resembling an adult that has been put through a washing machine! There is a shadow of the adults' necklace, and there are a few assorted flank stripes.

Flight: Coveys of Red-legs fly quite readily, and often scatter in several directions. The wings are slightly rounder than those of the Grey Partridge, but the species both show chestnut sides to the tail – a useful distinguishing mark from other gamebirds.

Voice: Rhythmic, harsh "clucks" and "chucks" like the puffing of a steam engine or the sound of an agitated hen.

Adult: Head and neck are orange, not showing the contrast of the Red-leg. A large, brown, horseshoe-shaped blob on the breast is peculiar to this species.

 adult male

juvenile *adult*

 adult

Blob size varies, smallest on summer females, but it is always present. The legs and small bill are grey; the back is barred and streaked, undertail is white.

Juvenile: Looks blander than a young Red-leg, completely lacking any stripes on the flanks.

Flight: Coveys of Grey Partridges are difficult to flush, but stick together when they do fly. The darker, subtly-streaked back might be visible.

Voice: Male makes a penetrating, hoarse sound like the creaking of a key in a rusty lock. Mostly heard at dusk and dawn.

---

adult male

adult female

adult male

 juvenile

There is usually a white eyebrow and crown-stripe, and a black throat, collar, cheek-stripe and outer crown. **Female:** No black throat; browner, less clear-cut markings on the rest of the head. The upper breast often looks spotted.

Juvenile: The streaks on the upperparts are barely discernible; very small spots on the breast. Tiny.

Flight: If it ever flies, it is usually to avoid being stepped upon. It makes off with the typical gamebird's whirring wings, but glides little or not at all. The Corncrake, which occurs in similar habitats (although it is very rare), can be distinguished by its larger size and chestnut wings. Partridges have chestnut tail-sides and broader wings. The impression given by the Quail is Snipe-like, but the Snipe has a very long bill.

Voice: The unique song is rendered "Wet-my-lips", with the first syllable longest. Mostly heard at night.

Habitat and breeding behaviour

Habitat
Only the Grey Partridge and the Quail are native to Britain. The Pheasant was introduced by the Normans in the late 11thC (or possibly earlier by the Romans), and the Red-legged Partridge was first released here in about 1790. The Pheasant came from Asia and the Red-legged Partridge from France.

Pheasant – the easiest gamebird to see, since it is large and conspicuous. Although usually seen in fields, it needs woodland with good ground cover in which to breed. They feed on many types of food, both animal and vegetable, which are obtained on the ground by searching and scratching. Many individuals take to the trees at night, to escape predation by foxes.

A mixed group of feeding pheasants

Partridges – are more tied to open country than Pheasants. Although the Red-legged Partridge sometimes occurs in wooded areas, and may even perch and roost in trees, it is happiest in complexes of fields and hedges. The Grey Partridge concurs with this, but never leaves the ground for perching or roosting. Grey Partridges prefer moister conditions than Red-legs, and also more open areas; Red-legs are happiest on fields that warm up in the sunshine, and have at least some cover. Both Partridges feed on plant material, and their chicks rely on insects; apparently, the Red-leg is alone in enjoying the roots of sugar-beet. The Grey Partridge is a quieter bird, calling less often, and it tends to be most active at dawn and dusk.

Quail – while our other game birds are rigidly sedentary, the Quail is a long-haul migrant, wintering in West Africa south of the Sahara. Rare in Britain, the Quail favours low-lying fields with dense stands of crops, such as winter wheat and clover. It is an omnivore which feeds, nests and roosts on the ground. Look for it especially on the downs of Wiltshire and Dorset.

Breeding and social strategies
Our gamebirds exhibit great variation in their breeding strategies.

Grey Partridge – is solidly monogamous, one male mating with one female. They make their nest in the cover of hedges, often well-concealed, and lay what is probably the largest average clutch of any British bird, 14 eggs. When the chicks hatch both parents guard them. As the season progresses these youngsters grow and remain in the parents'

Grey Partridge pair

other broods in late summer. Red-legged Partridges form winter coveys, but these are not based on a pair and their family, and so are less cohesive in their movements.

Quail – sometimes monogamous, but at other times both male and female will mate with several of the opposite sex – indeed, the behaviour of this elusive species has not yet been fully worked out! The female tends the nest and chicks alone, and they may well migrate as a family, joining up with others en route to Africa.

territory, and so on into the winter, when the family group stays together as a "covey".

Red-legged Partridge – also normally monogamous, and also makes its nest in a hedgerow, but does not always have just one nest. Sometimes the female will lay two separate clutches, and she will incubate one, and the male the other: this is a rare strategy among British birds. Once the chicks (an average of two per nest) hatch, they accompany their single parent for a while, but may well join up with

Pheasant – sometimes monogamous, but more often polygynous (one male mates with a number of females). Females live on the male's territory, and are bonded to him exclusively. Most males have only two or three mates, but a few have ten or more. Sometimes the male will help to guard hatched chicks, but really his gaudy plumage is a liability when it comes to the vulnerable stages of incubation and brooding. In winter, Pheasants often divide themselves into single-sex flocks, within which there is an established hierarchy for feeding and roosting activities.

Red-legged Partridges (the bird on the right is a hybrid with another species)

WATER RAIL
Rallus aquaticus
28cm. Rails have long legs with large feet, and creep around in undergrowth. The Water Rail, in particular, is a difficult bird to see. The body appears squashed from the sides, and it is able to squeeze between the reeds. Like all rails, it nods its head when walking, and tends to flick its tail. It runs and probes with dainty movements.

Where found: Widespread but uncommon resident in wet areas.

adult

Adult: The long, red bill and black and white bars on the flanks are distinctive. Look also for the grey on the neck, brown streaks on the back, and for the partly white undertail.

SPOTTED CRAKE
Porzana porzana
23cm. This elusive species is smaller than the Water Rail, and even shier. It has a shorter bill, reddish at the base and yellow-green at the tip, and tends to live up to its name by being spotted. In contrast to Water Rail, the undertail is always buff, never white, and the legs are green, not pink.

Where found: Rare breeding bird in large wetland areas.

adult male

Male: Males usually look greyer than females on the head and neck, and sport some black colour around the base of the bill.

CORNCRAKE
Crex crex
27cm. "Crex crex" says it all for this rare, elusive bird of hay-meadows which shouts from thick cover but is hardly ever seen. A summer visitor from April–September. Once common it has declined dramatically.

Where found: Rare, found in Irish and Scottish hay-meadows.

adult male

Male: If seen, it will appear much as any "normal" rail, but is rich chestnut around the wings and flanks. The supercilium is blue-grey.

MOORHEN
Gallinula chloropus
35cm. The commonest and most widespread member of the Rail family, the Moorhen is found everywhere from town ponds to isolated marshlands – wherever there is fresh water. Its characteristic deliberate walk, jerky movements and hard-pressed swimming action are familiar to most birdwatchers. Legs are green.

Where found: Common in lowland freshwater habitats.

adult

Adult: Mostly dark, slightly browner above, with a white line along the flanks. Bill waxy red, yellow tip. White undertail with central black stripe is easy to see as tail flicks constantly. their tails.

COOT
Fulica atra
38cm. Another very common rail, often thought of as a duck since it floats around on the water with ducks, and dives like some ducks do. However, it has a straight, unflattened bill and long legs with lobed toes. It is similar to the Moorhen, but always looks more rotund. Lobed feet and legs are blue.

Where found: Common in areas with open water.

adult

Adult: All-over coal-black except for the unmistakable white frontal shield – "as bald as a Coot". No white flank line or white undertail.

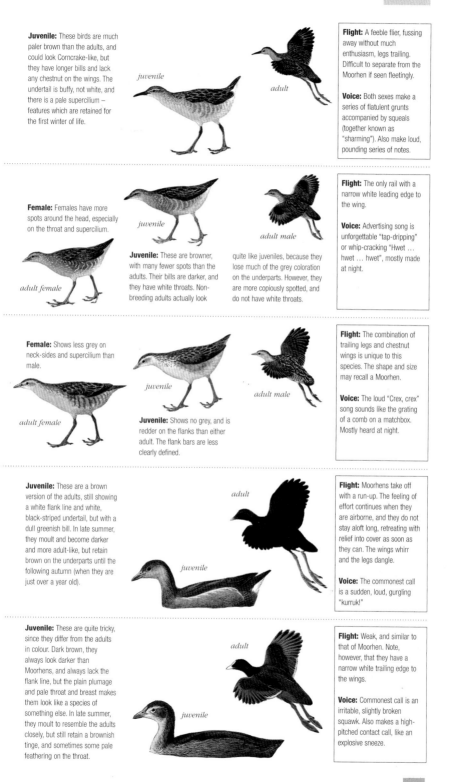

Juvenile: These birds are much paler brown than the adults, and could look Corncrake-like, but they have longer bills and lack any chestnut on the wings. The undertail is buffy, not white, and there is a pale supercilium – features which are retained for the first winter of life.

juvenile

adult

Flight: A feeble flier, fussing away without much enthusiasm, legs trailing. Difficult to separate from the Moorhen if seen fleetingly.

Voice: Both sexes make a series of flatulent grunts accompanied by squeals (together known as "sharming"). Also make loud, pounding series of notes.

Female: Females have more spots around the head, especially on the throat and supercilium.

juvenile

adult male

adult female

Juvenile: These are browner, with many fewer spots than the adults. Their bills are darker, and they have white throats. Non-breeding adults actually look

quite like juveniles, because they lose much of the grey coloration on the underparts. However, they are more copiously spotted, and do not have white throats.

Flight: The only rail with a narrow white leading edge to the wing.

Voice: Advertising song is unforgettable "tap-dripping" or whip-cracking "Hwet … hwet … hwet", mostly made at night.

Female: Shows less grey on neck-sides and supercilium than male.

juvenile

adult male

adult female

Juvenile: Shows no grey, and is redder on the flanks than either adult. The flank bars are less clearly defined.

Flight: The combination of trailing legs and chestnut wings is unique to this species. The shape and size may recall a Moorhen.

Voice: The loud "Crex, crex" song sounds like the grating of a comb on a matchbox. Mostly heard at night.

Juvenile: These are a brown version of the adults, still showing a white flank line and white, black-striped undertail, but with a dull greenish bill. In late summer, they moult and become darker and more adult-like, but retain brown on the underparts until the following autumn (when they are just over a year old).

adult

juvenile

Flight: Moorhens take off with a run-up. The feeling of effort continues when they are airborne, and they do not stay aloft long, retreating with relief into cover as soon as they can. The wings whirr and the legs dangle.

Voice: The commonest call is a sudden, loud, gurgling "kurruk!"

Juvenile: These are quite tricky, since they differ from the adults in colour. Dark brown, they always look darker than Moorhens, and always lack the flank line, but the plain plumage and pale throat and breast makes them look like a species of something else. In late summer, they moult to resemble the adults closely, but still retain a brownish tinge, and sometimes some pale feathering on the throat.

adult

juvenile

Flight: Weak, and similar to that of Moorhen. Note, however, that they have a narrow white trailing edge to the wings.

Voice: Commonest call is an irritable, slightly broken squawk. Also makes a high-pitched contact call, like an explosive sneeze.

Habitat and breeding behaviour

Moorhen and Coot

These two species are by far the best known of their family; indeed, many observers would more naturally assume they were ducks because of their preference for swimming around on park lakes and ponds. But neither have flattened bills or webbed feet like ducks.

Moorhen – the more amphibious species, often seen clambering around emergent vegetation, and even among the branches of trees. Feet are long, without webs or lobes, making them great for climbing and wading but less good for swimming. Moorhens make the latter activity look like hard work, bobbing their heads busily as they move forward. The Moorhen is extremely aggressive, constantly bickering, calling and posturing. The most common aggressive posture is "Head-down" performed mainly on land. At times of extreme territorial aggression, both the Moorhen and the Coot may fight their rivals with their feet, splashing in the water, toes interlocked. When nesting Moorhens tend to build among thick vegetation, on the island in a small pond, for example. They lay an average of seven eggs. Both Moorhens and Coots can be double or even triple-brooded; in the Moorhen, the young of early broods sometimes help with feeding young of later broods.

Coot – prefers to stick to open water, although it will happily graze in areas of open ground. In contrast to the Moorhen, the Coot is a fine swimmer. Its toes are lobed, opening out on the power (backward) stroke, and closing on the return (forward) stroke. The feet also help them to dive with ease, which they do far more often than the Moorhen. Both species take animal and vegetable food, although the Coot is probably more of a vegetarian. Also very aggressive, the Coot adopts the "Head-down" posture, but mainly on the water. For their nests Coots build a floating structure which is often in open water, attached to an overhanging branch. Six eggs are are usually laid. Coots build special rafts for their youngsters when they hatch, sometimes with a ramp to help them climb up out of the water.

Other rails

The other rail species are very secretive, being confined to dense vegetation, and rarely coming into view.

Corncrake and *Spotted Crake* – as well as being secretive these birds are also very rare, being found in Hebridean and Irish hay-meadows and a few large marshes respectively; both are summer visitors to Britain. Although even a glimpse of either is a privilege, both make memorable sounds, mostly at night. The peak calling time for the Corncrake is between midnight and 3am. The Spotted Crake sometimes calls continuously right through the hours of darkness.

Water Rail – quite common in freshwater marshes that have reeds, open water and mud. It is shy and unobtrusive, but can often be seen from hides, wandering along the border between open mud and dense reedbeds. They are easiest to see at dawn and dusk, but when the ground is frozen, they are forced to stay out in the open longer. At such times the diet, normally restricted to plants and small animals, may stretch to carrion, or even to live birds, which they catch by stealth.

Moorhen

Water Rail

Spotted Crake

Coot

OYSTERCATCHER
Haematopus ostralegus

43cm. One of the easiest waders to identify among the mass of estuarine birds: showing big, bulky and black and white. The neck and legs are rather short, adding to the thickset impression. The long orange-red bill suggests that it is carrying a carrot. Very noisy.

Where found: A common breeding bird in the north, mostly on the coast, but also inland. Rarer and more coastal further south. Very common in winter around all our coasts.

Flight: Flies strongly on bowed wings with shallow wing-beats, always calling loudly. The broad white wing-bar and black-banded tail are obvious.

Voice: Main call is shrill, urgent "ke-BEEK", often very loud. Song can be deafening: single piping notes accelerate into a fast trill, sometimes sounding like treble castanets. Often several birds sing together.

BLACK-WINGED STILT
Himantopus himantopus

38cm. This unmistakable bird looks faintly ludicrous, with its small body on unnecessarily long legs. The bill is long and needle-sharp.

Where found: A rare visitor to marshes and lagoons in southern Britain, most often seen in spring. It has bred here several times.

Flight: The legs trail far behind as the bird flies with a low, direct course. It glides in to land. The wings are black underneath, contrasting with the gleaming white underparts.

Voice: Commonest call is "kyik-kyik-kyik", with many variations, mostly sounding rather tinny.

AVOCET
Recurvirostra avosetta

43cm. Another unmistakable black-and-white wader, this time a picture of elegance with its long legs on well-balanced body, and its long, uptilted bill, which is swished from side to side.

Where found: A rare breeding bird on shallow, coastal lagoons, mostly in East Anglia. A few winter on southern estuaries or lagoons, with a concentration on the Exe Estuary in Devon.

Flight: This bird is a fast flier with stiff, but fairly full wing-beats. The trailing legs should eliminate confusion with Oystercatcher.

Voice: The commonest call is a fluty, liquid "kluit, kluit", with variations.

Migration and moult

An understanding of the movements of waders, and of what plumages they attain at different times, is extremely useful in identification. Here are a few principles.

A few weeks after hatching out from its egg, a wader chick will fledge – that is, obtain its first set of feathers – and thus become what is termed a juvenile (it will show juvenile plumage).

Juvenile waders almost invariably leave their "home" soon after fledging, beginning their southward migration on their own or with flocks of other juveniles. Many waders are long-distance migrants, so these young birds might well have to travel from the Arctic tundra to the tropics, or even further, when they are just a few months old. They do not complete the journey in one go, but have many different stopovers, and may stay for some time in each. Many waders of the far north stopover in Britain, so it is common to see groups of juvenile waders in many British wetlands in autumn, including those of species that do not breed or winter here, such as Curlew Sandpipers and Spotted Redshanks. At some time during the autumn and early winter (either before, during or after their migration), these juveniles will moult into a plumage that is closely similar to the adults' non-breeding appearance.

Many waders spend the winter (in non-breeding plumage) on British estuaries. Some remain for the whole season in one place, others move from estuary to estuary. But

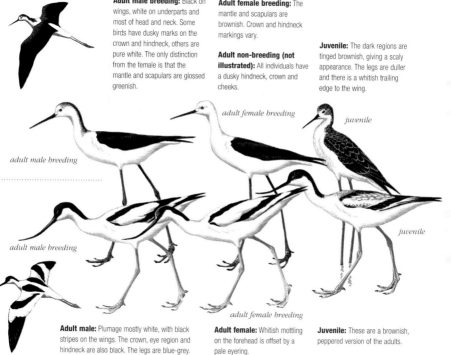

Adult non-breeding: The throat shows a white collar. The plumage is less black, the legs are less pink, and the bill tip is often darker.

adult non-breeding

Juvenile/immature: Young birds are sooty where the adults are black, and have dull-coloured bills, brown eyes and grey legs. A variably broad neck-collar is gained during their first winter.

adult breeding

Adult breeding: Black above, white below, with a long red bill, red eyes and pink legs. The throat is black.

juvenile

Adult male breeding: Black on wings, white on underparts and most of head and neck. Some birds have dusky marks on the crown and hindneck, others are pure white. The only distinction from the female is that the mantle and scapulars are glossed greenish.

Adult female breeding: The mantle and scapulars are brownish. Crown and hindneck markings vary.

Adult non-breeding (not illustrated): All individuals have a dusky hindneck, crown and cheeks.

Juvenile: The dark regions are tinged brownish, giving a scaly appearance. The legs are duller and there is a whitish trailing edge to the wing.

adult female breeding

juvenile

adult male breeding

adult male breeding

juvenile

adult female breeding

Adult male: Plumage mostly white, with black stripes on the wings. The crown, eye region and hindneck are also black. The legs are blue-grey.

Adult female: Whitish mottling on the forehead is offset by a pale eyering.

Juvenile: These are a brownish, peppered version of the adults.

eventually, as spring arrives, they must once again head back to their breeding grounds. Spring migration is often quick; the birds are in a hurry to get there before their rivals. Once they have arrived, waders breed quickly. Often only one parent carries out the nuptial duties, leaving the other to get on with its post-breeding moult. The non-breeders, failed breeders and unemployed parents tend to complete their moult before starting on their southward migration. The occupied birds may have to wait until a stopover, or to the end of their migration, before they can moult.

By late June the first individuals are on their way south again. The autumn migration lasts much longer than the spring migration, since it is staggered: non-breeders and unemployed parents set off first, followed by adults that have bred fledged young, and finally by juveniles themselves, the products of the year's breeding season. In the Dunlin, adults mainly pass through Britain in July and early August, and juveniles pass through mainly in late August and September. In this and all species there of course is a degree of overlap.

The autumn flocks of waders are often confusing, including as they do, mixtures of adults and juveniles in all stages of moult. It is quite possible to see flocks of Dunlins, for example, containing juveniles, non-breeding adults, and breeding plumage adults, all at the same time. Such puzzles are probably best left to the enthusiasts!

Wader identification

Over 30 species of waders regularly breed in or visit Britain. Many look very similar, and each may present a formidable variety of plumages – breeding, non-breeding, juvenile, and so on – that deter those new to birdwatching from even attempting identification. This section provides a few basic hints to help you take the plunge.

Imagine you are on an estuary, and in front of you is a seething mass of waders. There are three features that you must pay particular attention to when making an identification.

1. Size – some waders are clearly bigger than others. A Curlew is huge compared to a Dunlin, for example. More subtly, a Knot is only slightly larger than a Dunlin.

2. Shape and length of the bill – this is critical: it determines what the wader eats, and what technique it uses. The Curlew has a downcurved bill, the similarly-plumaged Bar-tailed Godwit has a slightly uptilted bill. The Grey Plover has a straight, thick bill; the Redshank has a straight, long bill.

3. Length of the legs – some waders have short legs and cannot wade much; other have long legs and are excellent paddlers. The Redshank, here, has much longer legs than the Knot, although both are similar in size and plumage.

Other useful identification characteristics are:

Flight – how the birds fly is also important. Some fly singly, others in small bands or large flocks. Look for characteristic pointers. The Redshank is the only species with a large white trailing edge to the wing, the Grey Plover is the only one with black armpits (axillaries), and the Turnstone has every flight field-mark in the book!

Plumage and colour – can pick out some waders straight away, eg. Turnstone and Oystercatcher, but this is often variable and is less useful to those just starting out than shape and behaviour.

Feeding technique – this behaviour can be so distinctive that certain species can be identified simply by using this clue (see also pp.102–103 and pp.106–107). In particular the Plover family has a special feeding technique all their own. They find their prey by sight and grab it in their short bills: first they watch from a stationary position; then, once they spy something, they run towards it and, if it is still available, they peck. This "stop-run-peck" system is highly distinctive (see below), and is somewhat similar to the progress of a Blackbird over a lawn. It will help to pick out any plovers in the mass of feeding birds.

The plovers' "stop-run-peck" feeding technique is characteristic

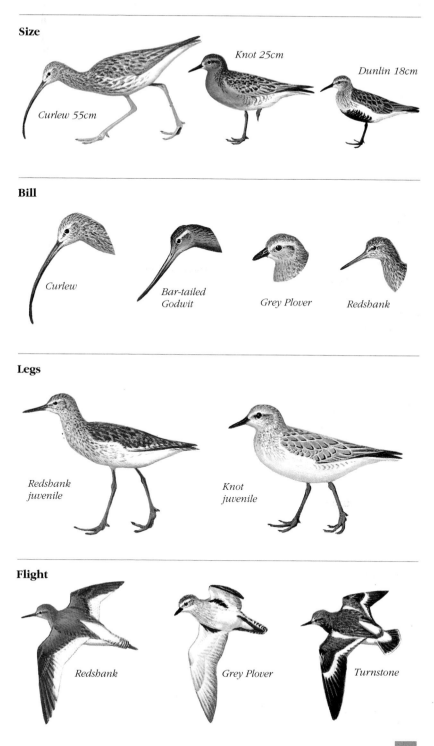

Size

Knot 25cm

Dunlin 18cm

Curlew 55cm

Bill

Curlew

Bar-tailed
Godwit

Grey Plover

Redshank

Legs

Redshank
juvenile

Knot
juvenile

Flight

Redshank

Grey Plover

Turnstone

WADERS *Plovers, Charadriidae: Charadrius*

LITTLE RINGED PLOVER
Charadrius dubius

15cm. The "Ringed" plovers are small, sandy-brown waders with bold black-and-white markings on their heads and necks. This is the smallest, slimmest species, with a distinctively horizontal posture and pointed rear end. It is not present in winter.

Where found: Uncommon summer visitor March–October. Small numbers breed in man-made habitats such as reservoir banks and gravel pits. Passage migrants are more widespread.

Flight: Dashes away with a jerky flight action on narrow wings. The Little Ringed Plover is distinctive in that it shows no obvious white wing-bar.

Voice: Main call is a shrill, down-slurred "piew". The song is an insistently repeated, grating "Gree-a", rather tern-like.

RINGED PLOVER
Charadrius hiaticula

19cm. This is a plumper, larger-headed bird than Little Ringed Plover, with a thicker bill and shorter legs. It is common, and present abundantly in winter, often in large flocks.

Where found: A fairly common resident on many coasts; breeds on sandy or shingle beaches. A few nest inland on gravel pits and river shingle. Common on coasts and estuaries during the winter.

Flight: Flies quickly but with deliberate beats, often glides before alighting. Look for the white wing-bar, not found on Little Ringed Plover.

Voice: Main call is soft, liquid, upslurred "tooip". The song is a rolling, murmured yodel based on "Too-wee-er" notes, stressed either on the "Too" or the "Er".

KENTISH PLOVER
Charadrius alexandrinus

16cm. A dumpy, big-headed, short-tailed wader set on legs that seem too long for it. It always looks much paler than the other two "Ringed" plovers.

Where found: Once bred here, but now a rare spring (occasionally autumn) visitor to muddy coastal areas in the east and south of Britain.

Flight: Another quick, fluttery flier, it shows a white wing-bar, thinner than that of Ringed Plover. The tail sides are more prominently white than those of the Ringed Plover.

Voice: Makes short "kip" calls, which elaborate into a rolling song quite similar to that of a Dunlin.

DOTTEREL
Charadrius morinellus

22cm. A medium-sized, plump wader of the mountaintops, usually above 700m (2300ft), with a unique combination of features – a broad white eyestripe and a thin pale breast-band. It perches upright on surprisingly long legs.

Where found: Scarce summer visitor (May–August) to mountaintops with short cover and scree. On migration it visits selected fields and hills for a few days each.

Flight: Flies with fast wing-beats, unhesitantly. The wings look remarkably plain except for the outermost primary, which has a white leading edge (can be quite visible).

Voice: Main call is a quiet, sweet whistle or series of whistles, a little like someone calling their dog; sometimes more trilling.

adult male breeding

Adult male breeding: Distinguished from Ringed Plover by its yellow eyering. Note also the black (thinner) bill, dull yellow (longer) legs, and narrow white line behind the black on the forehead.

Adult female: These are browner where the males are black (especially the breast band), and have a less prominent eyering.

Juvenile: Has brown, not even blackish, breast bands, often incomplete. They look scaly above. The Little Ringed juvenile has a relatively unpatterned head, with only a hint of an eyering, and with a barely discernible eyebrow. The forehead is often buffy.

adult female

juvenile

adult breeding

adult non-breeding

juvenile

Adult breeding: This species lacks the yellow eyering of Little Ringed Plover. It also lacks the white stripe on its relative's forehead, but has a more prominent eyebrow instead. The legs are orange-yellow, and the bill is yellow with a black tip.

Adult non-breeding: All the black parts look duller, and so does the bill.

Juvenile: Easily distinguished from Little Ringed Plover by white marks on the face: a white forehead runs into a prominent white eyebrow.

Adult male: In breeding plumage, both sexes have an "interrupted" breast band that hardly reaches beyond the shoulders. Both also have black legs and a black bill. The male possesses a black eye-stripe, a black band on the forehead, and a pleasing caramel-brown tinge to his crown and nape.

Adult female: The female lacks all black and toffee coloration, and looks more like a juvenile "Ringed" plover type, but with less scaling on the back.

Juvenile: Resembles adult female, but is paler, with a buffy wash to the crown and breast-patches.

adult male

adult female

juvenile

Adult female breeding: Unusual below, with a white throat, grey breast, black-bordered white breast-band, and deliciously red-chestnut belly. Further down, this gives way to black, and finally white on the undertail. The white eye-stripe on both sides reaches all the way to the back of the head to form a "V".

Adult non-breeding: Pale brown plumage is acquired from July onwards; all the grey, black and chestnut is lost. They retain their eyebrow and breast-band and this can aid identification.

Juvenile: Similar to adults in winter, but with a darker, more mottled breast. The back is darker, with more contrasting buffy scaling.

juvenile

Adult male (not illustrated): Males are less boldly marked, and have streaks on their crown.

adult female breeding

adult non-breeding

Good places for wader watching

Top areas

Here is a list of some of the species that are most likely to be seen at each of the top ten locations. Some may be seen in summer when they breed, some spend the winter in this country, while others may just be passing through during spring and autumn. (Autumn passage migrants may arrive here as early as late June.)

1. Firth of Forth
Grey Plover, Bar-tailed Godwit, Knot, Sanderling, Wood Sandpiper, Spotted Redshank, Greenshank, Little Stint.

2. Lindisfarne/Northumberland coast
Ringed Plover, Oystercatcher, Golden Plover, Lapwing, Sanderling, Knot, Dunlin, Bar-tailed Godwit, Redshank, Curlew, Black-tailed Godwit, Greenshank, Spotted Redshank, Wood Sandpiper, Curlew Sandpiper, Little Stint.

3. Solway Firth
Snipe, Redshank, Golden Plover, Lapwing, Dunlin, Oystercatcher, Curlew, Whimbrel, Sanderling, Black-tailed Godwit, Spotted Redshank, Ruff, Little Stint, Curlew Sandpiper.

4. Morcambe Bay
Dunlin, Ringed Plover, Oystercatcher, Golden Plover, Grey Plover, Lapwing, Knot, Sanderling, Black-tailed Godwit, Bar-tailed Godwit, Curlew, Redshank, Turnstone, Purple Sandpiper, Greenshank, Whimbrel, Spotted Redshank, Green Sandpiper, Common Sandpiper, Wood Sandpiper, Little Stint, Curlew Sandpiper, Ruff.

5. Ribble Estuary
Black-tailed Godwit, Green Sandpiper, Wood Sandpiper, Common Sandpiper, Ruff, Spotted Redshank, Dunlin, Redshank, Lapwing, Snipe, Whimbrel, Curlew, Little Ringed Plover, Greenshank, Little Stint, Golden Plover.

6. Dee Estuary
As above.

7. The Wash
Curlew Sandpiper, Wood Sandpiper, Black-tailed Godwit, Ruff, Redshank, Dunlin, Knot, Oystercatcher, Curlew, Bar-tailed Godwit, Grey Plover, Greenshank, Whimbrel.

8. Severn Estuary
Oystercatcher, Golden Plover, Grey Plover, Ringed Plover, Lapwing, Knot, Snipe, Bar-tailed Godwit, Black-tailed Godwit, Curlew, Redshank, Turnstone, Dunlin, Curlew Sandpiper, Little Stint, Greenshank, Whimbrel.

9. Thames Estuary
Oystercatcher, Ringed Plover, Snipe, Redshank, Green Sandpiper, Curlew Sandpiper, Dunlin, Spotted Redshank, Black-tailed Godwit, Avocet, Little Stint, Spotted Redshank.

10. Langstone/Chichester Harbour
Oystercatcher, Redshank, Ringed Plover, Grey Plover, Golden Plover, Knot, Dunlin, Ruff, Snipe, Black-tailed Godwit, Bar-tailed Godwit, Avocet, Curlew Sandpiper, Little Stint, Little Ringed Plover, Spotted Redshank, Greenshank, Whimbrel, Wood Sandpiper.

Other good estuaries
A. Moray Firth
B. Clyde Firth
C. Lough Foyle
D. Strangford Lough
E. Tees
F. Mersey
G. Conwy
H. Humber
I. Burry Inlet
J. Wexford Slobs
K Orwell
L. Blackwater
M. Camel
N. Exe

Top areas
Other good estuaries

1 Firth of Forth

2 Lindisfarne,
Northumberland Coast

3 Solway Firth

4 Morecambe Bay

5 Ribble Estuary

6 Dee Estuary

7 The Wash

8 Severn Estuary

9 Thames Estuary

10 Langstone/Chichester Harbour

GOLDEN PLOVER
Pluvialis apricaria

28cm. A large, rounded plover that always shows attractive golden coloration, hence its name. The bill is short and relatively thin compared to the Grey Plover's. Often common inland. Gregarious.

Where found: A fairly common breeding bird on moorlands. In winter it leaves upland areas to inhabit farmland, grassland and sometimes estuaries all over Britain and Ireland.

Flight: Rapid flight, showing pointed wings, beaten quickly and fully. Flocks bunch together closely. Look very white from below. From above, note the indistinct wing-bar and dark rump.

Voice: Main call is a clear, mournful whistle, often just one note "piou", sometimes "too-ee". The song is a pure, rhythmically repeated "Tirr-PEE-oo", followed by a rolling "Churilee, churilee".

GREY PLOVER
Pluvialis squatarola

28cm. The coastal Grey Plover is slightly larger than Golden Plover, with a larger head, much thicker bill and bigger eyes. It perches in a hunched posture, looking fed up. It is resolutely grey when adult, not showing any golden colour (but beware juveniles). Uniquely it shows obvious black "armpits" in flight.

Where found: A common migrant and winter visitor to muddy estuaries and some sandy beaches. It is rare away from the coast.

Flight: The flight action is similar to that of Golden Plover, but it forms smaller, looser flocks. The black armpits (axillaries) are unique, and an absolute giveaway; from above, it has a more obvious wing-bar than Golden Plover, and a white rump.

Voice: Gives a gorgeous, mournful flight call which is usually of three notes: "plee-OOOee".

LAPWING
Vanellus vanellus

30cm. This very common wader of farmland and grassland is easy to recognise, having a unique combination of wispy crest and glossy-green upperparts. It moves more slowly than other waders, and often stands still for long periods.

Where found: A common but declining breeder on fields and meadows and moorland. Extremely common on farmland and coastal areas in winter, often in large flocks.

Flight: Distinctive floppy flight, with deliberate beats. The wings are very rounded, almost like an owl's; in fact, the male has almost bulging wing-tips. As they flap, Lapwings show black above, white below. In display, they tumble and tilt and roll over.

Voice: The main call is a whining "pee-wi", hence the country name "peewit". The amazing song is full of yelping calls.

RUFF
Philomachus pugnax

23–29cm. A strange, sandpiper-like wader that shows great variation in plumage and size. However, it always looks characteristically small headed and pot-bellied. The bill is of medium length and mildly decurved, the legs are long and the small size of head is accentuated by a longish neck.

Where found: Rare nester on a few lowland meadows, notably the Ouse Washes. Widespread passage migrant to mainly fresh-water habitats. Winters in small numbers on fields in the south.

Flight: This bird exhibits an almost pigeon-like flight, with slow beats of its long wings. Look for the white ovals on the side of the rump.

Voice: Mostly silent (including during display), but sometimes utters a strange muffled croak when flushed.

adult non-breeding

adult non-breeding

adult non-breeding

Adult non-breeding: All black is lost, and the birds are golden-washed almost all over. The belly and undertail, however, are whitish.

Southern form: The white border dividing black from golden is less clear-cut, invaded by some gold and speckling. There is much less black on the face. Most British breeding birds look like this.

Juvenile: Similar to the winter adult, but with light barring on the flanks and belly.

Adult breeding: A stunning combination of the golden peppering above, and jet black below, reaching to cover the face.

Northern form: The black on the underparts is more extensive, enhancing the contrast with the white bordering it.

adult breeding northern

adult breeding southern

adult non-breeding

juvenile

---

adult non-breeding

Adult non-breeding: Quite a few waders are grey like this, but not with such a short, thick bill. Some adults retain black on their underparts well into winter.

Juvenile: Like adult winter plumage, but with more clearly-defined spotting on upperparts, and some clear streaks on the underparts. The deceptive creamy wash to the back feathers may suggest Golden Plover, but the latter is always warmer in colour all over.

Adult breeding: A Golden Plover in black-and-white. There tends to be slightly more black on the belly, however, cutting off the white line between upperparts and underparts.

lt non-ding

adult breeding

adult non-breeding

juvenile

Adult female breeding: Mottled with white on the forehead and throat, eroding the black there.

Adult non-breeding: The throat turns white above the breast-band, and there is less black on the face. The face, indeed, often has a buffy wash, and there are a few "scales" on the back.

Juvenile: Have much shorter crests, and are distinctively scaled (feathers are fringed) with buff on the back.

adult non-breeding

adult

Adult male breeding: Greenish-purple gloss on back and wings, black-and-white around the face and throat, black breast-band, clean white belly, chestnut under-tail coverts.

adult male breeding

adult female breeding

juvenile

---

adult non-breeding

Female (see below right): 23cm. Smaller than male. Dark, almost black above with rufous feather fringes; breasts are mottled. Plumage varies but not to the same extent as the males'.

Adult non-breeding: Legs are often reddish, so beware of confusion with Redshank. Ruffs are much more scaly on the back, usually with a large amount of white on the head.

Juvenile (not illustrated): Resembles breeding female, but with paler (buffy) feather fringes, and a relatively unpatterned breast.

Male breeding: 29cm. From April–June, males sport "ruffs" of various colours. These three examples are not shown at correct size.

adult males breeding

adult female

adult male non-breeding

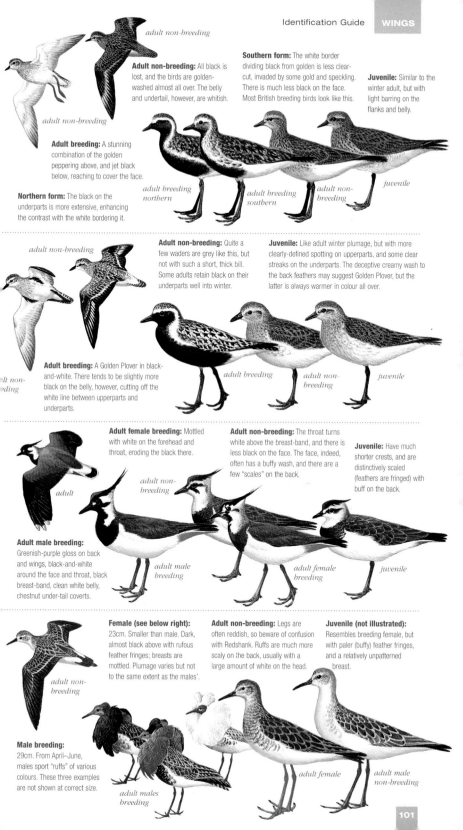

Estuarine and saltwater feeders

Plovers – have a characteristic "stop-run-peck" feeding method: from the motionless stop position, they cast their eyes over the mud for surface food. If no food is seen, they run to another spot and stop again, but if food is seen, they run towards it and peck, catching it by surprise.

Oystercatcher – probes in the mud for many foods, and also forages over mussel-beds and rock pools. They have an especially thick, powerful bill, ideal for dislodging and damaging shellfish (although they rarely take oysters). Individuals use one of two different methods to attack shellfish: hammerers apply blows to weak spots, and stabbers insert their bills between the shell valves and cut away the muscle keeping the shell shut.

Curlews and Whimbrels – have long, curved bills which are used for probing deep down in the mud. Prey is located by sight, by the evidence of their excretions from the burrow, or by touch while probing. Apart from deep-burrowing worms, they also take many of the larger crabs, which smaller waders are unable to tackle.

Dunlin – as with many other smaller waders this species feeds principally from near the surface, and uses mostly touch to locate the prey. Touch feeding on abundant, densely-packed prey allows for the birds to work in tightly-packed flocks. In such conditions "stitching" is a common technique, in which the bill is probed several times in a small area, giving the appearance of a sewing action.

Knots – probe and stitch, and a further favoured technique is called "ploughing", in which the bill is inserted and then thrust forward slightly, to make a short furrow in the soft mud. This method also relies on touch, and is well suited to the Knot's fairly short, but sturdy bill. Knots successfully harvest tellins this way, and may take 700 of them in a day.

Godwits – also stitch and probe, often doing so in quite deep water, where Dunlins could only swim!

Redshank – probes, stitches, feeds from the surface and can also detect prey by "swishing", moving its bill from side to side in the water or very soft mud until touching something.

Dunlins coming in to roost

Plovers use a "stop-run-peck" feeding technique

Avocet

Grey Phalarope spinning

Redshank

Avocet – one step ahead of the Redshank, the Avocet is a professional swisher, or "scyther". Avocets walk in shallow water, sweeping their heads from side to side, in a very distinctive movement.

Turnstone – feeds mainly on rocks, shingle and places covered with seaweed. Living up to its name, it literally lifts up stones and other items with its thick, sturdy bill, to reveal whatever is hidden underneath. It lives on a catholic diet of unearthed discoveries.

Purple Sandpipers –also have a broad diet, which can include plant material.

Sanderlings – specialise in feeding from sandy beaches, where the waves break. They run at a great pace when feeding, picking and probing like clockwork toys, constantly challenging then retreating from the breaking waves.

Phalaropes – feed in, rather than beside, the water, swimming like ducks. In the winter, they live far out to sea feeding on plankton. They are famous for their own special feeding technique, "spinning", during which they revolve in circles, picking off any prey disturbed by their action. Insects and their larvae are the main quarry during the breeding season when Phalaropes live on freshwater pools.

KNOT
Calidris canutus

25cm. One of three medium-sized waders that look very grey on the winter estuary, the others being Redshank and Grey Plover. This one has shortish legs, short neck and medium length bill. It always looks thickset, but at the same time appears long-bodied.

adult breeding

Where found: A widespread passage migrant in reasonable numbers to muddy, sandy coasts. Winter visitor to some estuaries in huge numbers, especially Morecambe Bay and the Wash.

Adult breeding: The brick-red colour is shared only by the Curlew Sandpiper, which is smaller and has a longer bill and neck.

SANDERLING
Calidris alba

20cm. A plump sandpiper, slightly larger than Dunlin. In winter, its ghostly-white appearance is distinctive. It runs around on sandy beaches like a clockwork toy, just dodging the breakers.

Adult breeding: The Sanderling is patterned black and rufous above and below, except for the white belly.

adult breeding

Where found: A common passage migrant and winter visitor to sandy shores and estuaries.

DUNLIN
Calidris alpina

18cm. This is the "benchmark" species against which all small waders should be checked, since it is the most abundant. It is also quite variable in plumage. It is typically hunched in appearance, and has a bill which curves down at the tip. Some birds have longer bills than others. Dunlins are usually seen in flocks, often very large.

adult breeding

Where found: A fairly common breeding bird, mostly in the north, on upland moors with standing pools; some coastal marshes. Abundant passage and winter visitor to muddy estuaries

Adult breeding: The black belly is an absolute giveaway; the bird looks as though it has been kneeling in oil. The amount of black varies between individuals, sexes and races.

PURPLE SANDPIPER
Calidris maritima

21cm. A plump wader, slightly larger and thicker-necked than a Dunlin, and almost always found on rocks, not mudflats. The thickish bill is yellow at the base, and the short legs are also yellow.

adult breeding

Where found: A few pairs breed in Scotland, having colonised in 1978. Otherwise, a fairly common winter visitor to rocky shores, groynes and piers. Commonest in Scotland.

Adult breeding: It looks dark, without much distinctive patterning, but there is a pleasant chestnut wash to the back.

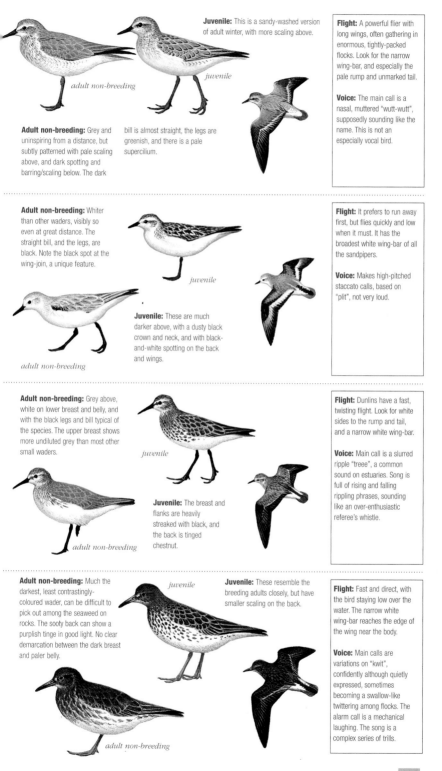

Juvenile: This is a sandy-washed version of adult winter, with more scaling above.

juvenile

adult non-breeding

Adult non-breeding: Grey and uninspiring from a distance, but subtly patterned with pale scaling above, and dark spotting and barring/scaling below. The dark bill is almost straight, the legs are greenish, and there is a pale supercilium.

Flight: A powerful flier with long wings, often gathering in enormous, tightly-packed flocks. Look for the narrow wing-bar, and especially the pale rump and unmarked tail.

Voice: The main call is a nasal, muttered "wutt-wutt", supposedly sounding like the name. This is not an especially vocal bird.

Adult non-breeding: Whiter than other waders, visibly so even at great distance. The straight bill, and the legs, are black. Note the black spot at the wing-join, a unique feature.

juvenile

Juvenile: These are much darker above, with a dusty black crown and neck, and with black-and-white spotting on the back and wings.

adult non-breeding

Flight: It prefers to run away first, but flies quickly and low when it must. It has the broadest white wing-bar of all the sandpipers.

Voice: Makes high-pitched staccato calls, based on "plit", not very loud.

Adult non-breeding: Grey above, white on lower breast and belly, and with the black legs and bill typical of the species. The upper breast shows more undiluted grey than most other small waders.

juvenile

Juvenile: The breast and flanks are heavily streaked with black, and the back is tinged chestnut.

adult non-breeding

Flight: Dunlins have a fast, twisting flight. Look for white sides to the rump and tail, and a narrow white wing-bar.

Voice: Main call is a slurred ripple "treee", a common sound on estuaries. Song is full of rising and falling rippling phrases, sounding like an over-enthusiastic referee's whistle.

Adult non-breeding: Much the darkest, least contrastingly-coloured wader, can be difficult to pick out among the seaweed on rocks. The sooty back can show a purplish tinge in good light. No clear demarcation between the dark breast and paler belly.

juvenile

Juvenile: These resemble the breeding adults closely, but have smaller scaling on the back.

adult non-breeding

Flight: Fast and direct, with the bird staying low over the water. The narrow white wing-bar reaches the edge of the wing near the body.

Voice: Main calls are variations on "kwit", confidently although quietly expressed, sometimes becoming a swallow-like twittering among flocks. The alarm call is a mechanical laughing. The song is a complex series of trills.

Freshwater and land feeders

Snipe – a marsh-loving species, is the most adept at probing (using touch only), and has an amazingly long bill to match.

Greenshank – also probes, but not so deeply and not exclusively; it is one of the few waders to hunt fish regularly, which it captures with a short, dashing chase and strike.

Spotted Redshank – feeds mostly from the surface of mud, not only where the water is shallow, but also in the deeps, where it will wade on its long legs, or even swim and up-end, catching prey by touch. Sometimes, groups of Spotted Redshanks hunt co-operatively in packs, chasing after and "herding" shoals of small fish or invertebrates (using sight).

Little Ringed Plover – is mostly a surface feeder, and chases after prey that has been detected by sight.

Little and Temminck's Stint – the stints have a similar feeding technique to the Little Ringed Plover. More specifically, stints feed with rapid, non-stop pecks, mainly on insects and other small invertebrates.

Green Sandpiper – feeds while walking steadily, pecking at prey on the surface, taking items such as insects, worms, crustaceans and molluscs.

Common Sandpiper – lives on rivers and chases after insects and their larvae, even grabbing at low-flying prey.

Lapwings – are most commonly found on farmland and short grassy areas, but also on saltmarshes. They feed on earthworms and other invertebrates.

Golden Plover – occupies similar habitats to the Lapwing, detecting invertebrates by sight, and using the typical plover "stop-run-peck" feeding technique (see p.94).

Woodcock – is a prober, working over damp patches of woodland soil and rooting in the leaf-litter by night. Earthworms are favoured among a variety of other food items taken by this bird.

Stone Curlew – a nocturnal species that takes a variety of ground-living prey. Also, when a moth flutters past, the Stone Curlew is able to catch it with a running jump. Such skill depends on excellent night vision, which of course the Stone Curlew has with its huge, staring eyes.

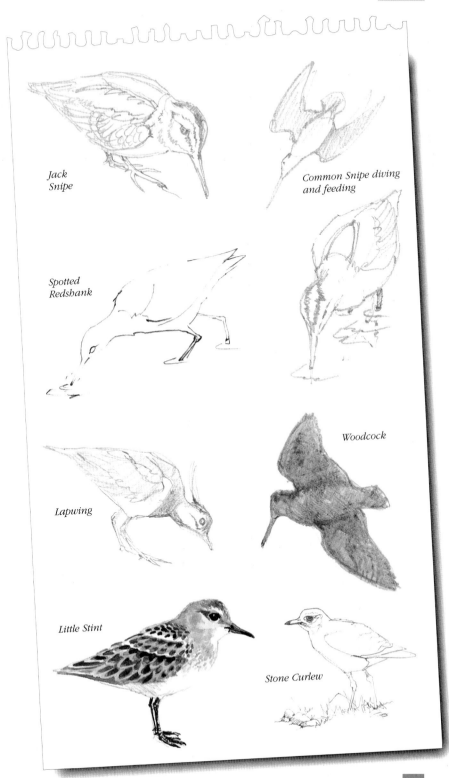

Jack
Snipe

Common Snipe diving
and feeding

Spotted
Redshank

Woodcock

Lapwing

Little Stint

Stone Curlew

LITTLE STINT
Calidris minuta

13cm. This looks like a small Dunlin with a short, straight bill. It is so lively and hyperactive, it can be exhausting to watch. A tiny, tame bird. The legs are black.

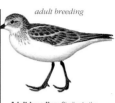

adult breeding

Where found: An uncommon passage migrant to inland and coastal mudflats and beaches. The main passage is in August and September. A very few birds winter on estuaries.

Adult breeding: Similar to the Sanderling in this plumage, but much smaller, with more white on the throat, and only a narrow band of light rufous across the breast. Also shows two pale yellow stripes on the mantle.

TEMMINCK'S STINT
Calidris temminckii

14cm. A small sandpiper with a crouched, almost horizontal posture. Although plump, it looks longer in body than its close relative, the Little Stint. The legs are yellow-green.

adult breeding

Where found: Rare breeding bird in a few Scottish bogs. Mostly a rare passage migrant in May, and then in August and September, to sheltered marshes and lakes in eastern England.

Adult breeding: Grey-brown above, always with some black and rufous markings. The white underparts meet the grey-brown breast to make an obvious band. Much duller than Little Stint.

CURLEW SANDPIPER
Calidris ferruginea

19cm. As its name implies, the Curlew Sandpiper has an unusually long, curved bill. This, along with its longer legs and larger body, distinguishes it from the Dunlins with which it so often associates. Look also for the slightly longer neck and more upright stance.

adult breeding

Where found: Regular passage migrant, mostly in autumn, to muddy places, usually on the coast. Commonest in the east, south and north-west of England. A few pass through in spring.

Adult breeding: The colour recalls Knot in summer, but this bird is much smaller and longer-billed. It also sports a white chin.

Diet and feeding technique

The food available to an estuarine wader depends on:
1) The depth to which it can probe with its bill
2) The depth to which its legs allow it to wade
3) The part of the estuary/shore over which it feeds
4) The technique employed to secure prey

On these pages we look at the first of these factors and the types of food eaten by estuarine feeders; the other three are discussed on pp.112–113.

1) Bill length
It is this that initially determines what food is available to a wader; this is because, within the muddy intertidal zone (the ground between high tide and low tide), certain types of prey are available at certain depths in the mud. More food types are within the range of the Curlew, for example, with its long bill, than are available to the Ringed Plover, with its short bill. Curlews can even reach the deep-living Lugworms, which are large and nutritious. Ringed Plovers cannot.

There are three main food types available in the intertidal zone:

Burrowing molluscs (shellfish): among many others, particular favourites of waders include the Cockle *Cardium edule* and Laver Spire Shell *Hydrobia ulvae* which live near

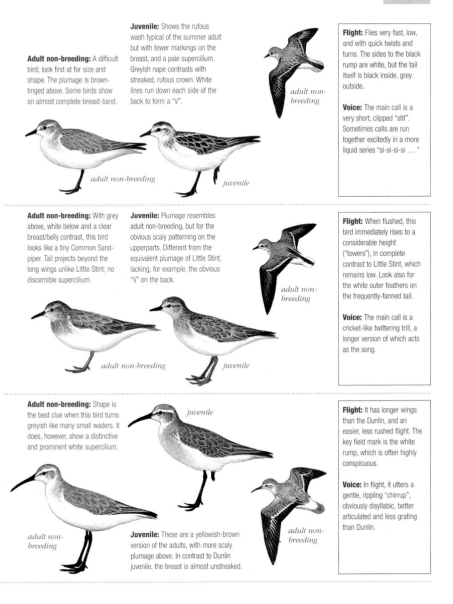

Adult non-breeding: A difficult bird; look first at for size and shape. The plumage is brown-tinged above. Some birds show an almost complete breast-band.

Juvenile: Shows the rufous wash typical of the summer adult but with fewer markings on the breast, and a pale supercilium. Greyish nape contrasts with streaked, rufous crown. White lines run down each side of the back to form a "V".

adult non-breeding

adult non-breeding

juvenile

Flight: Flies very fast, low, and with quick twists and turns. The sides to the black rump are white, but the tail itself is black inside, grey outside.

Voice: The main call is a very short, clipped "stit". Sometimes calls are run together excitedly in a more liquid series "si-si-si-si ... "

Adult non-breeding: With grey above, white below and a clear breast/belly contrast, this bird looks like a tiny Common Sandpiper. Tail projects beyond the long wings unlike Little Stint; no discernible supercilium.

Juvenile: Plumage resembles adult non-breeding, but for the obvious scaly patterning on the upperparts. Different from the equivalent plumage of Little Stint, lacking, for example, the obvious "V" on the back.

adult non-breeding

adult non-breeding

juvenile

Flight: When flushed, this bird immediately rises to a considerable height ("towers"), in complete contrast to Little Stint, which remains low. Look also for the white outer feathers on the frequently-fanned tail.

Voice: The main call is a cricket-like twittering trill, a longer version of which acts as the song.

Adult non-breeding: Shape is the best clue when this bird turns greyish like many small waders. It does, however, show a distinctive and prominent white supercilium.

juvenile

adult non-breeding

Juvenile: These are a yellowish-brown version of the adults, with more scaly plumage above. In contrast to Dunlin juvenile, the breast is almost unstreaked.

adult non-breeding

Flight: It has longer wings than the Dunlin, and an easier, less rushed flight. The key field mark is the white rump, which is often highly conspicuous.

Voice: In flight, it utters a gentle, rippling "chirrup", obviously disyllabic, better articulated and less grating than Dunlin.

---

the surface; the Baltic Tellin *Macoma balthica* which lives about 5cm down; and the Peppery Furrow Shell *Scrobicularia plana* which is a deep burrower. The short-billed Ringed Plover is a great fan of the Spire Shell, the longer-billed Knot greatly favours the Tellin, and the Curlew likes to take the Furrow Shell.

Worms: the Lugworm *Arenicola marina* lives in a burrow up to 15cm (6in) down, where it is only available to a very long-billed wader. However, it must regularly come to the surface to excrete, and there can be snapped up by many species. Another worm delicacy is the Ragworm *Nereis diversicolor*, with a similar lifestyle, and there are many others.

Crustaceans: a great favourite among waders is the tiny shrimp *Corophium volutator*, over which Redshanks and Ringed Plovers drool. It is tiny, living in a shallow burrow near the mud surface, sometimes at a density of 11,000 per square metre. Other larger and much less abundant Crustacea include the Crabs (eg. Shore Crab *Carcinus maenus*), which also do not burrow very deep down.

Daily movements and flocks

On a beach or estuary, the life of a wader is dominated by the tides. When the tide is out the bird must spend much of its time feeding; at high tide, when the feeding grounds are covered by water, it must rest and preen. These rules still apply even if low tide occurs at night, and high tide during the day.

Even among waders that do not live on estuaries, there are certain places to feed, and different places best for roosting. Lapwings and Golden Plovers, for example, often gather to roost on particular fields that appear unremarkable, but obviously comply with the right criteria.

Most waders are sociable, to a lesser or greater extent, when feeding, roosting, or travelling.

When feeding, the smaller, touch-feeding waders, such as Dunlins, Knots and Sanderlings gather into tightly-packed groups. Others space out more widely, especially the plovers, Curlew and Oystercatcher. Some Grey Plovers even defend their own personal territory on the mudflats or creeks. In some species, the degree of sociability can be important in identification: Snipe often feed in groups, Jack Snipe do not; Little Stints are sociable, Temminck's Stints are not; Redshanks are gregarious, Greenshanks prefer their own company.

When roosting, some waders such as Knots, Dunlins and Redshanks, tend to pack tightly (see below right). Others leave more space, especially Curlews and Oystercatchers, although they will often have an army of smaller species scuttling around their feet. Wader roosts always look packed; in fact, the centre of the roost provides a certain amount of shelter from the prevailing elements. The amount of personal space available will obviously depend on the size of the roosting site. Often, islands and jetties are chosen, with their limited space, so personal preferences have to be abandoned.

In flight, from feeding grounds to roosts, different species behave in different ways. Small species nearly always gather in fast-moving, low-flying, manoeuvrable flocks: these include Dunlins, Turnstones, Sanderlings and, in particular, Knots. The latter often indulge in impressive aerial manoeuvres over the roost, reminiscent of a plume of smoke. As they turn, a glistening pale streak runs

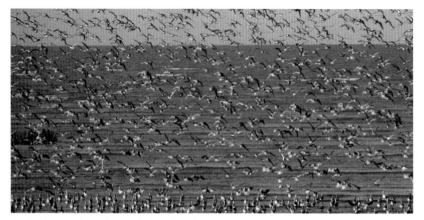

A mixed group of waders in flight and at the roost

A mixed flock of waders in flight

through the flock as the dark upper-sides tilt to reveal pale undersides. It is one of the great sights of British birdwatching. During this aerobatic feat, the individual birds must react very quickly to prevent collisions.

Curlews and Bar-tailed Godwits are also given to some aerobatics, and can be seen twisting, turning and tumbling over the roost. But by and large they fly in smaller, and less tightly-packed formations. Curlews will generally remain in groups of about 20, while Grey Plovers will settle for about half that number, and Redshanks about double, but of course this does vary. Oystercatchers are notable for the way in which they fly in single file over the sea.

How to watch waders

How can the birdwatcher be a witness to these spectacular movements? When visiting an estuary, choose to arrive on-site about two or three hours before high tide. Select a place where you can be reasonably concealed but can see clearly – a hide is perfect. As the tide rises the birds will be forced closer to land as they take advantage of the last mud to be

covered by the sea. It is easy to get very close views in these circumstances, making it possible to appreciate the waders' different feeding techniques, and even to see what they are feeding on.

Near to high tide, the waders will be forced to abandon feeding in favour of roosting. Hundreds of birds will be flying this way and that, and many will start to perform their aerial convolutions.

Of course, the same pattern will happen, in reverse, as the tide begins to drop again.

A winter pack of Knots

TURNSTONE
Arenaria interpres

23cm. A solidly-built, short-legged and short-billed wader with a unique plumage pattern. It prefers rocky shores, and sometimes shares these with the Purple Sandpiper. The legs are orange.

adult male breeding

adult female breeding

Where found: A common winter visitor to coasts, preferring rocky shores. Also found on mudflats in estuaries. It is also a common passage migrant; in May, small numbers are often found inland.

Male breeding: These are a mixture of black, white and vivid chestnut, with clear, well-defined markings: unmistakable.

RED-NECKED PHALAROPE
Phalaropus lobatus

18cm. Phalaropes swim on the water surface, buoyant as corks, busily picking around them for tiny fragments of food, self-absorbed and dizzy. Often they spin in circles in mechanical fashion. Identification as a Phalarope is never a problem. This is the smaller of our two species, with a "hypodermic" thin bill.

adult female breeding

adult male breeding

Where found: Rare breeding bird in marshy areas in northern Scotland (mostly Shetland), occurring around shallow pools. It arrives in May. Birds return south from mid-July onwards.

Male breeding: Essentially a brownish-grey bird, with an orange-brown streak beginning behind the eye and flowing, ever widening, down the side of the neck. The back is heavily streaked and striped with the same colour.

GREY PHALAROPE
Phalaropus fulicarius

20cm. This species is larger than Red-necked Phalarope, with a noticeably stouter bill.

adult female breeding

adult male breeding

Where found: An extremely scarce passage migrant, mostly to the south-west of England and Ireland, when it is seen mostly in late September and October. Birds are usually blown in by

Male breeding: The bill is yellow, black-tipped. "Grey" Phalarope seems a ridiculous name for this richly coloured bird.

Female breeding: Phalarope finery reaches its zenith. The female is more cleanly marked on the face than the male.

Diet and feeding technique

Continued from pp.108–109.

2) Length of legs
The length of the legs, and also the neck, determines how far into the water a wader can go to feed. The Curlew and Godwits can continue to feed in areas which the tide has partially covered, and Avocets can even swim when feeding.

3) Feeding Site
Not all waders feed exclusively on the mud of the intertidal zone. Turnstones, Oystercatchers, Ringed Plovers and Purple Sandpipers all feed on the rocky shores and beaches, and the Sanderling specialises on feeding over sandy beaches.

4) Feeding Technique
The feeding technique not only determines where a wader can feed and on what, it is also extremely useful in identification. Here are some examples. More feeding techniques are featured on pp.102–103 and pp.106–107.

Plovers: Plovers have a unique "Stop-run-peck" feeding method. From the motionless stop position, they cast their eyes over the mud for surface food. If no food is seen, they run to another spot and stop again, but if food is seen, they run towards it and peck, catching it by surprise. The Grey Plover, with the larger bill, is able to attack larger items than the smaller-billed Ringed Plover, but both obtain all their food

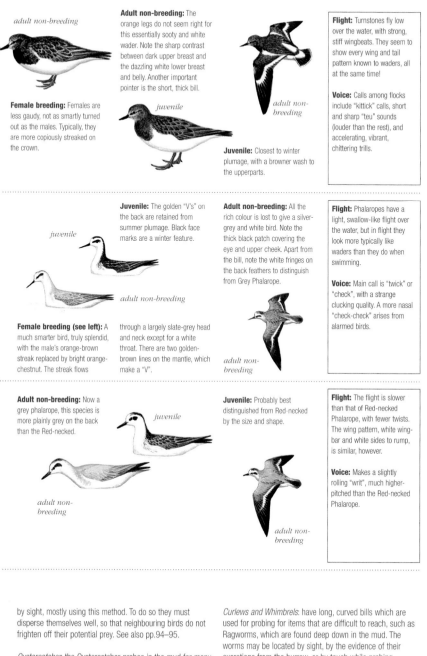

adult non-breeding

Adult non-breeding: The orange legs do not seem right for this essentially sooty and white wader. Note the sharp contrast between dark upper breast and the dazzling white lower breast and belly. Another important pointer is the short, thick bill.

Female breeding: Females are less gaudy, not as smartly turned out as the males. Typically, they are more copiously streaked on the crown.

juvenile

adult non-breeding

Juvenile: Closest to winter plumage, with a browner wash to the upperparts.

Flight: Turnstones fly low over the water, with strong, stiff wingbeats. They seem to show every wing and tail pattern known to waders, all at the same time!

Voice: Calls among flocks include "kittick" calls, short and sharp "teu" sounds (louder than the rest), and accelerating, vibrant, chittering trills.

Juvenile: The golden "V's" on the back are retained from summer plumage. Black face marks are a winter feature.

juvenile

adult non-breeding

Female breeding (see left): much smarter bird, truly splendid, with the male's orange-brown streak replaced by bright orange-chestnut. The streak flows through a largely slate-grey head and neck except for a white throat. There are two golden-brown lines on the mantle, which make a "V".

Adult non-breeding: All the rich colour is lost to give a silver-grey and white bird. Note the thick black patch covering the eye and upper cheek. Apart from the bill, note the white fringes on the back feathers to distinguish from Grey Phalarope.

adult non-breeding

Flight: Phalaropes have a light, swallow-like flight over the water, but in flight they look more typically like waders than they do when swimming.

Voice: Main call is "twick" or "check", with a strange clucking quality. A more nasal "check-check" arises from alarmed birds.

Adult non-breeding: Now a grey phalarope, this species is more plainly grey on the back than the Red-necked.

juvenile

adult non-breeding

Juvenile: Probably best distinguished from Red-necked by the size and shape.

adult non-breeding

Flight: The flight is slower than that of Red-necked Phalarope, with fewer twists. The wing pattern, white wing-bar and white sides to rump, is similar, however.

Voice: Makes a slightly rolling "writ", much higher-pitched than the Red-necked Phalarope.

---

by sight, mostly using this method. To do so they must disperse themselves well, so that neighbouring birds do not frighten off their potential prey. See also pp.94–95.

Oystercatcher: the Oystercatcher probes in the mud for many foods, and also forages over mussel-beds and rockpools. They use their thick, powerful bills to attack shellfish and will use one of two methods: hammerers apply blows to the mussel's weak spots; stabbers prise their bills in between the shell valves and cut away the muscle which keeps the shell shut. No one Oystercatcher uses both methods; hammerers have thick, blunt bills, and stabbers have more pointed bills.

Curlews and Whimbrels: have long, curved bills which are used for probing for items that are difficult to reach, such as Ragworms, which are found deep down in the mud. The worms may be located by sight, by the evidence of their excretions from the burrow, or by touch while probing. Experiments have shown that a curved bill is better than a straight one for searching among nooks and crannies in saltmarshes and mudflats. With such long, useful bills Curlews have numerous options for feeding, but tend to specialise to avoid competition with other waders. Apart from deep-burrowing worms, they also take many larger crabs, which present too formidable an opponent for smaller waders to tackle.

JACK SNIPE
Lymnocryptes minimus

19cm. Members of the Snipe group are famous for their long, straight bills which probe deep into the mud or soil, and also for their cryptic, straw-coloured plumage. The Jack Snipe has the shortest bill of the group. When feeding the bird can be identified by the way in which it bobs its body up and down, as if on springs – the Snipe does not do this.

adult

Where found: A widespread, but local, passage migrant and winter visitor, favouring inland marshy sites with copious vegetation.

Adult/juvenile: The bill is only slightly longer than the head. The crown is black in the centre, and there is an extra black stripe over the eye, within the pale

SNIPE
Gallinago gallinago

27cm. The Snipe has an amazingly long bill, almost as long as its body, and about twice the length of its head (a proportion greater than on any other British bird). The Snipe is noticeably larger than the Jack Snipe. The Snipe is very nervous and will fly away if you come within 10m (30ft).

adult

Where found: A fairly common breeding species in marshes, wet meadows and bogs throughout the country. Also a common passage migrant and winter visitor.

Adult/juvenile: The dark crown has a pale stripe along the top of it, and the wide supercilium lacks the Jack Snipe's extra stripe. The Snipe is also strongly barred along the flanks, unlike its relative.

WOODCOCK
Scolopax rusticola

34cm. This wader lives in woodland, probing for food in the soil and litter. It is usually seen flying over the trees at dawn and dusk on its "roding" display flight. The long bill is broader than that of the Snipe, and the body is larger and plumper.

adult

Where found: Our only woodland wader, favouring deciduous woods with plenty of cover, but also with damp open areas. It occurs throughout our area, but is commoner in winter.

Adult/juvenile: The all-over pattern affords astonishingly effective camouflage among the leaf-litter. The crown is dark, with three narrow rings dividing it.

STONE CURLEW
Burhinus oedicnemus

41cm. The Stone Curlew stares at you with its huge, yellow eyes, in reptilian fashion. It stands very erect and often motionless, melting into its surroundings. Sometimes it will "rest on its haunches", feet pointing forwards. This species is most active at dusk and at night.

adult

Where found: A rare summer visitor (March–October) to a few chalk downlands, arable fields and lowland heathlands in East Anglia and southern England.

Adult: Face is very white, otherwise plumage is streaked in various browns. The bill is yellow, black at the tip, and the legs are yellowish-brown. Adults show a contrasting wing-pattern.

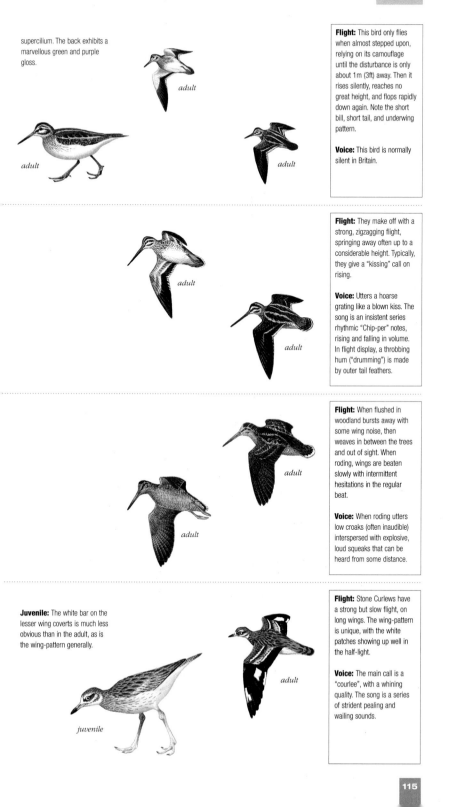

supercilium. The back exhibits a marvellous green and purple gloss.

adult

adult

adult

Flight: This bird only flies when almost stepped upon, relying on its camouflage until the disturbance is only about 1m (3ft) away. Then it rises silently, reaches no great height, and flops rapidly down again. Note the short bill, short tail, and underwing pattern.

Voice: This bird is normally silent in Britain.

adult

adult

Flight: They make off with a strong, zigzagging flight, springing away often up to a considerable height. Typically, they give a "kissing" call on rising.

Voice: Utters a hoarse grating like a blown kiss. The song is an insistent series rhythmic "Chip-per" notes, rising and falling in volume. In flight display, a throbbing hum ("drumming") is made by outer tail feathers.

adult

adult

Flight: When flushed in woodland bursts away with some wing noise, then weaves in between the trees and out of sight. When roding, wings are beaten slowly with intermittent hesitations in the regular beat.

Voice: When roding utters low croaks (often inaudible) interspersed with explosive, loud squeaks that can be heard from some distance.

Juvenile: The white bar on the lesser wing coverts is much less obvious than in the adult, as is the wing-pattern generally.

juvenile

adult

Flight: Stone Curlews have a strong but slow flight, on long wings. The wing-pattern is unique, with the white patches showing up well in the half-light.

Voice: The main call is a "courlee", with a whining quality. The song is a series of strident pealing and wailing sounds.

CURLEW
Numenius arquata

55cm. The Curlew is a large brown wader, named and famed for its enormously long, curved bill. Only the Whimbrel is genuinely similar, but smaller. Curlews walk and fly sedately, and make sounds that are out of this world.

Where found: Common breeding bird in upland and low-land heaths and moorland, with damp areas. Common and wide-spread (mainly coastal) passage migrant and winter visitor.

Adult: Curlews are big, with long legs. Pay attention to the bill shape, long and evenly curved; females have longer bills than males, often noticeably so. The head looks more or less unpatterned, but can show the hint of an eyebrow.

WHIMBREL
Numenius phaeopus

41cm. The Whimbrel is much smaller than the Curlew, with a less obviously curved bill. Its size is closer to that of the godwits, although Curlew remains the greatest identification pitfall.

adult

Where found: Breeds only on moorland in the very north of Scotland, mostly Shetland. A fairly common passage migrant (both spring and autumn) to various habitats on many coasts.

BAR-TAILED GODWIT
Limosa lapponica

38cm. Godwits are large, long-legged and long-billed waders closely related to curlews. However, in contrast to Curlew or Whimbrel their bill is not decurved, but straight or slightly upcurved. The Bar-tailed Godwit is the stockier of the two species, which has legs which seem too short for it (note the short distance between the belly and the "knees"). It also has the more uptilted, and shorter, bill.

Where found: A passage migrant and common winter visitor to many coasts, favouring muddy estuaries and sandy shores. Many migrants pass through the English Channel in April.

Adult breeding: The breeding male is richly coloured with red-chestnut on the whole of his underparts down to the vent; the female is much duller, not especially different from non-breeding plumage. However, both birds are darker brown on the back compared to Black-tailed Godwits, and neither have the strong belly and flank markings of that species. In both godwits, the female has the longer bill.

BLACK-TAILED GODWIT
Limosa limosa

41cm. This is a very elegant, long-billed, leggy bird, quite a contrast to its dumpy, short-legged relative. Note the longer distance between the belly and "knees". The bill is longer, and looks straighter.

Where found: Rare nester on meadows in scattered localities, notably the Ouse Washes. Much commoner in winter, at some estuaries in southern England and Ireland; also on passage.

Adult breeding: The brick-red coloration reaches only down to the breast, where it fades into the richly barred belly and flanks and disappears well before white belly and vent. (Birds nesting in Shetland show red going further down). The female is less barred on the underparts, but does show some red-brown colour on the head and neck.

Adult non-breeding: All the colour and patterning is lost, to give a very plain, uniform, grey-brown bird.

adult

adult

adult

Flight: They fly with characteristically slow, steady wing-beats, almost like a gull. Note the white, triangular rump.

Voice: The main call is a beautifully whistled "cour-lee!" It becomes more yelping if the bird is alarmed. For the song, loud, measured liquid notes rise in both pitch and tempo until they merge into a long, pulsating, bubbling, exultant trill.

Adult: The bill is shorter than that of Curlew, and tends to look straighter – drooped or even kinked mainly at the tip. On the head, a pale supercilium is offset by a somewhat diffuse dark eyestripe below and a much clearer black crown-stripe above. Whimbrels often look slightly darker-plumaged than Curlews, especially on the upperparts.

adult

adult

Flight: The Whimbrel flies with much faster wing-beats than the Curlew, looking less heavy. The tail, rump and wing-patterns are similar.

Voice: The main flight call is a tittering series of six or seven whistling notes. The song is similar to that of Curlew, but the fluty whistles accelerate into a straight, even, stammering trill, without the throbbing quality of Curlew.

Adult non-breeding: The upperparts look quite streaky, including the head and neck. The back shows pale fringes to the feathers, giving a strongly-patterned effect. The Black-tailed Godwit is relatively unpatterned on the back.

Juvenile: Warmer brown in tone than the adult; can look rather like a Curlew (but for the bill). It is streaked on the head and neck, in contrast to Black-tailed Godwit, shows a more distinct pale supercilium, and is slightly paler.

adult non-breeding

juvenile

adult breeding

adult non-breeding

Flight: In flight, this species is powerful and acrobatic. The colour pattern is more like the Whimbrel than Black-tailed Godwit. There are, of course, bars on the tail. The feet only just project beyond the tail.

Voice: Not a very vocal bird, mainly uttering nasal "Yak-yak" and "kirruk" notes.

Juvenile: In contrast to Bar-tailed Godwit, juveniles have an indistinct supercilium, very little streaking on head and neck, and a warmer brown wash all over.

adult non-breeding

juvenile

adult breeding

adult non-breeding

Flight: Another fast flier, with powerful, rapid wing-beats. Its flight pattern – white wing-bar, white rump, black tail – is utterly different to Bar-tailed Godwit's, and may even recall Oystercatcher. The legs trail well behind the tail.

Voice: The main flight call is a strong, nasal, creaking "wicka", much repeated. The song is an elaboration and embellishment of this basic theme.

SPOTTED REDSHANK
Tringa erythropus

30cm. The "Shanks" are medium-sized waders with long legs and long, mostly straight bills. The Spotted Redshank has longer red legs than the Redshank, giving it a taller and more elegant look. Often wades in deep water, and swims. Its bill is also noticeably longer, with the hint of a downward tilt at the tip. On Spotted Redshanks, the red on the bill is confined to the lower mandible.

male breeding

Where found: A fairly common passage migrant to muddy lakeshores and estuaries; commonest in east and south-east England in the autumn. Small numbers winter.

Adult breeding: Unmistakably sooty-black all over, except for constellations of white spots on the upperparts. Females are not as black.

REDSHANK
Tringa totanus

28cm. This very common species is shorter-legged than Spotted Redshank, and with a shorter, blunter bill. Diagnostically the bill is red at the base on both upper and lower mandible. The name "Redshank" refers to the red legs. This bird is exceedingly noisy. Sometimes the most common bird on a large estuary.

adult breeding

Where found: A common and widespread breeding bird in all kinds of marshes, freshwater and salty, and also other wet areas. A common passage migrant and abundant winter visitor.

Adult breeding: A brown-looking wader, copiously streaked. In breeding plumage, it is particularly heavily marked on the underparts.

GREENSHANK
Tringa nebularia

31cm. A taller bird than Redshank, also larger- and longer-bodied with colder coloration. The bill is much stouter, especially at the base, and it is slightly uptilted. The legs are not red; as the name implies, they are green.

Adult breeding: Against the cold-grey wash to the plumage, there are some black spots on the back, and rather strong streaks on the head, neck and breast.

Adult non-breeding: A very pale bird, whitewashed below. Any strong patterning on the wings and back has been lost, leaving grey feathers with narrow white fringes. The crown and hindneck are still peppered with black.

Where found: Rare breeder on bare, boggy moorland of northern Scotland (the Flow Country), but a common passage migrant to a variety of freshwater and coastal habitats. Small numbers winter.

Displays for courtship and territory

Although some waders form pair-bonds on their wintering grounds, usually a display is used to attract the attention of a mate. At the same time competitive males must also be repelled from the territory. Often both aims are achieved with a single, spectacular display, accompanied by loud calls.
Lapwing: The flight display involves a series of rising, falling, twisting and tumbling manoeuvres. that are accompanied by distinctive whining calls. In addition, the vigorously beaten wings make a throbbing sound.
Snipe: When falling earthwards the Snipe spreads its outermost tail feathers (one on each side), which vibrate in the current. A strange bleating sound is made. The display is known as "drumming", and often takes place at night.

Woodcock: Males perform a circuit around the woods where they live, at dawn and dusk. Flying with slow, interrupted wing-beats, they call to females with strange grunting and sneezing sounds. The display is called "roding". A quiet call of approval from below brings them down to a waiting mate.
Greenshanks: and others call loudly in flight while performing crazy "Switchback Flights", in which the momentum gained by the falling is used to gain height again.
Redshanks: and others make "Quivering Flights": wings are beaten with a different intensity to usual and with loud calls.
Dunlin: uses a subtle display on the ground; much information is conveyed in the brief lifting of one wing. It is a gesture of togetherness, like a knowing wink.

Adult non-breeding: It turns very white and grey. A prominent white patch between the bill (upper mandible) and the eye (which may reach behind the eye to make a supercilium) is characteristic of the species. This species is whiter and less streaked below than the Redshank.

adult non-breeding   *juvenile*

adult non-breeding

Juvenile: Youngsters are browner than their parents, with much white spotting on the back, and much barring below. Their legs are paler red. Look for those consistent "Spotshank" features – long bill, red only at base of lower mandible; white patch between eye and bill.

Flight: The Spotted Redshank is a very fast flier, on rapid wing-beats. It lacks the Redshank's white trailing edge to the wing, and the white "rump-triangle" appears to reach further up the back.

Voice: The flight call is a sharp, shrill, two-note "chew-it".

Adult non-breeding: It turns greyer above, and loses some of its streaking, above and below. In contrast to Spotted Redshank, there is at most only the hint of a pale patch either side of the eye, certainly not an obvious supercilium.

adult non-breeding   *juvenile*

adult non-breeding

Juvenile: Resembles adult breeding plumage, but with a profusion of buffy fringes to the back and wing-feathers. The legs are paler, more orange-yellow.

Flight: Fast, shallow beats, usually on a direct course but sometimes with much tilting and weaving. Broad white trailing edges to the wings are unique and easy to see.

Voice: In flight, it makes a fluty, ringing, melancholy, two or three-syllable "TEU-hu" or "TEU-huhu", with the first note stressed. For the song, repeated, slow single notes accelerate into a yodelling trill.

Juvenile: Darker above than birds in winter plumage, juveniles have very pale buff fringes to their back feathers. There is often a slight white indentation into the dark plumage at the shoulder.

adult non-breeding

adult non-breeding

adult breeding   *juvenile*

Flight: The flight is stronger than that of the Redshank, and less prone to perambulations. The Greenshank lacks any obvious white on its rather dark wings

Voice: In flight, it makes a deliberate, powerful, ringing "tew-tew" or "tew-tew-tew", with each note evenly stressed and pitched.

Ringed Plovers: a ruffle of feathers or a spread tail will equally convey a message of significance.
Oystercatchers: are less subtle. A familiar sight on their breeding grounds is the "Piping Display", which signifies mate ownership. The birds put their heads down and shout at the ground, side by side. Usually three, but 20 or more may join in, all piping excitedly at the top of their voices.
Ruff: has perhaps the most unusual wader display of all, made more remarkable for the silence that accompanies it. Groups of male Ruffs (up to 20) gather together on traditional display grounds ("arenas") to posture and fight over small territories within the arena. A gathering of displaying birds is called a "lek". The central position is the most desirable, and over time this will be achieved by the males best able to threaten and fight. The females, who visit the lek only briefly, will make straight for the "best" bird in the centre and mate with him or a bird nearby. The relationship is short and purely sexual: the female carries out all other parental duties alone.

Fascinatingly, some male Ruffs "cheat". They move around different leks, holding no territory, and not fighting. Instead, they make nuisance visits, attempting opportunistic sexual encounters while the territory-holding males are otherwise occupied. They are often successful. These opportunists are called "Satellites", and they usually have white ruffs and plumes. Territory-holding males are called "Independents", and usually have dark adornments.

GREEN SANDPIPER
Tringa ochropus

23cm. The "freshwater" sandpiperson this page are white-bellied, straight-billed waders that often bob their rear ends up and down. They are usually found on freshwater. The Green Sandpiper is the darkest of the three, and also the largest. It has dark green legs, which are shorter than those of its close relative, the Wood Sandpiper. It flies off showing a startling white rump.

adult breeding

Where found: A fairly common passage migrant, especially autumn (peak in August), to muddy margins and marshes, not only freshwater. A few winter, mostly in the south.

Adult breeding: Dark olive-green above with glistening white spotting on the back and wings. The heavily streaked breast is sharply demarcated from the white belly.

WOOD SANDPIPER
Tringa glareola

20cm. This is smaller, slimmer, more delicate, and longer-legged than Green Sandpiper. It is generally paler, and has yellow-green, not dark green legs. The white rump is less obvious.

adult breeding

Where found: Rare breeder since 1959 on Scottish lochsides. A scarce passage migrant, mostly autumn, to mainly south and east coasts.

Adult breeding: Browner on the back than Green Sandpiper, and larger spots create less contrast with the belly. Streaks from breast to belly mean there is little contrast in this area too.

COMMON SANDPIPER
Actitis hypoleucos

20cm. The constant bobbing of the rear end of this bird, a more exaggerated habit in this species than any other wader, is a good pointer. It is shorter legged, more tapered, and plainer brown above than its immediate relatives. The white notch at the shoulder is a good distinction from the other species on this page.

adult breeding

Where found: Commonly breeds by rivers, lakes and lochs in the north and west (including Ireland). Widespread passage migrant, and uncommon, mainly coastal winter visitor.

Adult breeding: White on breast and belly contrasts with the brown streaked upper-breast but not as sharply as on Green Sandpiper. Upperparts are olive-brown with black streaks. White on the belly forms a notch, not seen on the *Tringa* sandpipers.

General breeding behaviour

Pair-bonds

Waders form a great variety of "working relationships" when it comes to breeding. Although many of our most familiar species, including Redshank, Curlew, Dunlin and Oystercatcher form monogamous partnerships (one male, one female) which are sometimes sustained over several years, many other species exercise different options. The Woodcock, for example, can be polygynous (one male, several females), and a number of other species can be polyandrous (one female, several males). The latter include the Dotterel and Red-necked Phalarope, which also exhibit "role-reversal": the male undertakes all the breeding duties after the eggs are laid, and the more colourful female takes

much of the initiative in display behaviour.

In the Temminck's Stint, the female mates with two males and lays two clutches, of which she will incubate one, and one of her partners will incubate the other. In Dotterels and possibly Common Sandpipers, it goes further; a female may lay three or even more clutches, and she will incubate none of them, just relying on a succession of paternal males to do the work! This "rapid multi-clutch system" ensures maximum egg production in the shortest possible time.

To complete all the available options, Ruffs are promiscuous. The pair-bond is short-lived, not progressing beyond copulation. Both males and females mate with several different partners.

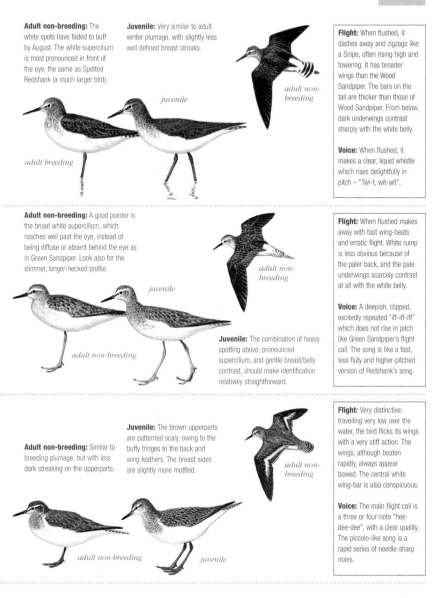

Adult non-breeding: The white spots have faded to buff by August. The white supercilium is most pronounced in front of the eye, the same as Spotted Redshank (a much larger bird).

Juvenile: Very similar to adult winter plumage, with slightly less well defined breast streaks.

juvenile

adult non-breeding

adult breeding

Flight: When flushed, it dashes away and zigzags like a Snipe, often rising high and towering. It has broader wings than the Wood Sandpiper. The bars on the tail are thicker than those of Wood Sandpiper. From below, dark underwings contrast sharply with the white belly.

Voice: When flushed, it makes a clear, liquid whistle which rises delightfully in pitch – "Twi-t, wit-wit".

Adult non-breeding: A good pointer is the broad white supercilium, which reaches well past the eye, instead of being diffuse or absent behind the eye as in Green Sandpiper. Look also for the slimmer, longer-necked profile.

juvenile

adult non-breeding

adult non-breeding

Juvenile: The combination of heavy spotting above, pronounced supercilium, and gentle breast/belly contrast, should make identification relatively straightforward.

Flight: When flushed makes away with fast wing-beats and erratic flight. White rump is less obvious because of the paler back, and the pale underwings scarcely contrast at all with the white belly.

Voice: A deepish, clipped, excitedly repeated "iff-iff-iff" which does not rise in pitch like Green Sandpiper's flight call. The song is like a fast, less fluty and higher-pitched version of Redshank's song.

Adult non-breeding: Similar to breeding plumage, but with less dark streaking on the upperparts.

Juvenile: The brown upperparts are patterned scaly, owing to the buffy fringes to the back and wing feathers. The breast sides are slightly more mottled.

adult non-breeding

adult non-breeding

juvenile

Flight: Very distinctive: travelling very low over the water, the bird flicks its wings with a very stiff action. The wings, although beaten rapidly, always appear bowed. The central white wing-bar is also conspicuous.

Voice: The main flight call is a three or four-note "hee-dee-dee", with a clear quality. The piccolo-like song is a rapid series of needle-sharp notes.

Nests and eggs

Most waders make no more than a scrape in the ground for their nest. "Scraping", indeed, can form an important part of display. While some waders nest in the open (eg. Lapwing), others have more hidden nests secreted among vegetation (eg. Snipe). The Green Sandpiper (and sometimes Wood Sandpiper) are unusual in choosing sites above ground, in the old nests of thrushes and other birds.

Almost all wader eggs are camouflaged. Most waders lay four eggs, which fit together into a small area and are easy to incubate. Incubating adults usually sit very tight, and are just as well camouflaged as the eggs. The sitting Woodcock simply melts into the pattern of the leaf-litter, while the

"disruptive" camouflage of the Ringed Plover disrupts the outline of the incubating bird, making it difficult to detect.

Chicks and parental care

Wader chicks are able to run around and feed themselves very soon after hatching, and keeping them safe can therefore be a problem. If a predator approaches parents can react in three ways: they can lure the intruder away from the nest with a "Distraction Display", such as pretending to have a broken wing; they can attack it to divert its attention; or they can take the young away bodily. There is circumstantial evidence that the Woodcock takes the latter course, carrying the young in its feet as it flies away to safety.

POMARINE SKUA
Stercorarius pomarinus

51cm. Skuas are gull-like, but darker all over, with distinctive, powerful, menacing flight. They are pirates, harrying other birds (mainly gulls and terns) mercilessly until they are forced to disgorge their food. The Pomarine Skua is larger, heavier-headed and more deep-chested than its commoner relative, the Arctic Skua. It is comparable in size to Lesser Black-backed Gull.

adult dark summer

adult pale summer

Where found: An uncommon migrant to most coasts, seen mostly in May, and again from September to the end of the year. The peak season is October and early November, later than other Skuas.

Adult (pale phase) summer: Dark-brown above, whitish below, dark cap, often with a creamy wash to the nape and cheeks. Long, twisted tail feathers give a distinctive spoon shape.

Adult (dark phase) summer: Rare; dark brown all over.

ARCTIC SKUA
Stercorarius parasiticus

46cm. This, the commonest skua, is smaller than Pomarine, and much less deep-chested. It is about the size of a Common Gull. The wing-flashes are smaller than those of Pomarine and Great Skua.

adult dark summer

adult pale summer

Where found: Breeds on coastal moorlands in western and northern Scotland. A regular passage migrant off most coasts, April–May, August–September. The most common Skua.

Adult (pale phase) summer: Similar to Pomarine but with smaller head and thinner neck. Tail is pointed.

Adult (dark phase) summer: In contrast to Pomarines, dark phase Arctics are common, and become commoner southwards.

LONG-TAILED SKUA
Stercorarius longicaudus

50cm (including tail). The Long-tailed is the smallest, narrowest-winged and slimmest of the skuas. It is only about the size of a Kittiwake or a Black-headed Gull. Its smaller bill makes it look gentler.

adult pale summer

adult intermediate summer

Where found: A rare migrant to offshore locations, in May, then August–September. Many pass the Outer Hebrides and English Channel in May.

Adult summer: Long, flexible tail that gets blown about in the wind. The length varies individually, however, and there is some overlap with Arctic Skua. Look also for the much greyer-brown back, which contrasts with the darker flight feathers, and for

GREAT SKUA
Stercorarius skua

58cm. This is the largest skua, very heavily built, with broad-based wings and a short, wedge-shaped tail, almost without projections. It approaches the Herring Gull in size.

adult

Where found: Breeds on north-western and northern Scottish coasts. Arrives in late March. A passage migrant in spring, and autumn (September and October), to most coasts.

Adult: It is all-over dark brown with paler streaking. The neck is streaked golden-yellow (in summer), and the cap is always diffuse and ill-defined. The underparts are always dark.

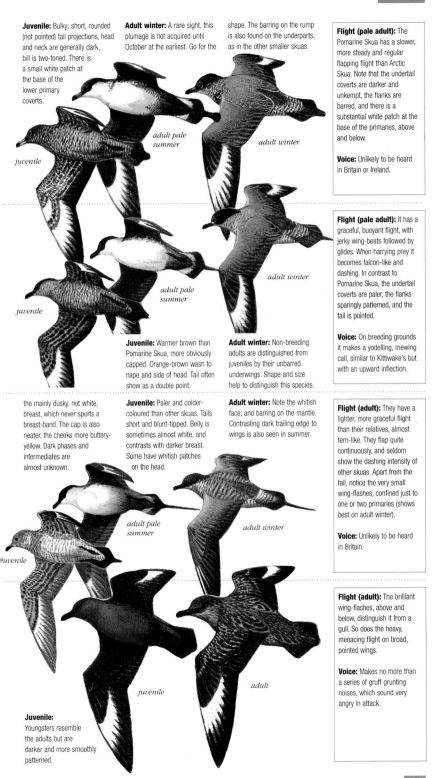

Juvenile: Bulky; short, rounded (not pointed) tail projections, head and neck are generally dark, bill is two-toned. There is a small white patch at the base of the lower primary coverts.

juvenile

Adult winter: A rare sight, this plumage is not acquired until October at the earliest. Go for the

adult pale summer

shape. The barring on the rump is also found on the underparts, as in the other smaller skuas.

adult winter

Flight (pale adult): The Pomarine Skua has a slower, more steady and regular flapping flight than Arctic Skua. Note that the undertail coverts are darker and unkempt, the flanks are barred, and there is a substantial white patch at the base of the primaries, above and below.

Voice: Unlikely to be heard in Britain or Ireland.

juvenile

adult pale summer

adult winter

Flight (pale adult): It has a graceful, buoyant flight, with jerky wing-beats followed by glides. When harrying prey it becomes falcon-like and dashing. In contrast to Pomarine Skua, the undertail coverts are paler, the flanks sparingly patterned, and the tail is pointed.

Voice: On breeding grounds it makes a yodelling, mewing call, similar to Kittiwake's but with an upward inflection.

Juvenile: Warmer brown than Pomarine Skua, more obviously capped. Orange-brown wash to nape and side of head. Tail often show as a double point.

Adult winter: Non-breeding adults are distinguished from juveniles by their unbarred underwings. Shape and size help to distinguish this species.

the mainly dusky, not white, breast, which never sports a breast-band. The cap is also neater, the cheeks more buttery-yellow. Dark phases and intermediates are almost unknown.

Juvenile: Paler and colder-coloured than other skuas. Tails short and blunt-tipped. Belly is sometimes almost white, and contrasts with darker breast. Some have whitish patches on the head.

Adult winter: Note the whitish face, and barring on the mantle. Contrasting dark trailing edge to wings is also seen in summer.

adult pale summer

adult winter

Flight (adult): They have a lighter, more graceful flight than their relatives, almost tern-like. They flap quite continuously, and seldom show the dashing intensity of other skuas. Apart from the tail, notice the very small wing-flashes, confined just to one or two primaries (shows best on adult winter).

Voice: Unlikely to be heard in Britain.

juvenile

juvenile

adult

Flight (adult): The brilliant wing-flashes, above and below, distinguish it from a gull. So does the heavy, menacing flight on broad, pointed wings.

Voice: Makes no more than a series of gruff grunting noises, which sound very angry in attack.

Juvenile: Youngsters resemble the adults but are darker and more smoothly patterned.

Feeding and nesting behaviour

A Great Skua in aggressive flight

When first seen, a skua may recall an immature gull, but it soon betrays its identity by its bulky, compact shape, and by the menacing edge to its flight action. This menace is well founded. Skuas are best known for two highly aggressive aspects of their behaviour: their violent robbery of other birds' food, and by their attacks on intruders near the nest.

Feeding

Our breeding skuas, *Great* and *Arctic*, both habitually attack other seabirds in order to rob them. Most attacks are against parent birds returning to the nest to feed fish to their young. A victim is approached in low level flight, and chased fiercely and relentlessly, with the clear threat of physical violence, until it is forced to disgorge its catch. Most attacks are carried out over the sea, often resulting in the victim ditching into the water. If food is dropped in flight, the robber will often catch it before it reaches the water surface. The sheer skill and persistence of the attack, often made by two birds working in tandem, is both impressive and unnerving to behold.

Where both skuas occur, they will sometimes divide victims of their muggings between them. Great Skuas tend to tackle larger birds, such as the larger gulls and even Gannets (they may even seize a Gannet's wing in flight), whereas the Arctic Skua jousts with smaller birds such as Arctic Terns, Kittiwakes and Puffins. Puffins, indeed, suffer greatly at the hands of skuas: one study revealed that a Puffin could expect to be robbed by Arctic Skuas once in every 25 fishing visits. But Great Skuas are worse; they do not always bother to rob Puffins, they just eat them instead.

Food-robbing (or kleptoparasitism) does not cater for the needs of skuas all the time, however. Great Skuas take offal from fishery vessels, and even deign to catch some fish for themselves. Some Arctic Skuas take small birds, small mammals and even berries during the breeding season, and both species are partial to eggs from seabird colonies.

Nest defence

Skuas nest on coastal moors and islands in the extreme north and north-west of Scotland. The *Arctic Skua* chooses heathery moorlands, sometimes some distance inland, whereas the *Great Skua* prefers grassy moors with more cover and boggy places, always close to the sea. Both nest on the ground, in colonies with rather large spacings. They proclaim their territory with various displays, including an heraldic lifting of the wings. All skua territories contain mounds or hummocks, where the birds keep a look-out.

The skills honed in the practice of food-robbing are transferred to vigorous nest-defence. If any intruder should approach the nest, be it a bird, sheep, dog or human being, a series of lunge-attacks begins. The birds

An Arctic Skua (light phase) attacking

sweep towards the intruder with low, purposeful flight, uttering brief, gruff calls; they only turn away at the last moment, usually enough to cause a flinch. When attacking people, they can make physical contact by foot or bill. Occasionally, blood can be drawn. To some people, a skua attack can be a frightening experience. To others it is one of the thrills of birdwatching. Whatever your perception, make sure you wear a hat!

An Arctic Skua on its nest

KITTIWAKE *Rissa tridactyla*

41cm. Named for its call, the Kittiwake is a coastal and ocean-going gull. Uniquely, the wing-tips of adults are completely black, as if dipped in ink. It is about the same size as a Common Gull, but is slimmer, with narrower and more pointed wings. At all ages, the legs are black. Adults have yellow bills, first years black.

adult summer

adult winter

Where found: Breeds on precipitous cliffs (also buildings and piers) around most coasts, often in vast colonies. It takes to the ocean in winter, arriving back at the cliffs in early spring.

Adult summer: Mantle and wings are grey, the rest of the body white. Note diagnostic wing-tips. **Adult winter:** August to early spring, there is grey on crown and hindneck, and a dark ear spot (a little behind the eye).

LITTLE GULL *Larus minutus*

28cm. This gull is simply tiny, and dainty with it, so identification is usually easy. The adults, and to a lesser extent immatures, have the most rounded wings of any gull. The legs are usually reddish.

adult summer

Where found: Mostly a passage migrant offshore, but also seen inland on large lakes. The majority are seen from July–October.

Adult summer: The combination of truly black head, plain grey upperwings, and small size is unique. In addition the adults' underwings are dark grey, with a broad white trailing edge (no other gull has largely dark underwings).

SABINE'S GULL *Larus sabini*

33cm. A small, long-winged, small-headed gull, usually seen offshore. A three-colour wing-pattern is characteristic at all ages, and it also has a distinctive forked tail (but this can be difficult to see).

adult summer

adult winter

Where found: A rare but annual visitor offshore, mostly in September and October. Seen on seawatches, especially after westerly gales.

Adult summer: Grey hood bordered by a black collar. Bill is black with a yellow tip. Triangular white trailing edge is bordered on outer wing by black, on inner wing by grey. The mantle is grey. **Adult winter:** After October, the grey hood is largely lost.

BLACK-HEADED GULL *Larus ridibundus*

36cm. This is by far the commonest small gull, and most numerous of all gull species inland. It is often seen on fields in large numbers, and follows the plough. A slimline, "skinny" gull, with long, thin, pointed wings. Its most important feature is the triangular white "flash" on the forewing. The bill and legs are red or orange-red.

Where found: It breeds on coastal marshes and inland lakes, the latter often in moorland. In winter it is everywhere.

Adult summer: Wing-tips are black-bordered, and offset a white triangle on the outer wing, more obvious in adults than immatures. Hood is chocolate-brown, rather than black, with white eye-rings.

adult summer

1st summer

juvenile

First Winter: From autumn onwards, the juvenile's black half collar fades. The crown is pale grey compared with the blackish coloration seen in the Little Gull.

1st winter

First summer: From early spring the juvenile's half collar has been totally lost, and the wing-markings have faded. The previously black bill begins to turn yellow.

Juvenile: One of three species on this page whose juveniles show "W"-shaped, triangular patterns on upperwings. Note smart white trailing edge to the inner half of the wing, and the black bar across the wing.

Flight: In light winds, the Kittiwake has a busy but graceful flight, with rapid wing-beats. In strong winds, it pretends to be a Shearwater, hugging the waves with stiff, angled-down wings.

Voice: The whining wail is rendered "Kitti-waaake" as if the last notes fall in pitch. It is a constant, atmospheric sound heard on many sea cliffs.

Adult winter: The black head markings are reduced to an ear-spot and a dark crown. (Second Winter individuals look like this, but have black smudges behind the white wing-tips.)

1st summer

1st winter

adult winter

First Winter: From autumn most of the brown patterning on mantle is lost. An ill-defined dark cap is retained. **First summer:** After an early spring moult, a variably black hood is acquired.

Juvenile: In contrast to juvenile Kittiwake, has a dark crown and a heavily-marked brown, not clean grey, mantle. The dark "W"-shaped wing-pattern is less clear-cut than that of Kittiwake, because the secondaries are grey, with some light barring.

juvenile

Flight: On its tiny, blunt wings it has a buoyant, though erratic flight, rather like a tern. Note that immatures so not show the dark underwings so characteristic of the adults.

Voice: In alarm it makes a high-pitched "kep", often uttered in series.

1st summer

First summer: In early spring, the hood acquires some grey coloration, and the tail loses its immature black band.

First Winter: The inner wing triangle is grey after November, although sprinkled with a few juvenile brown feathers.

1st winter

Juvenile: In place of all the grey, juveniles show scaly brown, including on the inner wing triangle. On the head, only the forehead, throat and eye regions are white.

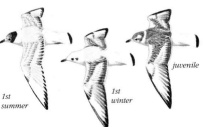

juvenile

Flight: It has a tern-like flight, buoyant but rather weak.

Voice: This species is unlikely to be heard in Britain.

adult winter

Adult winter: From August–March, adults lose their smart hoods, leaving a smudge behind the eye. As in summer, the legs are red; this is the only common species of gull with red legs.

1st summer

First Winter: From autumn the head assumes the adult's dark ear-smudge; wings have a faded juvenile pattern. **First summer:** Hood brown from February but not as smart as adult's.

1st winter

Juvenile: Head, mantle and wing-bar brown-bread-coloured. Otherwise wings are dark grey and white, with the white flash. The legs and bill are orange-yellow, the latter with a black tip.

juvenile

Flight: Black-headed Gulls often share flocks with Common Gulls, and show a quicker, more buoyant flight action. They are able to soar and glide and wheel like the larger species.

Voice: A variety of grating, churning screams, sometimes uttered in a challenging sequence. In disputes (eg. over bread) they make an irritable "kek" call.

Understanding the plumages of gulls

If you have ever been confused by the bewildering range of gull plumages, read on. Here is an explanation:

Rule 1 – All gulls change their feathers twice a year – the head and body feathers (partial moult) in spring, and all their feathers (complete moult) in the autumn. In spring they moult into summer plumage, and in autumn they moult into winter plumage.

Rule 2 – Gulls take several years to acquire adult plumage, the precise period depending on the species. During this period of immaturity, however, they still change their feathers twice a year. Each moult produces a slightly different plumage, which is termed according to age and season eg. "Second Winter". With each moult, they become more like adults. All gulls except adults are given the umbrella term "Immatures".

The sequences of plumages adopted by three common species of gull to show moult and aging are shown here.

1. All gulls start life as fluffy chicks in early summer.

2. They gain their first feathers, to acquire juvenile plumage, a little later.

3. In late summer, they begin to moult into the plumage that will cover them for their first winter of life – appropriately called "First Winter" plumage. The moult is complete by about October.

4. Early next spring, they will all start to moult their head and body feathers. They will not moult wing or tail feathers, but the pattern made by these will be fading. After beginning in February, the moult will be complete by April to reveal First Summer plumage.

5. By next autumn, our birds will be over a year old, and will be facing their second winter of life. In order to cope with the ravages of winter, they change all their feathers in a complete moult, to reveal Second Winter plumage. However, the Black-headed Gull is now mature, and its Second Winter plumage is no different from

Black-headed Gull **Common Gull** **Herring Gull**

juvenile

1st winter

1st summer

any other adult's. Therefore it is described as having adult winter plumage (Second Winter = adult winter). Common and Herring Gulls carry on to acquire Second Winter plumage, different from the adults'.

6. The Black-headed Gull moults early next spring into its fine adult summer plumage. The Common Gull and Herring Gull acquire Second Summer plumage. Birds showing Second Winter or Second Summer plumage are referred to as "Second Years".

7. In the autumn, our gulls are just over two years old. The Black-headed Gull moults into adult winter plumage again. The Common Gull has now matured, and it now acquires its first adult winter plumage (Third Winter = adult winter). Still not fully mature, the Herring Gull enters into a distinct Third Winter plumage, although it is becoming more like an adult all the time.

8. Next spring, our Black-headed and Common Gulls moult into adult summer plumage. The Herring Gull enters its last immature stage, Third Summer plumage.

9. Just after their third birthdays, all our gulls now moult into adult winter plumage. For the Herring Gull Fourth Winter = adult winter.

10. Next spring, all our birds will show adult summer plumage.

Black-headed Gull   **Common Gull**   **Herring Gull**

2nd winter

adult winter

2nd summer

adult summer

3rd winter

adult summer

adult summer

Note
Kittiwake follows Black-headed Gull's sequence. Little Gull and Mediterranean Gull follow Common Gull's sequence. Glaucous, Iceland and both Black-backs follow Herring Gull's sequence.

COMMON GULL
Larus canus

41cm. An easily overlooked species which is slightly larger than Black-headed Gull, but has Herring Gull-like plumage. It is darker on the mantle than Black-headed Gull, blue-grey rather than pale grey. In contrast to Herring Gull, it is much smaller and slimmer, with a dark (not pale) eye, a gentle (not fierce) expression, and with a different bill and leg colour.

adult summer

Where found: A common breeding species in Scotland and Ireland, found by inland freshwater lakes, and on the coast. Much more widespread in winter, and often common inland.

Adult summer: Distinguished by its yellow legs and large white markings on the black wing-tips. **Adult winter (not illustrated):** From autumn until early spring, the head acquires a degree of peppery streaking.

MEDITERRANEAN GULL
Larus melanocephalus

39cm. An uncommon species which resembles Black-headed Gull in adult plumage, but is similar to Common Gull in its immature stages. It is slightly larger and more heavily-built than Black-headed Gull, but slightly smaller and shorter-winged than Common Gull.

adult summer

Where found: Very rare breeding bird among Black-headed Gull colonies, mostly in south-east England. Uncommon visitor almost anywhere, coastal or inland, in any month.

Adult summer: Smart black head, otherwise very pale. Wings are white-tipped except for a thin black edge to the outer primary. Legs and bill are red. The latter is noticeably stout, and looks as though it droops at the tip.

GLAUCOUS GULL
Larus hyperboreus

70cm, but varies greatly. Mostly an Arctic gull, appropriately clad in very pale, icy plumage. Some birds are as big and lumbering as Great Black-backed Gulls, with broad wings, large heads and huge bills. The main confusion species is the smaller Iceland Gull.

adult summer

Where found: A scarce winter visitor in small numbers to coasts, harbours, rubbish tips and freshwater lakes.

Adult summer: Pale. White body, slightly darker grey back and wings. No black markings on wings, The legs are pink.

ICELAND GULL
Larus glaucoides

60cm. Another Arctic Gull, best distinguished from Glaucous by size and shape. Iceland Gull is smaller and slighter than Herring Gull, whereas Glaucous is always bigger and heavier than that species (usually much bigger). Compared to Glaucous, Iceland Gull also has proportionally longer wings, and a much smaller bill.

adult summer

Where found: Usually somewhat rarer than Glaucous Gull, but found in similar places. Our visitors actually come from Greenland, not Iceland.

Adult summer: A Glaucous Gull, one size down. Winter adults are streaked brown on the head and neck, as in Glaucous.

1st winter

1st summer

2nd winter

First Winter: The scaly brown mantle has begun to turn grey. The wing pattern has faded but still shows contrasting panels. Immature and adult Common Gulls often show grey-blue legs in the winter. The bills of First Winters are greyish, with darker tips.

First summer: The wing and tail patterns continue to fade. Some yellow colour appears on the bill.

Second winter: When just over a year old, immatures resemble winter adults, but have a little more black on the forewings.

Juvenile (not illustrated): Best distinguished by the panels on its wings – of which the middle one is the palest – and by the well-defined black tail-band. It lacks the Black-headed Gull's white "flashes" on the wings.

Flight: It has a more effortless, buoyant flight than the larger gulls, but has slower wing-beats than Black-headed Gull.

Voice: The main calls are typically gull-like, but with a cat-like, mewing quality, sometimes ear-splitting.

Adult winter: From August–March, the black head is lost, leaving only a black streak working backwards from the eye, and sometimes also up towards the crown. This "black eye" looks like the result of a fight. Leg colour fades to orange.

1st summer

1st winter

First Winter: From autumn onwards, the mantle turns grey, and much of the brown on the forewing is lost. The hindneck is white, not pale brown as in Common Gull.

adult winter

First summer: Much black is acquired on the hood from February onwards, although not enough to "complete" it. The wing pattern fades.

Juvenile (not illustrated): Juvenile plumage most resembles Common Gull, but it is browner backed and the wings are much more contrasting. The middle band is paler grey and the primaries have white streaks near the tip.

Flight: It has a heavier, stiffer flight than Black-headed or Common Gulls, with more deliberate beats.

Voice: A very distinctive "keeow!" sounding surprised.

1st summer

First/second summer: Becomes whiter as it grows older.

2nd summer

1st winter

Adult winter (not illustrated): October–March, the head and neck are very heavily streaked with brown.

First Winter: All over "coffee-coloured"; finely streaked, but with white wing-tips. The bill is obviously pink with a black tip (see Iceland Gull).

Flight: Has a heavy flight, most similar to Great Black-backed Gull.

Voice: The typical call is quite distinctive: a definitely two-syllable, high-pitched "k ... leel".

1st winter

First summer: Paler; the patterning on the back and wings is often neater than on similar age Glaucous.

1st summer

2nd summer

First Winter: There are no reliable plumage differences from Glaucous Gull. Billl looks all-dark, not black-tipped pink.

Second summer: The useful bill-pattern distinction from Glaucous is lost: both species have black-tipped pink bills.

Flight: Wings are beaten more quickly than Glaucous; this gives an effortless buoyancy.

Voice: Barely distinguishable from Herring Gull, and unlikely to be heard in Britain.

Identifying perched gulls

On these pages are some comparisons between similar gull species. As a general rule, always look for structure, leg colour, and size and colour of the bill.

1. Black-headed Gull – adult winter
Black smudge behind eye. Thin dark-red bill. Black wing-tips.
Mediterranean Gull – adult winter
Larger head, thicker neck. Thick, "droop-tipped" bill. Larger smudge or streak works back from eye. Longer red legs. White wing-tips.

2. Mediterranean Gull – adult summer
Black head, white eye crescents. White wing-tips. Red legs.
Black-headed Gull – adult summer
Brown hood, white eye-rings. Black wing-tips. Red legs.
Little Gull – adult summer
Tiny size, short neck. Black head, no eye marks. White wing-tips. Red legs and bill.
Sabine's Gull – adult summer
Small head. Grey hood, black collar. Red eye-ring. Black, white-spotted wing tips. Bill black with yellow tip. Legs black.

3. Kittiwake – adult summer
Yellow bill, dark eye. Black wing-tips. Black legs.
Common Gull – adult summer
Yellow bill, dark eye. Black wing tips, white-spotted. Yellow legs.
Herring Gull – adult summer
Yellow bill heavier, with red spot. Yellow eye and "frown" giving mean expression. Bulky. Black wing-tips, white-spotted. Pink legs.

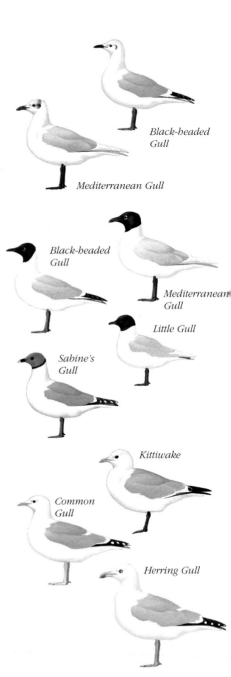

Black-headed Gull

Mediterranean Gull

Black-headed Gull

Mediterranean Gull

Little Gull

Sabine's Gull

Kittiwake

Common Gull

Herring Gull

4. Black-headed Gull – adult winter
Thin neck, small head. Black smudge behind eye. Light-grey wings and mantle. Black wing-tips. Red or orange legs and bill.

Common Gull – adult winter
Thicker neck, larger head. Peppered brown on head and neck, no distinct smudge. Blue-grey wings and mantle. Black wing-tips, white spotted. Yellow bill, often with dark ring. Yellow or blue-grey legs.

Black-headed Gull

Common Gull

5. Glaucous Gull – adult winter
Large-headed, bulky. Bill half length of flat-crowned head. Wings barely project beyond tail, and certainly by less than length of bill.

Iceland Gull – adult winter
Smaller headed. Bill less than half length of rounder head. Long wings project well beyond tail, certainly by more than the length of the bill.

Glaucous Gull

Iceland Gull

6. Great Black-backed Gull – adult summer
Huge, plump, bulky. Fearsome, oversized bill, kinks down at red spot. Very black-backed. Blunt rear end, marked white "tertial step". Large white spots on wing-tips. Pink legs.

Great Black-backed Gull

Lesser Black-backed Gull – adult summer
20% smaller, not so bulky – quite elegant. Much smaller bill, straighter. Dark-grey backed. More tapered rear end. Smaller white spots on wing-tips. Yellow legs.

Note: Passage Lesser Black-backs from the north pass through in spring and autumn, and are as dark on the back as Great Black-backs.

Lesser Black-backed Gull

Herring Gull – adult summer
Slightly larger than Lesser Black-back. Bulky. Bill intermediate between two Black-backs. Silver-grey on back. Blunt rear-end, quite short wings. Pink legs.

Herring Gull

GREAT BLACK-BACKED GULL
Larus marinus

70cm. A huge, plump, large-billed, large-headed gull, fierce in demeanour and behaviour. It has shorter, broader wings than other large gulls. It is much larger than the similarly-plumaged Lesser Black-backed Gull, and has pink, not yellow legs.

3rd winter

adult summer

Where found: Breeds mainly on western and northern rocky coastlands, favouring islands and headlands. Found much more widely, and sometimes inland, in winter.

Adult summer: Jet-black back is only shared by Northern Lesser Black-backs (see below). Large blobs of white on wing-tips.
Third winter: Still has a slight tail-band. Head is white, with limited streaking. White wing-tips less prominent than on an adult.

LESSER BLACK-BACKED GULL
Larus fuscus

55cm. Smaller than Great Black-back and Herring Gull. It has longer wings than both, and a smaller, slighter body. In contrast to the others, adults have yellow, not pink legs. Lesser Black-backs from Scandinavia pass through in Spring and Autumn and a few winter. These birds are as dark as Great Black-backs but show the typical Lesser wing-pattern, yellow legs and small size.

3rd winter

adult summer

Where found: Mostly a summer visitor (February–October); breeds on coasts and inland moorland. Most depart to the Mediterranean in winter, but some (mostly adults) remain.

Adult summer: Dark-grey, not black on the back. Small blobs on wing-tips.
Third winter: As Adult Winter but for faded tail-band and a little brownish colour in the wings.

HERRING GULL
Larus argentatus

60cm. Usually the commonest gull on the coast, the Herring is most people's "seagull": its sounds create the seaside atmosphere. A large, pale-grey species, with a heavy body and broad wings. It has pink legs.

3rd winter

adult summer

Where found: Very common on coasts, breeding on cliffs, rocky areas and sand-dunes. A resident species, it disperses more widely in winter, and can be found inland.

Adult summer: Paler on the mantle and wings than Lesser Black-back, but with similar wing-tips. Larger than Common Gull.
Third winter: As Adult Winter but less clean-cut black wing-tips, brown on wings and tail.

Feeding techniques

Herring Gull: A master of the "dropping" habit. Shellfish are dropped from a height to break them open. They also take live prey such as rabbits and can be seen foraging in rubbish tips.
Mediterranean Gull: Takes prey in a variety of ways, including aerial pursuit, from the ground, surface plunging and surface feeding.
Common Gull: The Common Gull, together with other species, often foot-paddles in beach pools and inland puddles, an action designed to stir up edible particles.
Great Black-backed Gull: The largest of the gulls, the Great Black-back can be a voracious predator; some individuals are specialists on certain mammals or seabirds.

They may also forage on rubbish tips for carrion and other items. Often takes live prey like the Herring Gull.
Kittiwake: Typically "picks" from the water surface for fish and other items. Occasionally they will plunge-dive into the water.
Black-headed Gull: Often hawks for flying insects high in the sky.
Little Gull: Catches prey, mainly insects, in flight. May dip to surface of water or land to snatch prey, and may land on water.
Sabine's Gull: Uses a variety of different feeding techniques to pick up its preferred foods: plunge-diving, surface-feeding, foot-paddling, picking and scavenging.

1st summer

Second summer: The identity should be clear from the black coloration that now appears on the back. The bill begins to turn yellow.

1st winter

juvenile

Flight: Flies heavily on huge, bowed wings, and can even recall a Heron.

Voice: Belts out a fearsome, gruff challenge, slower than the crowing of the other large gulls. In addition, it makes a range of menacing, deep-throated calls.

2nd summer

First Winter/summer: The head and underparts whiten, and the bill acquires a pale base (as Herring). The white head contrasting with the mantle is a useful distinguishing feature from Herring. At this age, Lesser Black-back has darker, plainer wings.

Juvenile: Apart from size, can be distinguished from LLBG by a paler "window" on the outer wing (also seen in Herring Gull), less clear-cut tail-band, and generally paler plumage. Juvenile Herring Gulls have a more clear-cut tail band and less chequered backs.

2nd summer

First Winter: The head whitens, but is still darker than on Great Black-back. The dark tail band contrasts strongly with the whitish rump, much more so than on Herring Gull.

juvenile

Flight: Much less heavy than Great Black-back's.

Voice: The crowing, or "long-call", has a more laughing and less triumphant quality than Herring Gull's. Most of the other calls are quite nasal in tone.

1 summer

First summer: The wings are still plainer than on any other large gull. **Second summer:** Pale grey at last appears on the mantle, and yellow appears on the bill.

1st winter

Juvenile: Plain, dark wings. The outer wing is all-dark, with no paler brown "window". Mid-panel on the inner wing (formed by the greater wing coverts) is darker than on the other species. Note dark ear-coverts.

2nd summer

1st winter

Juvenile: Pale brown intrudes into the wing-tip forming a "window". Fewer chequered markings on the mantle than Black-backs. The tail-band is less well-defined than the Lesser's, but better defined than the Great's. Bill is pink at the base.

Flight: It flies effortlessly on slightly bowed wings, often soaring and gliding.

Voice: Makes a variety of crowing calls, ringing calls, moans and mutters. The crowing "long call" is very triumphant.

1st summer

Second summer: Grey intrudes on to the mantle and wings.

First Winter/summer: These are generally less contrastingly pale-headed than either Black-back.

juvenile

Glaucous Gull: Is a predator, scavenger and may also steal food, eggs and young from other birds.
Iceland Gull: Takes food (carrion, eggs and young of other birds) from the surface and by plunge-diving in shallow waters. Also picks and scavenges on land.

The following plumages are not illustrated above but should be mentioned.

Great Black-backed Gull
Adult winter: From June–January, there is a limited amount of streaking around the head and neck (much more on Lesser Black-back). This also applies to Third Winters.

Lesser Black-backed Gull
Adult winter: The white head of summer changes to give a much-freckled appearance on the face, crown and neck. Great Black-back is much less freckled.

Herring Gull
Adult winter: Similar to adult summer, but strewn with brown streaks on the head and neck, à la Lesser Black-back.

ARCTIC TERN
Sterna paradisaea

35cm. This is a very graceful, delicate species, with shorter wings but a longer tail than Common Tern.

adult summer

Head (summer): It has a rounder crown than Common Tern. The shorter bill is all blood-red.

Where found: Very much a northern bird; breeds mostly in Scotland; also widespread in Ireland. Late April–October. Almost always breeds on the coast. Also seen on passage.

ROSEATE TERN
Sterna dougallii

38cm. Together with the next two species, this is one member of a famously tricky trio, that are all much smaller and daintier than Sandwich Tern. Roseate is by far the whitest-looking, with no marks at all on the underwing. It has the shortest wings and the longest tail.

adult summer

Head (summer): It has a long, mostly black bill. As the summer progresses, more red coloration can show at the base.

Where found: A rare summer visitor, May–September, breeding on a very few offshore islands among other terns. Very rare on passage.

COMMON TERN
Sterna hirundo

35cm. This is the most widespread of the difficult trio, and the only white tern that commonly breeds inland. It has the shortest tail, and the longest wings of the three: Roseate, Common, Arctic. It is larger and more "solid" looking than the Arctic Tern.

adult summer

Head (summer): The crown is flatter than on Arctic or Roseate Tern. The bill is orange-red, with a black tip. It is significantly longer than the bill of Arctic.

Where found: Summer visitor, April–October. Breeds in colonies at a variety of coastal and inland habitats (islands, shingle banks and saltmarshes). Common around all coasts on passage.

Migration

All our terns are summer visitors; they breed here (although the Black Tern does so only occasionally) and spend the rest of the year well to the south of us.

Sandwich Tern
Spends the winter in West Africa, with some birds continuing further down the African coast, stopping only when they run out of land at South Africa. The earliest return to our coasts in late March or early April. They are common passage migrants to all coasts.

Roseate Tern
Leaves us in the autumn and travels southward to the coasts

of West Africa, where it spends the winter. The journey is undertaken in leisurely fashion; the birds tend to follow coastlines and fish as they go.

Common Tern
Arriving in April and leaving in October, the Common Tern spends the winter in West Africa in similar areas to the Sandwich Tern.

Arctic Tern
The Arctic Tern flies south without worrying about running out of land. They head for the immensely rich feeding grounds of the Antarctic, where they plunge-dive around the

adult summer

Adult winter: As usual, the forehead whitens and the bill blackens. No changes to the wings will be apparent as Arctic Terns do not moult until much later in the autumn (October), by which time they have left us.

Adult summer: All the flight feathers are translucent, showing little contrast. The wing tips, above and below, are fringed with a neat black line (diffuse in Common, absent in Roseate's underwing).

adult winter

juvenile

Juvenile: In contrast to Common Tern, the secondaries are all-white (no dark bar), and the forewing is much less strongly smudged with black.

Flight: The Arctic Tern has a shorter "arm" than Common, and the sharply pointed wings are less angled back. The Arctic Tern flies on shallower, more rapid wing-beats.

Voice: Most of the calls are higher pitched than Common Tern's, with a whistling or piccolo-like quality. "Peet-peet" notes are often heard, and the alarm call "kee-aah" is stressed on the second syllable.

---

adult summer

Adult winter: The forehead goes white, as in other terns. The tail becomes shorter, and the primary "triangle" darkens.

Adult summer: A white looking tern with an extremely long tail. There is an exotic pink wash to the breast, hence the name. The outermost primaries make a dark "triangle" on the outer wing.

adult winter

juvenile

Juvenile: Juvenile plumage is similar to the larger Sandwich Tern, and different to Common or Arctic. The back looks scaly (quickly lost = First Winter). Wing has a complete white trailing edge. Bill is black.

Flight: On shorter, blunter wings, it has a stiffer flight action than Common or Arctic.

Voice: Main call is an abrupt, two-note "chivy" or "chew-it", the latter recalling the Spotted Redshank's call. Other calls can be so rasping as to recall, if vaguely, a Jay.

---

adult summer

Adult winter: From July onwards, any black on the forehead disappears, and often the bill blackens somewhat, as if burnt. The leading edge to the forewing acquires a diffuse blackish bar.

Adult summer: Note the wing pattern, above and below: the outer primaries are darker than the inner primaries, showing an obvious contrast. In fact, the inner primaries and secondaries are translucent, while the outer primaries are not.

adult winter

juvenile

Juvenile: Head pattern similar to adult winter. Mantle and back are washed with brown, with subtle scales. Distinguished from Arctic in flight by a large, dark bar on the leading edge of the inner wing and dark bar on the trailing edge of the inner wing.

Flight: The inner part of the wing (the "arm") is longer than on Arctic, and the outer half (the "hand") points backwards more. The Common Tern has a slightly easier, more relaxed flight pattern.

Voice: There are many calls, almost all lower pitched than Arctic's, and more grating. One distinctive call is the alarm note "kee-aah", with the first note stressed.

---

pack ice. They do not necessary stay in the same place all winter (summer in the Antarctic), but sometimes even undertake a circular tour of the entire Antarctic continent. Having travelled all the way from Britain, northern Europe or even the Arctic in the first place, the scale of their movements defies the imagination. It is estimated that most Arctic Terns travel around 30,000km (18,500 miles) a year, and some probably travel 50,000km (30,000 miles) or more. It is the longest migration of any bird in the world, and is virtually equivalent to a circumnavigation of the globe. Since this journey is undertaken annually, some long-lived Arctic Terns probably break the million-kilometre barrier in their lifetime.

Little Tern
Arrives in Britain in April and begins its journey to West Africa around September, spending the winter in the rich fishing grounds along the African coast. Although they do not breed in large numbers in this country, they are widespread on passage, occasionally inland.

Black Tern
Rarely breeds in Britain, but can be seen on passage in spring (May) and autumn (late July–September) when it visits inland lakes and marshes as well as coastal areas with calm waters. In some years they may pass through in quite large numbers.

A guide to terns

Gulls and terns look superficially similar, but terns have the following features:

1. long, usually strongly-forked tails
2. long, pointed bills
3. long, angular, pointed wings
4. much more buoyant, elegant flight, often with deep wing-beats
5. thin bodies
6. most have black caps.

Sandwich Tern – all terns (except the Black Tern) plunge-dive for their fish; the Sandwich Tern dives from a greater height than the others. Young Sandwich Terns (not the others) often form into crèches. On perched adults (see below), notice the black, yellow-tipped bill, shaggy crest and black legs. Sandwich Terns often nest close to Black-headed Gulls for protection.

Roseate Tern – note the clean white underside of this bird in flight. Roseates form special, private "sub-colonies" of their own when sharing breeding ground with other terns. Unlike all the other species, they nest under vegetation or some other cover. Notice how far the tail streamers project beyond the wings.

Common Tern – on the underside of the wing, there is smudged black on the trailing edge of the tip, and it "cuts in" near the wing-angle. All species of tern perform a display in which male birds present fish to their mates. When perched, the Common Tern's tail-streamers project only as far as the wing-tips.

Arctic Tern – on the underside of the wing, the tips are bordered by a neat black line, and all the flight feathers are translucent. The Arctic Tern nests in very open habitats. It has shorter legs than the other species, so sometimes avoids grassy cover. When perched, the tail streamers project beyond the wings, but not so far as those of the Roseate.

Little Tern – these birds are tiny: note the permanent white forehead, and yellow, black-tipped bill. Little Terns hover more than the other species, and for longer. Little Terns form smaller colonies than the others, more dispersed, and usually away from the other species. Like all terns, the Little Tern camouflages its eggs well.

Common Tern

Arctic Tern

Little Tern

Sandwich Tern

Roseate Tern

These terns have all been drawn to the correct scale

Little Tern

Arctic Tern – sharp black trailing edge

Sandwich Tern – whiter than other terns

Common Tern – smudged black trailing edge

Black Tern

Roseate Tern – clean white underside

SANDWICH TERN
Sterna sandvicensis

41cm. Terns resemble gulls but are smaller, more graceful, have longer, narrower wings, forked tails and thinner, more pointed bills. Most have black caps. The Sandwich Tern is our largest species. It looks whiter than all the others except Roseate.

adult summer

Head (summer): It has a long, angular head, crowned with a distinctive shaggy crest. The bill is black, with a yellow tip (adults only).

Where found: Summer visitor March–October. Breeds on scattered coasts with sand-bars and shingle beaches, usually with Black-headed Gulls. Common passage migrant to all coasts.

LITTLE TERN
Sterna albifrons

24cm. A distinctive species characterised by its faster wing-beats and diminutive size. A tern in miniature.

adult summer

Head (summer): The long bill is yellow with a black tip (reverse of Sandwich), and the forehead is permanently white, although bordered on its lower edge by a black eyestripe.

Where found: Nests in small colonies on sand or shingle beaches. Arrives in April, leaves in September. Not very common; more widespread on passage, occasionally inland.

BLACK TERN
Chlidonias niger

24cm. While the other five, whiter-looking terns are called "Sea Terns" (Sterna), this is a "Marsh Tern", which in summer feeds on insects and lives in freshwater marshes. However, in Britain it is only a passage migrant, and is frequently seen on the sea. Note the dark appearance, shallowly-forked tail and small size. Although nearly as small as a Little Tern, it looks heavier, with longer, broader wings.

adult summer

Head (summer): Unsurprisingly, this is black!

Where found: Has occasionally bred, but mostly a passage migrant in spring and autumn, to inland lakes and marshes, and on the coast.

Breeding behaviour

Sandwich Tern
In Britain breeds in scattered coastal areas with sand bars and shingle beaches, often with Black-headed Gulls. Forms monogamous pair-bonds that may continue from year to year. The nest is a scrape formed by both sexes with little or no lining material. Lays 1–3 mottled, buff-coloured eggs and incubation takes 21–29 days. After the eggs are hatched the young are cared for by both parents for 30–35 days, but within a colony the young may form crèches.

Roseate Tern
Nests in small to medium-sized colonies. Pair-bonds are established at some point before the birds reach their breeding grounds. Like many terns, Roseates may abandon their breeding sites if they are disturbed by predators. Nests are usually built at sites with cover or in the hollow of a rock. In Britain Roseates breed on a few offshore islands among other terns. Between one and three blotchy, buff-coloured eggs are laid; these are incubated by both parents for around 23 days. Providing the cover around the nest is good, the chicks may remain for 15–20 days, but they will move if it is not.

Common Tern
The Common Tern breeds in colonies at a variety of coastal and inland habitats, especially islands, shingle banks and

adult summer

Adult summer: A predominantly white-looking species, actually very pale grey on wings and back, with darker outer primaries. At all times, the legs are black.

Adult winter: From as early as June, the forehead turns white, and there are white flecks in the black crown.

adult winter

adult summer

Adult summer: One of the white terns or sea terns (Sterna), so it is white below and pale grey above. The wings are tipped with black, above and below. In contrast to all other species, the legs are yellow.

Adult winter: From late summer, the white on the forehead expands to most of the crown, but is still bordered with black down to the eye – the bird looks as though it is balding. The bill turns black.

adult winter

adult summer

Adult summer: Black on the underparts, except for the undertail, which is contrastingly white. The wings and back are dark smoky-grey above, whitish below. The rump and tail are very pale ash-grey. Legs are red.

Adult winter: The black underparts begin to moult in June, appearing blotchy at first and eventually white. The black on the head is lost, except for a remnant on the crown and cheeks. A black spot remains at the shoulder, where the wing joins the body. The wings are all-grey, except for a slightly darker leading edge.

adult winter

Juvenile: The all-black bill is shorter than the adult's. The bill is patterned with squiggles and "V"-shaped markings which overflow slightly on to the wings. Normally, the cap is all-black, but very soon reverts to the adult non-breeding pattern.

juvenile

Flight: With its long wings and short tail, this large tern has a heavier, stronger flight than its relatives. Juveniles have shorter wings than adults and can look in shape like a different species.

Voice: Main call is a distinctive, two-note "kay-yek", very grating and a little irritable.

Juvenile: The crown is flecked with white, and the mantle and back are chequered with brown. The wings are strongly marked on the leading edge with dark coloration. The bill is black, and the legs brown.

juvenile

Flight: Very obvious – the wings are beaten very fast, as if hurried. Little Terns are experts at hovering, much better than other terns, often staying suspended in the air for some moments.

Voice: The main call is an upbeat "quet-quet", often accelerating into a chatter.

Juvenile: The head pattern resembles Adult Winter, but the wings and back are very different, being heavily marked with dark brown.

juvenile

Flight: An elegant flier that swoops and dips with effortless ease. The wings do not beat as strongly as other terns', and Black Terns do not plunge into the water.

Voice: Not a particularly vocal bird, but it does give a rather nasal "kyep" or "kip-kip" in flight.

saltmarshes. They form monogamous pair-bonds that persist from year to year. Nests are built on the ground by the male and female who scrape the ground together to form a shallow depression. Eggs are laid from the end of May and incubation takes 20–23 days. Chicks are tended by both parents and fly after about four weeks.

Arctic Tern

Breeds in coastal sites, mostly in Scotland, and is also widespread in Ireland. Pair-bonds are monogamous, and the mates will build the nest together, often alternately. Eggs are laid from late May and range in colour from pale buff to olive, and are patterned with darker blotches. The parents

share the responsibility of incubation for 20–24 days. Once hatched the chicks stay on or near the nest for 1–3 days, after which they find shelter under stones or nearby vegetation. Fed by both parents, they fly after four weeks.

Little Tern

Nests in small colonies on coastal beaches of sand or shingle. Pair-bonds are essentially monogamous, but mate changes do occur. 2–3 blotchy, buff-coloured eggs are laid and these are incubated by both sexes for 19–22 days. Once hatched the chicks are fed and cared for by both parents, but they move away from the nest to the safety of nearby cover after about a day.

GUILLEMOT
Uria aalge

42cm. The Guillemot, like all auks except Black Guillemot, is dark above and white below. Typically the feet are set well back so the birds perch upright when out of the water. The Guillemot is the slimmest auk, with a thin, dagger-like bill. All auks swim on the sea like ducks, and dive expertly.

Where found: Colonies are on sheer cliffs and sea-stacks.

adult summer "Bridled"

adult summer

RAZORBILL
Alca torda

41cm. The large, thick bill gives this bird a heavy-headed appearance that is always distinctive given a good view. The bill looks thick from the side, but thin from above; adults always have a white band near the tip.

Where found: Breeds in rocky places in small colonies.

adult summer

BLACK GUILLEMOT
Cepphus grylle

34cm. A small auk which looks very different from its relatives at all times of the year.

adult summer

Where found: Northern and western rocky coasts all year.

Adult summer: Sooty-black all over except for a huge white patch on the wing. The legs are red.

LITTLE AUK
Alle alle

20cm. Much the smallest auk, only half the size of a Guillemot; in fact, it can be confused with a Starling in flight! The bill is so short and stubby that it looks more like a nose. They may be forced onto the east coast ("wrecked") by strong autumn northerly gales

adult summer

Where found: A scarce but regular winter visitor offshore.

Adult summer: A rare sight in Britain. The upperparts, including the head and neck, are black, with some white V-streaks on the back and a tiny white spot by the eye.

PUFFIN
Fratercula arctica

30cm. Another small, rotund auk, unmistakable at all times if seen well, because of its extraordinary triangular beak. The clown-like face and bright colours, together with its waddling walk, make the Puffin a great favourite of many people.

adult summer

Where found: Visitor March–August to isolated, grassy coasts.

Adult summer: Basically black above and white below, but white on the face and ornamented with

Adult summer: All the upperparts, including the head and neck, are dark chocolate-brown in most British birds, but many from southern Scotland northwards are almost black above. Diagnostically, all adult Guillemots have streaks on the flanks.

Adult summer "Bridled" form: Has a neat white eyering and white streak running from it.

adult winter

adult winter

adult winter

juvenile

Adult winter: Only dark colour left on head and neck is on crown, hindneck, around the eye, and in a streak running along the cheek. Some have an almost complete dark collar. "Bridled" birds retain the white eyering.

Juvenile: Like winter adults, but smaller with shorter bills. Brownish above, no flank streaks.

Flight: Fast, with rapid wing-beats. Secondaries have a white trailing edge. Holds head down in flight, appears hunch-backed. Underwings show dark "arm-pits". Legs protrude beyond the tail.

Voice: Colonies make a cacophony of rolling, braying sounds, like distant laughter.

adult winter

Adult summer: Razorbills are always black above, which distinguishes them from brown southern Guillemots, and they lack flank streaks. A white line runs from the top of the bill to the eye.

Adult winter: Transition similar to that of Guillemot, with much dark coloration being lost on the head and neck. More black remains below the eye (on the ear-coverts), leaving a smudge, not a neat dark line. Looks hunched on the water.

Juvenile: They are always much darker about the face than Guillemots, and the bill is quite different.

adult winter

juvenile

Flight: Holds its head up in flight, and the trailing feet are hidden by the tail. White trailing edge to the inner wing like Guillemot, but has clean white armpits.

Voice: Relaxed, deep, contented grunts and snores, like the creaking of a ship's timbers.

adult winter

adult winter

Adult winter: From July onwards, a transformation takes place, leaving only the wings, including the white patch, much the same as in summer.

Otherwise, the body becomes predominantly white, with much black barring on the upperparts. It looks plump on the water, with a pointed tail.

juvenile

Juvenile: Juveniles are darker on the crown and hindneck than winter adults, and have some dark patterning on the large white wing-patch.

Flight: Since it does not nest on cliff-ledges, this species always flies low over the water. The white upperwing patch is unmissable.

Voice: Utterly unlike any other auk: high pitched, mournful whistles and drawn-out "electronic" peeps, the latter often in trills.

---

adult winter

adult winter

Adult winter: Mostly white below, including the throat. The crown is black, covering the eyes and cheeks, but the black cheeks are bordered by a white collar which extends much of the way

round the neck. Look, if possible, for the white V-marks on the back, which remain. On the water, the tail is held as high, or even higher up, than the head.

juvenile

Juvenile: Unlikely to be seen in Britain. Browner than adult winter.

Flight: It has a white trailing edge to the inner wing, unlike the other small auks (Black Guillemot and Puffin). In this species and in Puffin, the underwing is dark.

Voice: Unlikely to be heard in Britain.

---

a huge bill. The eyes are set in a grey triangle, seemingly painted on. The outsize bill itself is grey, red and yellow, and the fleshy gape is also yellow. The feet are an incongruous brilliant red.

Adult winter: The bill becomes smaller and loses much of its colour and contrast, but retains the same basic colours. The white face is darker and the legs become yellow.

adult winter

juvenile

adult winter

Juvenile: With much smaller bills than the adults, young Puffins can be an identification problem. However, they do always show a pale face rimmed with black.

Flight: Needs fast wing-beats to propel its plump little body, but it is good at hanging in the air around the turbulent clifftops. Wings are black; no white trailing edge. Underwings are also dark.

Voice: Gentle moans often uttered in threes. Inside the burrow, their crooning sounds like a distant chainsaw.

Nest-sites and breeding behaviour

A Guillemot colony on cliff

Nest-sites

Guillemots – breed in huge colonies, sometimes up to 100,000 birds strong. They select tall, sheer cliffs with ledges, and flat-topped stacks on rocky coasts. Incubating and brooding Guillemots often sit so close together that they are actually touching their neighbours; the single egg is the centre of a tiny "territory" that can be less than 0.05m², the smallest breeding territory of any bird in the world. Rows of Guillemots adorning a cliff ledge are not only inaccessible to land predators, but also present a formidable array of bills with which to deter a potentially peckable aerial predator. The egg of a Guillemot is pear-shaped, so that, if it rolls, it will roll in a circle, and not straight off the cliff-ledge. Every egg is also individually patterned with its own "signature" so that the nest-site can be distinguished from those of other members of the colony.

Razorbill – has a very different strategy. It nests only in loose colonies, each pair often several metres from its neighbours. The site chosen is always more sheltered than a Guillemot site, usually with a roof over the head, and a wider, safer surface on which to put the round, not pear-shaped egg. Wide ledges, cliff cavities, scree slopes and other rocky places support Razorbills, always in much smaller numbers than Guillemots.

Black Guillemot – usually selects a site near the bottom of a cliff, or in a cave, in a boulder-covered beach, or even in the man-made wall of a harbour or building. These birds always nest close to the water. Small, well-spaced pairs, forming rather loose colonies, prefer properly sheltered places, with a good roof, and good protection from marauding predators. A secret hideaway under a boulder is a typical site.

Puffin – takes the idea of a hideaway one stage further, by excavating its very own burrow, or even borrowing one from a rabbit. The single egg is laid in the safety of darkness at the end of a passage 1–2m (3–6ft) long. It is white, and not individually marked. Not surprisingly, the burrowing habit confines Puffins to areas where suitably soft soil is found in close proximity to the sea; many clifftops fit the bill. In ideal areas, the birds may be found in very large colonies of up to 50,000 pairs.

A group of Guillemots on a ledge

Parental care

Guillemots, Razorbills and Puffins lay only one egg, so the parents of these species must invest their time in caring for it well.

Razorbills and *Guillemots* – feed their youngster, and brood it when necessary. It grows quickly, but its pampered life is a short one; when only a quarter grown, and still without its proper flight feathers, it must jump off the cliff encouraged by its parents. If the jump is successful, it will call to its father, and join up with him on the water. Leaving the mother behind, the two swim far out to sea, where the father feeds the chick for a week or two before leaving the offspring to fend for itself.

Puffins – young are fed in their burrow until they are about three-quarters grown. They must make that same cliff-top jump all by themselves, without help or encouragement. They leave at night, while the parents are away fishing, driven by instinct alone. If they reach the sea successfully, and then learn to fish self-taught, the chances are that they will live for up to 20 years.

Black Guillemots – lay two eggs, probably because their nest-site is closer to the sea, and commuting is easier, so allowing for more feeding visits to the young. The two chicks are fed until almost full-grown, and have a relatively angst-free trip to the sea when the time comes to leave the nest.

COLLARED DOVE
Streptopelia decaocto

32cm. A conspicuously creamy pink-grey dove with a neat but solid build, and a long tail. It is a familiar resident of many suburban neighbourhoods.

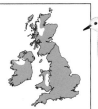 

adult

Where found: A widespread, often common resident of suburbs, settlements and farming areas. It is only been a British bird since "invading" from south-east Europe in the 1950s.

Adult: The ground colour is creamy pink-grey, but it is darker on the tail and wings. Diagnostically, there is a black half-collar around the neck (edged white).

TURTLE DOVE
Streptopelia turtur

27cm. A slimline species, more delicate than the Collared Dove and only a summer visitor. It has a shorter tail. It likes bushy places, including farmland hedgerows, but is generally uncommon.

adult

Adult: Quite different from the plainer Collared Dove. The breast has a strawberry wash, the head is bluish, and the back is richly scalloped with golden honey-brown edges to the feathers. On the neck is a black-and-white mark like a zebra crossing.

Where found: A summer visitor, April–September, migrating by day. It breeds in hedgerows, woodland edges and large gardens mostly in the south-east of England.

CUCKOO
Cuculus canorus

33cm. Everyone knows the Cuckoo's song, but few are familiar with the grey, hawk-like shape that flits unseen from perch to perch to deliver the sound of summer. The Cuckoo is long-bodied, with pointed wings that are often drooped, and with a long, graduated tail (ie. becomes thinner towards the tip). The tail is often twisted from side to side in a peculiar fashion. The bill is quite long, and slightly curved.

adult male

Where found: They arrive in April and stay in a variety of rural habitats (farmland, heathland, marshland, woodland) until they depart, the adults in August, the juveniles in September.

Adult male: Adults are all-grey above, but darker on the wings and tail, the latter studded with small white spots. The breast is white, with black barring all the way down.

The life of the Cuckoo

The Cuckoo lives a peculiar life because it has forsaken the burden of bringing up its own young, a burden which so dominates the lives and motivations of other species. Instead, eggs are placed in the nest of a foster-parent of a different, usually much smaller species, and left to their own devices. A young Cuckoo never meets its parents, and never meets its own young. Its relations with the opposite sex tend to be cursory, and primarily sexual, with most birds apparently being quite promiscuous. The Cuckoo is Britain's only exclusive brood parasite.

Female Cuckoos lay about a dozen eggs. She will place each one in a different nest, but generally belonging to the same species, usually the same species that raised her.

Therefore, a Cuckoo raised by a pair of Reed Warblers will grow up to lay its own eggs in Reed Warblers' nests, although any surplus eggs might find their way into the nests of other hosts. Although about 100 species are known to have been parasitised by Cuckoos in Europe, British Cuckoos tend to go for three main hosts – Dunnocks in woodland or scrub, Meadow Pipits in open country and moorland, and Reed Warblers in marshland. These are all much smaller birds, of course, so the Cuckoo lays unusually small eggs in order to mimic those of its victims.

Most species of birds lay their eggs in the early morning. but when in its egg-laying phase, the female Cuckoo spends its mornings watching the activity around, and leaves any

Juvenile: Youngsters lack the neck collar, and are more scaly on the back and wings.

juvenile

adult

Upperside: From above, this dove looks very pale. The long tail is white on its outer corners.

adult

Underside: The undersides of wings and body are both creamy-white, without much contrast between the two. The tail pattern is noticeable: black in front, white on the outside.

Flight: Both Collared Dove and Turtle Dove have fast, flickering flight, with interruptions to the rhythm of the wing-beats. When Collared Doves land they raise their tail and lower it slowly.

Voice: A rather monotonous coo often rendered "U-nit-ed", with stress on the middle syllable. On landing and in other situations, it gives a strange purring buzz.

Juvenile: The subtle colours on the head and belly have not yet developed, and the back and wing markings are duller. There is no neck mark.

juvenile

adult

Upperside: It looks dark because of the rich patterning. The white edges to the tail contrast with the darker inner parts, a particularly obvious feature when the bird is landing.

adult

Underside: The wings are dark on the underside, and contrast strongly with the pale belly – a distinction from Collared Dove and all others in the family. The tail is largely black, but white-tipped.

Flight: It flies rapidly on back-swept wings, giving a "flicking" action like Collared Dove, but regularly tilting from side to side as it goes, a habit peculiar to the Turtle Dove.

Voice: A deliciously soothing, soporific purr, "Tur-tur", appropriate for warm, sunny days. The singer is hard to locate.

Adult female: Most resemble males, but have browner breasts.

adult female rufous

Adult female (rufous): A few adult females have a rufous ("Hepatic") coloration: they are rufous-chestnut above, with copious barring above and below. They resemble juveniles more than other adults.

large fledging

Fledgling: The great gape of these oversize youngsters is often enough to identify them.

juvenile

Juvenile: heavily barred and patterned, with pale-fringed feathers, against a greyish, or much more reddish-brown (but never as reddish as Hepatic females) ground colour. All have a very distinctive white spot on the nape.

Flight: Distinctive: wing-beats are fast, but shallow, and never rise above the level of the body. The head is slightly uptilted. Most birds fly low over the ground. While superficially the Cuckoo may resemble the Sparrowhawk, the flight is very different (see pp.74–75).

Voice: The "Cuck-oo" is often elaborated into throaty coughs; female makes a loud, bubbling ringing, sound.

moves until the afternoon. As soon as the incubating host takes a break to feed and stretch, the Cuckoo steals in, removes an egg and replaces it with its own, all in a matter of seconds. When the host parent returns, it fails to notice any slight difference in the appearance of the eggs, and, beguiled by the same size of clutch, starts unwittingly to raise a new Cuckoo. Not all potential hosts can be duped in this way, however, and some do remove the newly-laid Cuckoo's egg.

When it hatches, the young Cuckoo has no mercy; it wipes out the rest of the host's clutch by heaving them, eggs or young, out of the side of the nest. Having guaranteed its "parents'" full attention, the young glutton soon outgrows its

nest, looking bloated and incongruous in the company of its diminutive providers. It may take the Cuckoo anything up to six week before it becomes fully independent.

Cuckoos are often mobbed by smaller birds, much in the way that an owl or other predator is harassed. Whether the mobbing is caused by the Cuckoo's striking resemblance to a hawk or falcon, or whether its misdeeds are known to the mobbers, is unclear.

Display, nesting and breeding behaviour

In this section we compare the display and breeding habits of the five British pigeons and doves. There is no real difference between a "pigeon" and a "dove", just the name.

Feral Pigeon (Rock Dove) – during the display flight this bird flies out from its perch (eg. on a building) and flies with deliberate, slow beats for a short while. It then performs a few wing-claps, and finally glides with its wings held in a V-shape, with the tail spread. These pigeons, unlike all their relatives, nest in colonies, albeit rather loosely scattered ones. They select ledges for nesting, in buildings or cliffs according to their habitat. It is easy to watch pigeons displaying. The familiar puffed-up posture, accompanied by a coaxing cooing, is called the "Bowing Display".

Stock Dove – the display is similar to the Feral Pigeon's, but the wing-claps are quieter and the wings are barely held above horizontal in the gliding stage. They tend to fly from tree to tree, often in a circle. Stock Doves select a hole for nesting, usually a tree-hole, but sometimes a hole in a ruin, a cliff or even a rabbit-hole. Where suitable sites are scarce, pairs will nest close together. All members of the pigeon family are able to suck up water when they drink, in contrast to most birds, which must raise their heads and let gravity do the work.

Woodpigeon – takes off and immediately rises steeply into the air with rapid wing-beats. As it reaches the summit of its climb, it performs

several loud wing-claps, then sails down on spread wings and tail. It builds a very flimsy nest of twigs, placing it in the branches of a tree. Sometimes, the eggs can be seen in the nest from below. All pigeons lay two eggs. When the young hatch, they are fed on "pigeon milk", a special concoction prepared in the gullet of their parents. Pigeons are one of the few groups of birds to feed their young on milk like mammals.

Collared Dove – leaves its elevated perch (eg. a rooftop aerial) and climbs into the air at an even steeper angle than Woodpigeon, using deep, powerful beats that sometimes produce wing-claps, and with tail spread. It reaches a good height, then glides down on spread wings and tail, usually in a spiral, not straight down like a Woodpigeon. The flimsy twig nest is constructed in a tree or shrub, often near the trunk. Garden conifers are often selected. The pigeon family can be amazingly productive, nesting all year round, brood following straight on from brood. If plenty of food is available, all our resident species have been known to raise five broods in a year.

Turtle Dove – a similar performance to the Collared Dove's, but the ascent can be quicker, even steeper, and with more wing-clapping. The gliding, or spiralling phase can last for a long while, up to a minute. It nests in thick hedges, especially of hawthorn, making the usual pigeon-type flimsy platform.

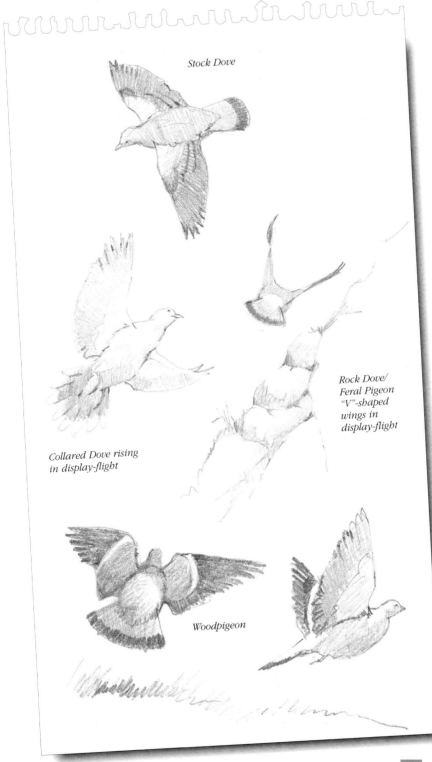

Stock Dove

Rock Dove/
Feral Pigeon
"V"-shaped
wings in
display-flight

Collared Dove rising
in display-flight

Woodpigeon

ROCK DOVE/STREET PIGEON/FERAL PIGEON
Columba livia

33cm. A species with a double life: "Wild Type" Rock Doves occur on wild, rocky coasts; "Feral Pigeons" live in close association with people, in towns and cities and wherever there are buildings. They are well-proportioned, sturdy pigeons with comparatively short tails, and are often easy to identify simply because every individual has a different colour or pattern.

adult

Where found: Rock Doves are found mostly in north and west Scotland, and in Ireland, confined to coastal regions. Feral Pigeons occur widely, mostly in areas of dense human population.

Adult: Adult Rock Doves are typically pigeon-grey, with an iridescent purple/green neck patch. They have red eyes. On the wings are two large black bars.

STOCK DOVE
Columba oenas

33cm. The Stock Dove is a well-organised, compact bird, with the shortest tail of any dove or pigeon. It is found mostly in farmland and woodland, usually in small numbers, never in overwhelmingly large flocks.

adult

Where found: A widespread resident of lowland woods and farmland, also occurring on cliffs and outbuildings.

Adult: Slate-grey all over with a subtle mauve wash to breast and iridescent green neck-patch. A series of spots make up two small wing-bars, and the primaries are dark. Eyes are black, tail is black-tipped.

WOODPIGEON
Columba palumbus

41cm. The largest pigeon, plump, with a small head and a deep, "beer gut" chest. With tiny head and long tail, it looks awkwardly proportioned. An extremely abundant species, especially in farmland and woodlands, where it is wary. It is also found in city centres and gardens, where it can become very tame.

adult

Where found: Mostly a woodland and farmland species, where it can be superabundant – and a pest. Found all year almost throughout Britain and Ireland.

Adult: On the neck is a large, untidy white mark next to a small iridescent green/purple neck-patch. The breast is washed purplish-pink. The eyes are white. Primaries are white-edged.

Feeding techniques and behaviour

Collared Dove
Takes seeds, grains and fruits of weeds and grasses, and will regularly flock to sites that offer this sort of food, such as farms, docks and distilleries. Can also be seen feeding in gardens, allotments and shrubberies. The Collared Dove feeds mostly on the ground, but is known to take berries from bushes and trees

Turtle Dove
A summer visitor found in hedgerows, woodland edges and large gardens, mostly in the south-east of England, the Turtle Dove feeds on weeds, seeds, cereals and leaves. Feeds mostly on the ground.

Rock Dove
Found on rocky coasts mostly in north and west Scotland and Ireland, Rock Doves feeds on cereals, seeds and buds found in the grassy areas above the clifftops.

Feral Pigeon
Feral Pigeons are abundant wherever there are human settlements living in large groups in buildings such as warehouses, church towers and factories. They eat similar items to Rock Doves, but will also take artificial foods in town and cities, particularly bread that is thrown to them in parks. They usually feed in flocks by walking and pecking. May feed in trees but appears very clumsy.

Juvenile: Drabber than their elders, lacking a proper neck patch. Eyes are dark.

feral variants

juvenile

adult

Feral variants: Through centuries of domestication, a wide variety of breeds have been established, which escape and intermix in the wild "feral" state. The three individuals illustrated are typical. However, many are still very similar in pattern to Rock Doves.

Flight: It flies rapidly on swept-back wings, with fast, steady wing-beats. The speeds attained are often worthy of the term "Racing Pigeon". Rock Doves (and many Feral Pigeons) have a white rump (not found in any other pigeons), a pale underwing, and two long black bars on the trailing edge of the inner wing.

Voice: A mild, stammering coo, "Look-at-the-MOOON".

Juvenile: Insipidly coloured, and browner than adults, without the neck gloss.

juvenile

adult

Flight: It looks very compact, and is surprisingly easy to pick out with practice. The wings are straighter than on other pigeons, and they seem shorter, almost triangular. The wing-beats are faster than Woodpigeon's, about equal with Feral Pigeon's. Look for they grey rump, grey (not white) underwings, and only small, interrupted, double black wing-bars. The best clue, however, is that the Stock Dove's wings are grey-centred and black

bordered, an arrangement not found on other pigeons.

Voice: A repeated, deep-throated "OO-oo-OO", repeated in an intensifying series, with a distinctly disapproving air. This is a quiet, easily overlooked sound, and the singer is hard to locate in the treetops.

juvenile

adult

Flight: The Woodpigeon is a powerful flier with quick, purposeful wing-beats. The wings are slightly backswept, and do not appear triangular like the Stock Dove's, and the tail is much longer. The large, white wing-crescents, visible on the wing-edge when perched, are usually unmissable in flight, making this an easy bird to identify.

Voice: A suggestive, throaty coo that is uttered in a slow,

deliberate rhythm as if to make a point. There is a sequence of five coos, three fast and two slow, as in "Take TWOOO COOOS Taffy".

Juvenile: Similar but dingier, without the obvious neck marks.

Stock Dove

A resident of lowland woods and farmland, also occurring on cliffs, outbuildings and in city parks with mature trees, the Stock Dove feeds on buds, flowers, leaves and seeds. Food is taken on the ground by walking and pecking. Sometimes feeds in flocks but more likely to be seen in pairs. Occasionally feeds in trees, usually alone.

Woodpigeon

Found almost throughout Britain and Ireland in woods, parks and farmland with trees, the Woodpigeon eats mainly berries, leaves, seeds, buds, flowers and root crops, and some worms and slugs. Food is mainly taken on the ground by

walking and pecking, but also in trees where, unlike other pigeons, it is very agile and is able to climb over small branches to reach food.

BARN OWL
Tyto alba

34cm. Much the palest owl, sandy-brown above and white below, looking ghostly in the half-light and bright in the headlamp beam from a car. This is the only owl species with a heart-shaped face, against which its small, black eyes are set. Mostly nocturnal.

adult light

Where found: Open country, such as farmland and marshes.

LITTLE OWL
Athene noctua

22cm. Introduced in the 19thC, this is by far our smallest owl, not much bigger than a thrush, but still obviously an owl with its broad head, chunky body and short tail. The Little Owl is often active by day, although it usually hunts in twilight or darkness.

adult

Where found: A locally common resident, mainly farmland areas.

TAWNY OWL
Strix aluco

38cm. This is the common owl of woodland, gardens and urban areas, which utters the familiar hooting. It is a large, compact species, with a very rounded head. It is seldom seen because of its nocturnal habits. In Ireland this species is replaced by the Long-eared Owl.

adult

Where found: Common where there are mature trees.

LONG-EARED OWL
Asio otus

36cm. The long ear-tufts (not actually ears) that give this species its name are not always very easy to see, as they can be raised or lowered as the bird reacts to situations. It perches in an upright position, often tight against the tree trunk. Largely nocturnal, it favours coniferous woods.

adult

Where found: Commonest Owl in Ireland; not so in Britain.

SHORT-EARED OWL
Asio flammeus

38cm. The Short-eared Owl does not sit upright, but at an angle as if leaning over. It has a much rounder face than Long-eared Owl, and just a hint of ear-tufts. Surprisingly for an owl, it is very often active in daylight. Continental birds may winter and are widespread.

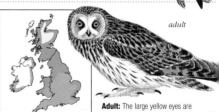
adult

Adult: The large yellow eyes are surrounded by a black rim, within a pale buffy facial disc. Warmer brown than the Long-eared.

Where found: Scarce breeder on moorland and sand dunes.

Adult (light): Almost all British Barn Owls are light-coloured. Pure white below, it is richly patterned above: light sandy-brown feathers are dusted with ash.

Adult (dark): Rare variants are much darker, with a red-brown, not white, underside, often with many spots. Intermediates exist between the two forms.

adult dark

adult light

Flight: On moderately long wings it has a buoyant, constantly shifting flight, often working along ditches or the edges of fields. The legs dangle, and are noticeably longer than those of other owls.

Voice: A drawn-out, blood-curdling screech. The young make ugly hissing sounds.

Adult: Its facial expression is distinctive: fierce yellow eyes are set below broad, pale eyebrows, giving an angry, frowning expression; the effect is accentuated by the rather flat head. Otherwise, the Little Owl is an earthy-brown colour, with a healthy smattering of white spots; the underside is paler, heavily streaked.

adult

Flight: Only the Little Owl flies with great undulating bounds, low over the ground. The flight pattern is closer to that of a Mistle Thrush or a woodpecker. With its blunt head and rounded wings this species looks dumpy in flight.

Voice: The male gives a high-pitched, questioning hoot with an upward inflection that is easy to imitate. Both sexes utter a cat-like, but somewhat abrupt mewing call "kiew!" Calls are and loud and clear.

Adult: It lives up to its name by being largely tawny-brown, richly patterned to resemble the tree-trunks and branches where it lives. The breast is patterned with crossed lines, and there are streaks and spots on the upperparts, but the effect is largely uniform. The eyes are black, and set in a large facial disc.

adult

Flight: Flies quite purposefully, with quick but regular flaps of its short, broad wings.

Voice: The male has a wonderful atmospheric hooting song, which has enlivened many a horror movie. A preliminary, haunting "Hoo" is followed by a pause, then a "Hu, hoo-ooo … ", the end broken and quavering. The female gives a few, less patterned hoots, and both sexes give a sharp "ke-wick". The young beg with a sound like some children's toys make when squeezed.

Adult: The characteristic ear-tufts are perched atop a slim facial disc with a peachy wash; the eyes are red, and have narrow white brows. The body is typically coloured for camouflage among tree-trunks, with a complex mixture of browns of various tints, but never with the warm hues of Tawny Owl. The breast is heavily streaked all down the front.

Underside: The tips of the wings are barred.

adult

adult

Upperside: Behind the dark patch at the wing-angle the primaries are a rich, peach colour, with finely-barred edges.

Flight: It flies on longer, narrower wings than Tawny Owl, with a more relaxed action.

Voice: The male's song is a series of low hoots, each the same, with long pauses in between. The female gives a nose-blowing buzz, and the young make loud squeaks like the rusty hinges of a gate.

Underside: Wing-tips are quite boldly black.

adult

Upperside: The whole wing is a colder buffy colour than that of the Long-eared, and more contrastingly marked. The barring all along the wing is solid and, compared to Long-eared Owl, unsubtle. A similar picture is seen on the tail. A white trailing edge to wing and tail is obscure but definite. The colour behind the carpal patch is much paler than on the Long-eared Owl's wing.

adult

Flight: Flies on longer, narrower, more swept-back wings than Long-eared. Flight is more haphazard; often climbs to a greater height.

Voice: The male utters a series of low hoots, repeated quickly like a laugh; often embellished with sharp wing-claps. The female replies with a distinctive "Chee-op".

Mobbing, feeding and breeding behaviour

Mobbing

Being generally nocturnal, owls are usually difficult to see in the wild. One of the best ways to locate them is to listen out for the agitated cries of smaller birds that are "mobbing" the larger predator. Blackbirds, in particular, are good indicators; their angry "chink, chink" calls are usually uttered only at dusk, so if you can hear them by day, it is likely that a predator, such as an owl, hawk or cat is around.

The Tawny Owl is the most frequent target of mobbing, especially if it is roosting on a branch. When the Blackbirds start their angry calls, others inevitably join in – Wrens, Great Tits, Robins and Chaffinches – to make quite a cacophony. All this attention will normally disturb the owl, so you will stand a good chance of seeing it.

No-one is quite sure why smaller birds risk their lives in order to mob owls. Perhaps it is to show the predator that they are aware of its presence, perhaps it is just to irritate it and move it on. There is also evidence that mobbing is educational, showing young birds which predators are dangerous.

If you are very lucky, the mobbing birds may lead you to a communal roost of Short-eared or Long-eared Owls. Migratory individuals of these species sometimes that gather in small groups, the Long-eared Owls in bushes and the Short-eared Owls on the ground. It is the only time that owls are ever remotely sociable.

Feeding

Owls have many adaptations to hunting in twilight, at night, or even in pitch darkness. They have huge eyes, with binocular (overlapping) vision to help them judge distance; they have incredibly sensitive ears to hear and locate the slightest rustle;
and they have soft plumage, with serrated edges to the primary flight feathers, to allow them to fly without a whisper of sound. Barn Owls can catch prey using only their hearing, in pitch darkness.

Short-eared Owl – a rodent specialist, preferring Short-tailed Voles, hunting them in wavering flight over rough ground.

Barn Owl – also prefers small mammals, and uses a similar technique.

Long-eared Owl and *Tawny Owl* – both prefer mammals, but take good numbers of birds too, most frequently dropping on their prey from a perch and catching it by surprise.

Little Owl – takes many invertebrates, enjoying large beetles, crickets and worms.

Breeding

Owls begin calling in the autumn, as territorial rights are restated or newly stated. Breeding commences early in the year, before the ground vegetation has grown up so much as to provide copious cover for the potential prey. For a nest-site, Tawny Owls and Little Owls usually select a hole in a tree, the Barn Owl finds a ledge in a building, the Long-eared Owl uses an old crow's nest, and the Short-eared Owl scrapes away a shallow hollow on the ground. Most species lay three to five white eggs. Young owls, or owlets, are covered with down and always seem to look harassed. They are cared for by the parents for a long time after they have left the nest, because it takes a lot of time and practice before they can start to fend for themselves.

Little Owl

Tawny Owl

Short-eared Owl

Barn Owl
perching

Barn Owl
in flight

Long-eared Owl

A Short-eared Owl
perched on a fence

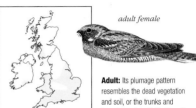

NIGHTJAR
Caprimulgus europaeus

27cm. This is a nocturnal species, which rests by day on the ground or along branches, protected by its marvellous camouflage. It has long, pointed wings, a long tail, and a long body. The bill is tiny, but its mouth is huge; the head is flat, and there is hardly any neck.

adult female

Where found: A scarce summer visitor, May–September, to lowland heaths and recently felled conifer plantations.

Adult: Its plumage pattern resembles the dead vegetation and soil, or the trunks and branches, where it sits. Overall, there is a greyish-brown ground colour.

RING-NECKED PARAKEET
Psittacula krameri

41cm. A long-tailed green parrot flying through the British countryside is unlikely to be mistaken for anything else. Although various species of captive parrots escape from time to time, only this species has managed to establish itself in the "wild".

adult male

Where found: A very local resident, relying mostly on suburban gardens for food and nesting; also found in open woodland.

Adult male: Large-headed, slim-bodied, with a long, pointed tail. Adults are green with red bills; their napes and tails have a dash of sky-blue. The male has a black chin, and a collar which is first black and then rose-pink as it goes around the neck.

HOOPOE
Upupa epops

28cm. As you will see from the picture, this is not a difficult bird to identify. The pink plumage and large crest make it unique.

adult

Where found: Regrettably, a very scarce passage migrant in spring and autumn, mostly to the south coast. It has bred here. It favours areas with lots of short turf or sandy ground.

Adult: The head and neck are pink, and are adorned with a huge fan-like crest, which is pink with black tips. Usually flattened (see above right), the crest is

KINGFISHER
Alcedo atthis

16cm. The dazzling colours of the Kingfisher make it a great favourite of many people. Usually, it is seen as a blue flash zipping low over the water. It is a small, large-headed, short-tailed bird with a huge, dagger-shaped bill. The tiny legs are red.

Where found: It is widely distributed on slow-flowing rivers and streams, and on lakes and ponds, throughout the lowlands of Britain and Ireland. It avoids fast-flowing streams.

Adult male: Basically, Kingfishers are blue-green above and orange below. There is white on the throat and on the side of the neck. The crown and moustache are turquoise, etched with darker, scaly bars. Running down the back, rump and tail is a streak of the brightest possible blue, giving the famous "blue flash" that sums up most sightings of this species. The male has a black bill.

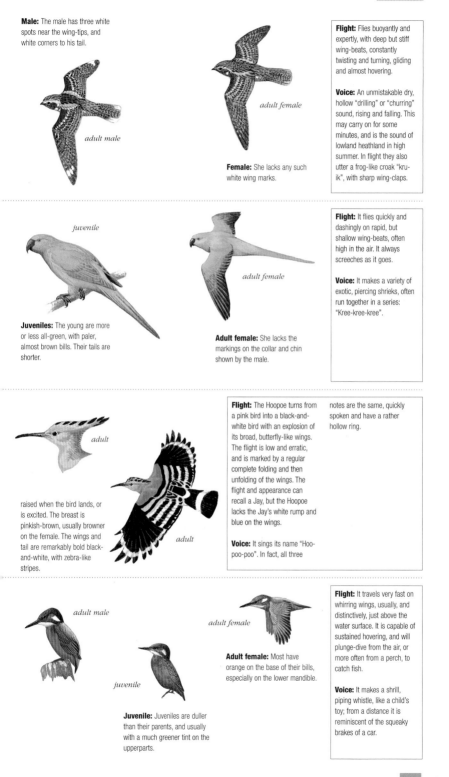

Male: The male has three white spots near the wing-tips, and white corners to his tail.

adult female

adult male

Female: She lacks any such white wing marks.

Flight: Flies buoyantly and expertly, with deep but stiff wing-beats, constantly twisting and turning, gliding and almost hovering.

Voice: An unmistakable dry, hollow "drilling" or "churring" sound, rising and falling. This may carry on for some minutes, and is the sound of lowland heathland in high summer. In flight they also utter a frog-like croak "kru-ik", with sharp wing-claps.

---

juvenile

adult female

Juveniles: The young are more or less all-green, with paler, almost brown bills. Their tails are shorter.

Adult female: She lacks the markings on the collar and chin shown by the male.

Flight: It flies quickly and dashingly on rapid, but shallow wing-beats, often high in the air. It always screeches as it goes.

Voice: It makes a variety of exotic, piercing shrieks, often run together in a series: "Kree-kree-kree".

---

adult

raised when the bird lands, or is excited. The breast is pinkish-brown, usually browner on the female. The wings and tail are remarkably bold black-and-white, with zebra-like stripes.

adult

Flight: The Hoopoe turns from a pink bird into a black-and-white bird with an explosion of its broad, butterfly-like wings. The flight is low and erratic, and is marked by a regular complete folding and then unfolding of the wings. The flight and appearance can recall a Jay, but the Hoopoe lacks the Jay's white rump and blue on the wings.

Voice: It sings its name "Hoo-poo-poo". In fact, all three notes are the same, quickly spoken and have a rather hollow ring.

---

adult male

adult female

juvenile

Adult female: Most have orange on the base of their bills, especially on the lower mandible.

Juvenile: Juveniles are duller than their parents, and usually with a much greener tint on the upperparts.

Flight: It travels very fast on whirring wings, usually, and distinctively, just above the water surface. It is capable of sustained hovering, and will plunge-dive from the air, or more often from a perch, to catch fish.

Voice: It makes a shrill, piping whistle, like a child's toy; from a distance it is reminiscent of the squeaky brakes of a car.

Habitat, feeding and breeding behaviour

Nightjar

The Nightjar is the only British bird that specialises in eating moths. It becomes active only after dark, when most moths fly, and is a summer visitor, staying with us only during the moth-rich months of May–September. It winters in tropical Africa. It catches most of its food in flight, apparently detecting it by sight, approaching from below so that the prey can be seen against the sky. Two special features – a wide gape and a row of bristles around the mouth – help the Nightjar to trap its prey.

To find Nightjars, go on to a lowland heathland at dusk in June or July. Choose a still, warm night. About half an hour after sunset, the first birds will begin churring, and may be approached silently. If they stop making this sound, and instead call "cruik", they are flying, and might be glimpsed as silhouettes, twisting and turning over rides or clumps of trees. Try waving a white handkerchief; in the darkness, this may be taken for the white wing-spots of a male, and cause the birds to approach you to have a look.

Ring-necked Parakeet

Most of the parrots flying wild in Britain belong to this species. They are not native to Britain, or Europe, but were introduced here accidentally at the end of the 1960s. They are most likely to be seen at bird tables in gardens, or flying in small groups over suburban rooftops. Amazingly, they seem well able to survive the winter here, and sometimes even breed in our coldest months, January and February. They seem to be dependent on garden scraps for their food at this and other times. They nest in holes in trees.

A Kingfisher landing with its catch

Hoopoe

Another exotic hole-nester is the Hoopoe, which uses tree-holes and also cavities in walls, but seldom does it do so here. A pair bred in Wales in 1996, but the previous British breeding record was in 1977. The bird's main foods are large insects and small reptiles, which are not common on these islands, so this charismatic bird is unlikely ever to be more than an occasional visitor.

Kingfisher

Not so the Kingfisher. It might seem too bright and tropical to be a British bird, but it is really quite common here, on lakes and slow-flowing streams. For breeding, Kingfishers have two requirements: an abundant supply of small fish, and an earth bank in which they can excavate their own nest-hole.

Most observers only see Kingfishers flashing past, just above the surface of the water. If you persevere you may see them stationary, scanning the surface of the water for movement, or you may even catch them in the act of fishing. They strike by plunge-diving; if successful they will beat the fish against something (eg. their perch) to render it motionless before swallowing it whole, head-first.

In spring, pairs often cement their relationship with a fish-presenting display, male to female. If the female takes the fish, the pair-bond is sealed.

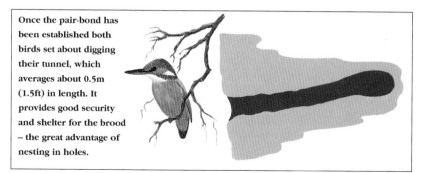

Once the pair-bond has been established both birds set about digging their tunnel, which averages about 0.5m (1.5ft) in length. It provides good security and shelter for the brood – the great advantage of nesting in holes.

WRYNECK
Jynx torquilla

16cm. This woodpecker does not look like a woodpecker; if anything, it resembles a thrush or a warbler, until the long, snake-like tongue is seen, lapping up ants and other insects. The Wryneck lacks the upright stance and short, stiff tail of other woodpeckers, often sitting crossways on a branch like any "perching bird". When feeding on the ground, it often holds it tail up.

adult

Where found: Rare summer visitor to orchards and woodland with dead trees, but now almost entirely a passage migrant in spring and especially autumn. Most frequent on the east coast.

GREEN WOODPECKER
Picus viridis

32cm. The largest and heaviest of our woodpeckers, with the longest bill, and the only one that has apple-green coloration. It most frequently feeds on the ground at anthills, rather than on trees.

adult male

Where found: An open-country species which needs mature trees for nesting, so it breeds in parkland, large gardens and open woodland. A resident, commonest in the south.

GREAT SPOTTED WOODPECKER
Dendrocopos major

23cm. Two of our woodpeckers are black-and-white, and this is by far the commonest and most widespread of the pair. It is about Starling-sized, and feeds mostly on the broader trunks and branches of trees.

adult male

Where found: It is a resident of woods of all sizes and types, and frequently comes into gardens to feed on nuts and suet. A common bird, except in the very north.

Adult male: Both sexes have a creamy-white breast, crimson-red undertail, and two white marks on the back/shoulder. Male has a black crown and red nape-patch.

LESSER SPOTTED WOODPECKER
Dendrocopos minor

15cm. A tiny black-and-white woodpecker, only the size of a sparrow. It is extremely unobtrusive and difficult to see, feeding mostly in the treetops and on the outermost branches and twigs of trees.

adult male

Where found: It needs woods with tall trees, or habitats with weak-barked trees such as willows, alders and birches, where it will often feed close to the ground but never on it.

Adult: It looks rather like a Nightjar in miniature as far as coloration is concerned, with a mixture of browns and greys giving a bark-like appearance. Stripes on the head, neck and back mimic the pattern of a snake, the effect being enhanced by the bird's habit of writhing its neck (hence the name "wry-neck"), and hissing when threatened.

adult

Flight (not illustrated): Like all woodpeckers it has an undulating flight, but with shallower dips than its relatives.

Voice: A loud, ringing "kiew-kiew-kiew" like a bird of prey, especially the Hobby. Uttered only in the spring.

Adult male: It is brighter green above than below, with an especially bright yellow-green rump. The crown is virulent red from forehead to nape. The pale, staring eye is surrounded by a black mask. In the male, there is a moustache below the eye which is red, bordered with black (sometimes difficult to see).

juvenile

adult female

Juvenile: A spotty, messy version of the adult.

Adult female: She differs in that her moustache is entirely black.

Flight: It bounds up and down like a rollercoaster, usually low over the ground. The wings close every few beats. When seen flying away, the bright yellow rump of this bird is very obvious.

Voice: A loud, ringing laugh which goes fractionally down the scale; in country areas this familiar sound is called "yaffling". When alarmed, the yaffle takes on a more yelping quality.

Adult female: The female lacks the red nape-patch, so her crown is entirely black. Usually there is less red on the belly.

adult female

Juvenile: Juvenile woodpeckers are confusing. Although sharing the adults' basic pattern, juveniles have all-red crowns (like a male Lesser Spotted Woodpecker). They also have pink, not red, on the undertail, and have streaks around the shoulders and flanks.

juvenile

Flight: It resembles a Starling in shape – pointed bill, dumpy body, short tail – but flies with a distinct undulating pattern, the wings being closed every few beats.

Voice: The main call is an excited "tchick", occasionally elaborated into a rattle. In early spring (February–May) both sexes drum, beating their bills against wood, in a quick drum-roll that fades rapidly away.

Adult male: All Lesser Spotted Woodpeckers differ from their larger relatives in having streaks on the breast, no red on the undertail, and in having a set of white stripes across the wings and back, like a ladder. They are also, of course, much smaller. The male of this species has a complete red crown.

adult female

Juvenile: The forehead is white, giving way to red and finally black on the crown. Young females show less red than males.

juvenile

Adult female: It differs by having a white crown, which gives way to a black nape.

Flight: Typical woodpecker undulations, but fluttery.

Voice: The male gives an excited ringing "kee-kee-kee ... ", all on one note. Both sexes give a very weak version of the Great Spotted Woodpecker's "tchick" call. The drumming is weaker than Great Spotted's, and longer, with sustained pressure and no fade. Often two drum-rolls are performed in close sequence.

Climbing and pecking behaviour

Climbing

Woodpeckers have a characteristic shape that readily identifies them. They cling to tree trunks in an upright posture, holding on with their strong feet, supported by their stiff tail; they have powerful, pointed bills, set on a large head on a stocky body, and have relatively long wings.

The woodpeckers specialise in obtaining invertebrates from the trunk and branches of trees, especially by chipping away at rotten wood or bark to reveal the creatures hidden beneath. All the features mentioned above are necessary to carry out these operations. The feet obviously need to be strong in order to hold on to the near-vertical surfaces of trees; they are also splayed, so that two toes point forward and two toes point back, an arrangement called "zygodactyl". To complement the zygodactyl feet, the tail is thick and strong, with special stiff feathers. It acts as a prop to keep the bird upright, and suffers great wear and tear in the line of duty.

The vertical, propped-up woodpecker is well adapted to cling on powerfully, but its movement up and down is restricted to a rather awkward-looking series of hops. The shape just does not allow for easy turns this way and that, especially in the downward direction.

By holding on tight, however, there is a great advantage to a bird with a powerful bill. Within reason, it can hit the wood or bark as hard as it likes without falling off. Herein lies the secret of the woodpecker's success – it can forage where no other bird can forage, under and among the wood and bark, by using its bill as a hammer. It can also, of course, carve out its very own nesting or roosting holes when the need arises. Woodpeckers do not just have large bills, they also have specially-thickened skulls so they can cope with the large forces involved in these processes.

Territorial behaviour

Two of our woodpeckers have put their ability to hit wood hard to a further use – territorial proclamation. Great and Lesser Spotted Woodpeckers tap their bills in special places, with special rhythms, to send messages. Each individual woodpecker has its own recognisable "drumming", its own code of beats, to declare ownership of a piece of territory and to advertise its presence. Very occasionally, the Green Woodpecker also drums, but this activity seems almost confined to the more arboreal species.

Wryneck

One woodpecker, however, breaks most of the rules. It has a much smaller bill and head than the others, and a long, unstiffened tail. Furthermore, it is a long-distance migrant from Africa. Most people would not take the Wryneck for a woodpecker at all, unless they noticed the arrangement of its feet, and that is unlikely. But this curious, brown bird does show one typical family characteristic – its tongue. All woodpeckers have long, sticky tongues which probe into the tiny, unseen fissures of bark and wood, "vacuuming up" insects as they go. The tongue is so long that it retracts into a special place in the skull, above the eye – just another special adaptation of these fascinating and attractive birds.

It is typical to see the Green Woodpecker perched on the ground (right) as well as on a tree (left)

Great Spotted
Woodpecker

Wryneck

The Wryneck will fly down from its perch and then hop along the ground

WOODLARK
Lullula arborea

15cm. Larks are "small brown birds" which live mostly on the ground (terrestrial), but sing in the sky. The Woodlark is our smallest species, with a distinctive short tail. Unlike the other two larks, it regularly perches on trees, bushes and wires.

Adult: A wide, whitish eyebrow extends all the way back to the nape, meeting its counterpart on the other side to make a V-shape at the back of the neck. The ears are chestnut-brown, bordered

adult

Where found: Uncommon, local species. Various open habitats with scattered trees, notably heathland and felled woodland. Some populations are resident, others disperse in winter.

SKYLARK
Alauda arvensis

18cm. For a bird of such famed vocal prowess, the Skylark is disappointing to look at, being largely brown and streaky. It is also larger than most people expect, approaching the Starling in size. Watch for the crouching run when it is on the ground, and for the often-raised crest; in the air it has characteristically fluttering flight.

Adult: Larger than Woodlark, with a thicker bill and much longer, white-sided tail. It lacks the head and wing-bend features of Woodlark, but does have a weak, buffy eyebrow.

adult

Where found: A widespread and abundant resident in all types of open country, but especially farmland fields.

SHORE LARK
Eremophila alpestris

16cm. An uncommon but distinctive lark, showing a yellow-and-black mask on the face. It is shy and unobtrusive.

Adult summer: Black horns can be difficult to see, but otherwise the bold yellow-and-black head markings are unmistakable. Unstreaked below. May have pinkish wash to upperparts.

adult summer

Where found: A scarce winter visitor to wild, windswept seashores and coastal marshes, mainly on the east coast.

Breeding behaviour

The Woodlark and Skylark breed regularly in this country. The Shore Lark is mainly a scarce winter visitor, found mostly on the beaches and marshes of the east coast, but has occasionally bred in Scotland.

Woodlark

The Woodlark is uncommon and local in this country, but can be found in open habitats with scattered trees, such as heathland and felled woodland. While the male is looking for a mate, and for a time after pairing has occurred, he will perform a song-flight. He makes an angled ascent, usually taking-off from the tops of trees, and will then circle at a reasonably constant height, up to a maximum of 100m

(300ft). Paired males tend to circle lower than single males. Another form of song-flight occurs when the male takes off from the ground. He will rise up to about 10–20m (30–60ft) before he starts to sing and will then move in irregular spirals, rising and falling, singing constantly. The final descent is silent. When building the nest the male and female will both excavate a hollow in the ground, in which the female constructs the nest from grass, and lines it with finer material such as hair. From the end of March 3–4 pale, brown-spotted eggs are laid, and these are incubated for 12–15 days by the female only. Once hatched, the young are fed by both parents, and will fly, badly at first, after 10–13 days.

adult

pale. A very distinctive buff-and-black mark can be seen at the bend of the wing. The Woodlark has a crest, but it is a feature which is often hard to see.

Flight: It flies with strong undulations, with regular wing-closures, almost like a small woodpecker. That similarity is reinforced by the very short tail. The tail itself is dark-brown-edged, with pale dots at the tip. The somewhat rounded wings lack the white trailing edge of Skylark.

Voice: The call is a distinctive "tit-loeet", slightly hurried. The song is fabulous: pure notes (some alternating high and low) descend and accelerate in a perfect, mellifluous, lilting refrain. The song, given from ground or air, is more pipit-like than lark-like. It is heard early in the year, from January–April.

adult

Juvenile (not illustrated): Juveniles are a strange sight, very scaly on the back and with no crest. They have moulted to look like adults by late summer.

Flight: The Skylark flies on a straighter course than Woodlark, although it still rises and falls when flying purposefully. However, much of the time it will simply be seen fluttering low over a field, chasing, or briefly rising into the air, to fall almost immediately. Look out for the white trailing edge to the slightly angled-back wings. When singing, it may rise to a great height, as its song cascades down.

Voice: The main call is a friendly "chirrup!", with obvious "R" sounds. It sings endlessly high in the sky, without pause, pouring out a fast, shrill stream of notes in warbling style. Although reminiscent of summer days, this song can be heard nearly all year.

adult winter

adult winter

Adult winter: The horns are all but lost, and the other black markings become sullied with yellow edges. Females, in particular, look more streaky above.

Flight: It usually flies low, but with a definitely undulating, and quite easy action. The pale underbelly contrasts with dark coloration on the undertail.

Voice: The commonest calls are a pipit-like, but confident "seep", often combined into a two-note "tsee-tsip".

Skylark

Common in all types of open country, the Skylark particularly favours arable land where it can be heard singing as it circles in the air, or seen walking on the ground. Once again the song-flight is important during pair-formation. The Skylark will take off silently, into the wind, and from 10–20m (30–60ft), makes a steep spiralling ascent with tail spread and wings fluttering, singing constantly. It can reach up to 100m (300ft). Monogamous pair-bonds are formed which often persist from year to year. The nest, made from grass and leaves with a lining of finer material, is built by the female inside a hollow depression on the ground or among short vegetation such as grass and crops. Between three and five eggs are laid from late April onwards, and these are incubated solely by the female for 11 days. Once hatched the chicks are fed and cared for by both parents for 18–20 days, but they usually leave the nest at 8–10 days.

Shore Lark

Pairs of Shore Larks have occasionally bred in the mountains of Scotland that offer a tundra-like habitat. The nest, a grass cup, is built on the ground. Eggs are laid from mid-May to June and the clutch usually consists of four greenish eggs speckled with yellow-brown. The female incubates the eggs on her own for 10–14 days and both parents then feed and care for the chicks for 9–14 days.

The rise and fall of the lark

A Skylark singing

Skylark

Few bird songs in all the world have been more celebrated, more appreciated, than the glorious song of the Skylark. The sheer exuberance of this bird's performance, its non-stop energy, and the musical quality of its outpourings, have inspired musicians and poets alike.

Most Skylarks sing for around two minutes at a time, but some individuals have been recorded singing for up to an hour continuously! When singing, they seem to take hardly a breath, but this is a false picture, since birds can sing equally well when breathing out and breathing in, owing to the nature of their vocal organs. Skylarks are also associated with the dawn, hence the familiar phrase "up with the Lark". The main singing period is indeed the very early morning; start times of 04.00 are regular in summer, and even 02.30 has been commonly recorded.

The Skylark usually delivers its song in flight. It rises at a steep angle, into the wind, and rises to a maximum of 100m (300ft) or so, singing all the while. When aloft, it usually just hovers on the spot, but may circle at a constant height, before beginning a slow descent with its wings held motionless. Usually it spirals down, stops singing before it reaches the ground, then touches down after a final, closed-wing plummet.

A Skylark hovering

A Woodlark singing

Woodlark

The Woodlark is no slouch when it comes to singing, either. It shows little of the Skylark's energy, but outdoes it in the sheer subtle beauty of the song. The pure phrases are well spaced, mellifluous and effortlessly fluent. They are often heard at night, to maximum aesthetic effect. Although Woodlarks sing from a perch more frequently than Skylarks, they give an equally polished flight performance. Rising in spirals, they tend to circle over the territory rather than hovering, and rise and fall in dizzy loops on fluttery wing-beats. The descent is slow, spiralling and accompanied by song.

Larks descending?

Sadly, the huge populations of Skylarks that once dominated the skies above our fields are in serious decline. In many areas, the overall numbers have dropped by a half or even more, threatening the Skylark's future as an abundant British bird.

Several theories for Skylark reductions have already been put forward: hard winters at the end of the 1970s; a loss of farmland weeds due to herbicide use; a decrease in the amount of rotational farming (the variety is good for Skylarks); a decrease in the amount of young ley (fallow) grassland; the trend towards autumn, not spring, tilling (with the resulting loss of winter stubble). Current research will hopefully determine which of these factors, if any, is the most important.

West Country Woodlarks also breed on farmland, but most of the population in the Home Counties breeds on heathland, another threatened habitat. The Woodlark has also decreased recently, at least in the number of sites where it can be found. The main threats to lowland heathland are development, fires, encroachment by trees and shrubs (some heaths are turning into woodland) and excessive disturbance.

SWIFT
Apus apus

16cm. This bird never perches and is almost always seen flying; it can, however, cling to the sides of walls. Presenting an anchor-shape in flight, with a cigar-shaped body and narrow, slightly curved-back wings, the Swift is easy to identify. The tail is quite short, and forked, although it is often held closed (the Swallow's never is).

adult

Where found: A bird of high summer, arriving in late April at the earliest, and leaving in August. A very common sight over built-up and many other areas.

Adult: Dark-brown all over, although usually appearing black, except for an unimpressive white throat.

SAND MARTIN
Riparia riparia

12cm. The smallest, slimmest member of the aerial Swallow and Martin family, always found near water. It has shorter wings than Swallow or Swift, and a much shorter, more shallowly forked tail.

Adult: It is very plain on the back, just brown, without a white rump. Below it is very clean – "whiter-than-white" – except for an obvious brown breast-band. Some brown from the underwings leaks down on to the flanks.

Where found: The first of our aerial birds to arrive; mid-March–October. Widely distributed, but local, breeding on riverbanks, sandbanks or wherever they can make their tunnel nests.

SWALLOW
Hirundo rustica

19cm. A popular herald of summer which dashes low over fields and meadows with panache. An effervescent species, rarely quiet, whether flying in long glides or perching on its favourite overhead wires. The long, swept-back wings and long tail-streamers readily identify it.

adult male

Where found: A summer visitor from late March–October. Often very common in farmland and lightly built-up areas, but it must have fields over which to forage.

HOUSE MARTIN
Delichon urbica

12cm. A small, compact aerial bird, much more common in built up areas than the Swallow. The wings are relatively short and stubby, and the tail is quite strongly forked. The white rump always gives this species away.

Adult: It is blue-black above, except for slightly browner wings and tail, and that benchmark white rump. Below, it has gleaming white underparts, which contrast with the darker underwings and tail.

Where found: A summer visitor, mainly from April–October. It needs buildings or cliffs on which to nest, so is a common sight in towns and villages.

adult

Juvenile: They are paler brown, slightly mottled. The white throat-patch is larger, and extends to the forehead.

juvenile

Flight: Performs long, sweeping glides at dizzying speed. Groups often dash around the rooftops, screaming their heads off. The wings are held stiffly, and beaten quickly. The impression gained is of speed and expertise.

Voice: A distinctive, piercing scream, with many variations. Screams from groups high in the air are typical of warm summer evenings.

adult

adult

Juvenile (not illustrated): Similar, but it looks scaly, and the throat is slightly tinged darker.

Flight: It is not a powerful flier like Swift or Swallow, but is still highly manoeuvrable, moving to and fro with flutters and short glides. Sand Martins tend to be seen over water, although all the aerial birds on this page also visit water regularly.

Voice: The main call is dry, buzzy and rasping, less up-beat and chirrupy than the House Martin's call.

Adult male: All adult Swallows are glossy royal-blue above, except for white spots at the base of the tail, and a spot of red-chestnut on the forehead. Below, they have the same red-chestnut on the throat, a royal blue breast band, and otherwise creamy-white underparts. The white tail spots are larger, and much more obvious from below.

Adult female (not illustrated): In the main, females have shorter tail-streamers than males, although there is some overlap.

juvenile

Juvenile: Juveniles have very short tail streamers, much shorter than those of any female. Otherwise, they are duller overall, with quite a different, pinker colour on the throat and forehead.

Flight: Easy to identify in flight: low, but buoyant swoops over the ground. There are longer movements in the same direction than the more haphazard flight of martins. In contrast to the House Martin there is no white rump.

Voice: Its main call is a cheerful "witt-witt". The song is a medley of grating twitters, interspersed (usually when perched) with buzzes.

adult

adult

Juvenile (not illustrated): Juveniles are duller everywhere, with less clear dark upperparts, and grey-tinged underparts.

Flight: It flies at moderate pace on shortish, stiff wings, with regular tight circling. Both martins give a more fluttery impression than the more purposeful Swallow and Swift.

Voice: It utters rather gravelly short trills which can be rendered "prrt". The song, usually delivered from the nest, is a surprisingly pleasant, gurgly adaptation of this basic call.

Feeding, nesting and roosting behaviour

Aerial Feeders

Members of the Swift family and Swallow family (not actually closely related) share the skies in the pursuit of flying insects. Each species uses a different part of the sky, a slightly different technique, and takes slightly different prey from the other, but there is nevertheless considerable overlap.

Swift – often flies the highest, taking the smallest prey – minute insects and spiders ("flying" on their webs), so small that they have been dubbed "aeroplankton". It flies in long, powerful sweeps.

House Martin – often flies high, but on average takes larger prey than the Swift. It seems to specialise in small flies and aphids, which are gathered in more circumspect, slower sweeps and glides. It often flies in fairly tight circles and semi-circles.

Sand Martin – usually flies at low altitudes, not far from the ground. Apparently, its prey averages larger in size than that of the House Martin, although the bird itself is smaller. The flight is more fluttery than any other aerial feeder. It is usually found near water.

Swallow – the lowest flier, usually just above ground, and over fields, using a slower, sweeping flight than that employed by the Swift. It takes the largest prey of any of our aerial feeders, eg. bluebottles.

Nest-sites

All these species commonly nest in colonies.

Swift – nests in the highest places, usually on a tall building such as a church tower. It selects a well-protected ledge, usually inside the eaves of a roof; since the Swift can barely perch at all it must have easy access from the air.

House Martin – also uses buildings, although generally nests lower down. It builds a mud nest which is stuck on to the side of the building, usually under the eaves.

Sand Martin – relies on the presence of sandy riverbanks and sand quarries for breeding. The birds burrow into the sand, making a tunnel about 0.5m (1.5ft) long.

Swallow – most nest inside buildings, such as barns (in North America this species is known as the "Barn Swallow", and the Sand Martin the "Bank Swallow"), sheds and garages. They select a ledge, normally building against a vertical surface.

House Martin at nest

Roosting

All our species usually sleep in the nest during the breeding season, but look elsewhere on migration. The Swallow and Sand Martin are found in reedbeds or other marshy vegetation at night on their travels, sometimes in enormous numbers. The House Martin apparently utilises unoccupied nests in colonies, but also roosts in trees. The Swift is famous for its sleeping habits: while some birds use conventional sites such as walls and trees, others undoubtedly catch quick naps in the night sky, while they are aloft.

Swallow at nest

MEADOW PIPIT
Anthus pratensis

14cm. The pipits are small, ground-living (terrestrial) birds that look like miniature thrushes because of their streaky breasts. The Meadow Pipit is our commonest species. Pipits walk along the ground and often wag their longish tails. In this species, its terrestrial lifestyle has given rise to very long hind claws.

Where found: An abundant resident in many treeless habitats, especially rough pasture and moorland. Many leave the high moors in winter and go downhill or to the coast.

Adult: The Meadow Pipit is basically olive-brown above and contrastingly whitish below, although the ground colour varies and many look much greyer, especially in summer. The breast streaking is strong from the upper breast to the upper belly and flanks. The face looks rather plain, because of the lack of a strong eyebrow or eyestripe.

TREE PIPIT
Anthus trivialis

15cm. The Tree Pipit is exceedingly similar to the Meadow Pipit, but is slightly larger and more robust. Its bill is broader, and it has a flatter crown. The hind claws are shorter than Meadow Pipit's, so much so that, if seen, they can clinch an identification. Importantly, the Tree Pipit is a summer visitor only to Britain.

Where found: A summer visitor, early April–October, to a variety of open country habitats with scattered trees, notably heathland.

Adult: The Tree Pipit looks a shade more buffy than Meadow Pipit, especially on the throat and breast (contrasting with the white belly). It looks smarter than the other species, with very well-marked breast streaks; these are thick and bold on the upper breast, suddenly becoming thin on the flanks. The face shows quite a well-defined buffy eyebrow, contrasting with a thin but noticeable dark eyestripe. On the wings, the pale wing-bars show more clearly than on Meadow, and the median wing-

ROCK PIPIT
Anthus petrosus

17cm. This is a relatively large, very dark pipit that is usually seen around rocky shores and cliffs. It has a longer bill than the Meadow Pipit, which is most likely to occur in related habitat. A good distinction is the leg colour, which is blackish, not flesh-pink.

Where found: Very much a bird of rocky coastlines all year round, not just cliffs, but also flatter beaches with plenty of shingle and seaweed.

Adult: It is dark brown above, much more so than any other pipit. The breast streaking is particularly heavy, set against light brown, thus making the whole bird look dusky. The wing-bars and eyebrow are obscure.

WATER PIPIT
Anthus spinoletta

17cm. Another large, dark pipit, a very close relative of Rock Pipit, and often considered to be the same species. In Britain, it is mostly found on freshwater. At all times, it is best told from Rock Pipit by the prominent white eyebrow.

Where found: Winter visitors from October–April, inhabiting freshwater, not saltwater habitats – especially watercress beds, lakesides and rivers.

Adult winter (not illustrated): Water Pipits are winter visitors to Britain, but attain summer plumage before they leave. The species is paler and greyer than Rock Pipit, and especially looks whitish below. The streaks on the breast are fewer, and the wing-bar is more prominent. Watch particularly for that white eyebrow. Note that the tail is white-edged, in common with Meadow and Tree Pipits.

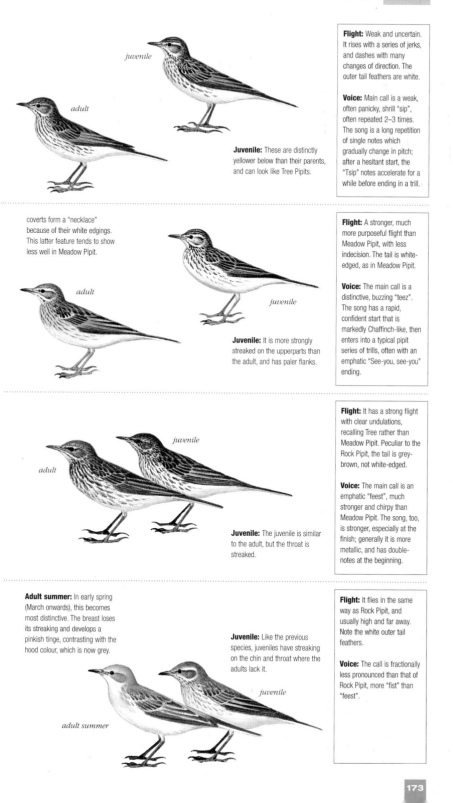

juvenile

adult

Juvenile: These are distinctly yellower below than their parents, and can look like Tree Pipits.

Flight: Weak and uncertain. It rises with a series of jerks, and dashes with many changes of direction. The outer tail feathers are white.

Voice: Main call is a weak, often panicky, shrill "sip", often repeated 2–3 times. The song is a long repetition of single notes which gradually change in pitch; after a hesitant start, the "Tsip" notes accelerate for a while before ending in a trill.

coverts form a "necklace" because of their white edgings. This latter feature tends to show less well in Meadow Pipit.

adult

juvenile

Juvenile: It is more strongly streaked on the upperparts than the adult, and has paler flanks.

Flight: A stronger, much more purposeful flight than Meadow Pipit, with less indecision. The tail is white-edged, as in Meadow Pipit.

Voice: The main call is a distinctive, buzzing "teez". The song has a rapid, confident start that is markedly Chaffinch-like, then enters into a typical pipit series of trills, often with an emphatic "See-you, see-you" ending.

juvenile

adult

Juvenile: The juvenile is similar to the adult, but the throat is streaked.

Flight: It has a strong flight with clear undulations, recalling Tree rather than Meadow Pipit. Peculiar to the Rock Pipit, the tail is grey-brown, not white-edged.

Voice: The main call is an emphatic "feest", much stronger and chirpy than Meadow Pipit. The song, too, is stronger, especially at the finish; generally it is more metallic, and has double-notes at the beginning.

Adult summer: In early spring (March onwards), this becomes most distinctive. The breast loses its streaking and develops a pinkish tinge, contrasting with the hood colour, which is now grey.

Juvenile: Like the previous species, juveniles have streaking on the chin and throat where the adults lack it.

juvenile

adult summer

Flight: It flies in the same way as Rock Pipit, and usually high and far away. Note the white outer tail feathers.

Voice: The call is fractionally less pronounced than that of Rock Pipit, more "fist" than "feest".

Song flights and pipit identification

Aerial Songsters

Although they are relatively unexciting to look at, pipits are good songsters and perform impressive, spectacular song flights that rival those of the larks (see pp.166–167), close relatives.

A pipit song flight may start from the ground or a perch (see below). The bird rises up at a steep angle, busily fluttering its wings, and gains a height of 10–30m (30–90ft); then it descends in parachute fashion, wings spread, tail up, legs dangling down. It sings from the early part of its ascent until just before landing.

Meadow Pipits – make the shallowest, slowest ascent, and have the longest, most drawn-out song. Sometimes they enter into a second song-flight before even completing the first. They almost always rise from the ground, or a very low perch, and return to the same spot, or another spot equally low down.

Tree Pipits – make the steepest ascent, and have more of an "attack" to the early part of their song than the other pipits. They almost always rise from a high perch, such as the top of a tree, and return to the same, or a comparable perch.

Rock Pipits – are said to have a steeper ascent than Meadow Pipits, but the difference, if any, is obscure. Otherwise, their song-flight is very similar to the Meadow Pipit's, beginning and ending on the ground or a low perch.

Meadow Pipit/
Rock Pipt

Tree Pipit

Tree Pipit   Skylark   Linnet (female)

House Sparrow   Corn Bunting   Yellowhammer   Dunnock
                                      (female)

Is it a pipit?

Birdwatchers in open country are often faced with a whole host of small brown birds that all look similar at first glance. Here we compare the Tree Pipit with a number of similar-looking birds, and give tips on how to distinguish them.

Pipit – small, resembling a "miniature thrush". Thin bill. Usually has white outer tail feathers and a long tail. Wing-bars are obscure. Bird walks, can run. Tail is wagged. Panicky flight.

Skylark – much larger than pipit. Has a crest. Thicker bill than pipit. White outer feathers on long tail. Bird walks and runs. Does not wag tail. Fluttering flight.

Linnet – female is dull-coloured, male often colourful. A small finch, pipit sized. Has tiny, fairly thick bill. Very slim. Long tail, white-edged. Wings have a silvery bar that continues down the wing. Hops on ground. Does not wag tail. Steeply undulating, purposeful flight, usually in tight flocks.

Sparrow – larger than pipits, finches and buntings, but smaller than Skylark. Thick, seed-eater's bill. No crest. Plump, with shortish tail, unmarked. White wing bars show up well. Hops on ground. Flicks tail but does not wag it. Very noisy and cheerful.

Corn Bunting – rather like sparrow, but very drably marked. Thick bill, short, unmarked tail and plump body are similar. No eyebrow or wing-bars. Hops on ground. Undemonstrative.

Other Buntings – eg. Yellowhammer, Reed Bunting – females are dull-coloured. Have white outer tail feathers on long tail. Larger than pipits, smaller than Skylark. Slim body, but more robust than pipits. Usually have stripes down moustache. Thick bill. Hop on ground.

Dunnock – small, brown-streaked, with a thin, insect-eater's bill. Tail quite long, unmarked. Rather slim, crouches along ground, Hops or shuffles, flicks wings and tail constantly, but does not wag tail. A quiet species. Does not flock.

YELLOW WAGTAIL
Motacilla flava

17cm. Wagtails are distinctive walking and running birds which constantly wag their tails; all are brightly or boldly coloured. The Yellow Wagtail has the shortest tail of the three species, making it resemble a pipit in shape. In contrast to the other wagtails, it is a summer visitor only to Britain. The Blue-headed Wagtail is an uncommon passage migrant that occasionally breeds.

Where found: Summer visitor, April–October. Prefers damp habitats, but also occurs in arable crops. In late summer especially, it is often seen feeding in company with cattle.

Adult male summer: It is bright yellow below, more greenish-yellow on the crown and mantle.

Adult female summer: The crown and mantle have a browner tinge, making them look darker. Below, the yellow is slightly paler than on the male.

Adult male "Blue-headed": On this subspecies, the crown, nape and cheeks are blue-grey instead of yellow-green, highlighting a white, not yellow, eyebrow.

GREY WAGTAIL
Motacilla cinerea

18cm. Although yellow below, this is not as yellow as a Yellow Wagtail; it is grey above, hence its name. The Grey Wagtail has the longest tail of the three species, making it look very attenuated. It is also the only species with flesh-coloured, not black legs.

Where found: Breeds mostly along fast-flowing rivers and streams, but also along slower or still water, always fresh. Wider habitat preferences in winter, such as lowland lakesides.

Adult male summer: The underparts are entirely lemon-yellow (not buttery-yellow as in Yellow Wagtail). Above, and on the cheeks, it is slate-grey; the cheeks are sharply defined above and below, by a white eyebrow and white moustache respectively, and below the moustache is a jet-black throat. The Yellow Wagtail has no such strong marks on its head, and the Blue-headed Wagtail lacks the black throat.

PIED WAGTAIL
Motacilla alba

18cm. This is the commonest wagtail, boldly black-and-white ("pied"), and the one most likely to be seen away from water. An easy bird to identify, although tricky to age and sex.

Where found: Common resident in many habitats, often by water. A familiar sight in towns and cities, especially on lawns. The White Wagtail is a visitor on spring and autumn passage.

Adult male summer "Pied": The head is black on all sides, including crown, throat and side of neck, leaving a white patch from forehead to cheeks. From crown to back it is solidly black, joining up with the black breast. The black terminates on the breast, with some dark colour dusting the flanks resembling leaked ink.

Ups and downs in the lives of Wagtails

No-one knows exactly why wagtails pump their tails up and down all the time. There must be a reason, of course – there may be several – but here are some of the suggestions that have been put forward.

The tail wagging makes them look conspicuous to us, and therefore, probably to each other, suggesting it may be a form of continuous display. Equally, the movements are said to coincide with the to and fro movements of waves of water, or with vegetation waving in the flow of a stream, thus affording a type of camouflage (this theory derives from the fact that other waterside birds, notably Common Sandpiper and Dipper, also wag their rear ends up and down). Another suggestion is that wagging disturbs insects around the bird, which it then snatches. Another is that the movements themselves actually attract insects. Whatever the real reason, the Wagtail wagging mystery is a good example of how much is yet to be discovered about even our commonest birds.

Adult female "Blue-headed":
Where the male is blue-grey, the female is dull grey-green, and this colour extends on to the back. The throat and breast are whitish (yellow in Yellow Wagtail).

Juvenile: The juvenile has a shorter tail, and is overall much browner than its parents (of either subspecies). The eyebrow is buff coloured, and bordered

above and below by dark stripes. There is a blotchy moustache which extends down to an equally blotchy band across the throat.

Flight: All wagtails have sweeping, undulating flight. This species has two white wing-bars.

Voice: The call is a musical "sweep". The song is a series of short, scratchy phrases based on the call-note; often two or three phrases are strung together haphazardly.

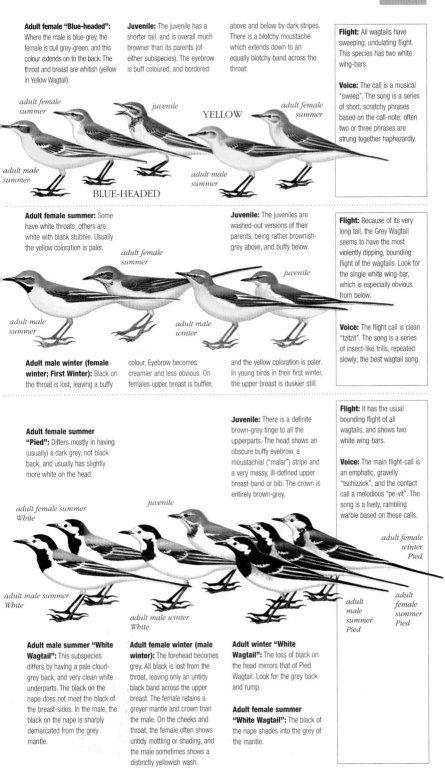

adult female summer

juvenile

YELLOW

adult female summer

adult male summer

BLUE-HEADED

adult male summer

Adult female summer: Some have white throats, others are white with black stubble. Usually the yellow coloration is paler.

Juvenile: The juveniles are washed-out versions of their parents, being rather brownish-grey above, and buffy below.

Flight: Because of its very long tail, the Grey Wagtail seems to have the most violently dipping, bounding flight of the wagtails. Look for the single white wing-bar, which is especially obvious from below.

Voice: The flight call is clean "tzitzit". The song is a series of insect-like trills, repeated slowly; the best wagtail song.

adult female summer

juvenile

adult male summer

adult male winter

Adult male winter (female winter; First Winter): Black on the throat is lost, leaving a buffy

colour. Eyebrow becomes creamier and less obvious. On females upper breast is buffier,

and the yellow coloration is paler. In young birds in their first winter, the upper breast is duskier still.

Flight: It has the usual bounding flight of all wagtails, and shows two white wing-bars.

Voice: The main flight-call is an emphatic, gravelly "tschizzick", and the contact call a melodious "pe-vit". The song is a lively, rambling warble based on these calls.

Adult female summer "Pied": Differs mostly in having (usually) a dark grey, not black back, and usually has slightly more white on the head.

Juvenile: There is a definite brown-grey tinge to all the upperparts. The head shows an obscure buffy eyebrow, a moustachial ("malar") stripe and a very messy, ill-defined upper breast-band or bib. The crown is entirely brown-grey.

adult female summer White

juvenile

adult female winter Pied

adult male summer White

adult male winter White

adult male summer Pied

adult female summer Pied

Adult male summer "White Wagtail": This subspecies differs by having a pale cloud-grey back, and very clean white underparts. The black on the nape does not meet the black of the breast-sides. In the male, the black on the nape is sharply demarcated from the grey mantle.

Adult female winter (male winter): The forehead becomes grey. All black is lost from the throat, leaving only an untidy black band across the upper breast. The female retains a greyer mantle than the male. On the cheeks and throat, the female often shows untidy mottling or shading, and the male sometimes shows a distinctly yellowish wash.

Adult winter "White Wagtail": The loss of black on the head mirrors that of Pied Wagtail. Look for the grey back and rump.

Adult female summer "White Wagtail": The black of the nape shades into the grey of the mantle.

Feeding, breeding and roosting behaviour

Pied Wagtail feeding

Feeding

All the wagtails feed on insects and other small invertebrates. These are obtained by three main techniques.

1. Flycatching, in which the wagtail catches airborne insects in short aerial sallies.

2. Picking, in which small items are literally picked from the ground as the wagtail walks along.

3. Run-picking, in which the wagtail sees some prey and darts after it at a run (the Grey Wagtail does not perform this last manoeuvre).

The three species tend to select different places in which to hunt food, although there is considerable overlap.

Grey Wagtail – usually forages only near water, on rocks in rivers or alongside the edges of streams or pools.

Yellow Wagtail – feeds mostly in wet meadows, and has a particularly close association with livestock, especially cattle. The tiny birds run around the grazers' legs, chasing after any insects that are disturbed.

Pied Wagtail – more of a generalist, and is happy living close to man. It will feed on roads, lawns and especially on roofs.

Breeding

Wagtails choose different breeding sites. The *Yellow Wagtail* nests on the ground, in grassy places, usually next to a tussock and often in the territory of a pair of Lapwings. The latter birds will help to drive away various intruders, including cattle, which may help the wagtails with feeding, but also trample on their nests. The *Grey Wagtail* always nests near water, often in a hole in a wall or in a riverbank,

Pied Wagtail at nest

or under a bridge, or in tree-roots not far from the water's edge. The *Pied Wagtail* also likes holes or crevices in which to place its nest, but prefers artificial sites: walls, barns, and even items of machinery. All wagtails lay clutches of about five eggs.

When breeding is over the Yellow Wagtail, the only exclusive summer visitor of the three, departs south to Africa to spend the winter there. The other two species stay with us, although they may journey some distance from their breeding sites. At such times, the Grey Wagtail, in particular, becomes much more common in lowland areas.

Roosting

All wagtails roost in groups. The *Grey Wagtail* is the least sociable, rarely gathering in groups of more than ten or 20, but *Yellow Wagtails* and *Pied Wagtails* may number into four figures at the roost. Grey Wagtails tend to select trees, but Yellow and Pied Wagtails are great users of reedbeds. In urban areas, the Pied

Yellow Wagtail at nest

Wagtail also gathers to roost in some unusual sites, including buildings and streetside trees. It is a strange sight to see a well-spaced group of these small birds sitting quietly in the branches, while the shoppers and commuters go about their business on the teeming streets below.

Grey Wagtail at nest

Bombycillidae, Cinclidae, Troglodytidae, Prunellidae

WAXWING
Bombycilla garrulus

18cm. A spectacular bird that is unmistakable if seen well. It is usually seen in groups, which feed on winter berries. The shape and size, if not the colour, are similar to that of Starling. The crest is always obvious.

Where found: Rare winter visitor, mainly in the east Inhabits gardens, hedgerows and anywhere there are berries. In some years ("Irruption Years") large numbers visit.

Adult: All adults have soft, silky, pink-brown plumage, broken only by a black mask and bib, chestnut vent, and by the gaudy wings and tail. Normally, the female has a less clear-cut black bib, and has slightly duller wing and tail markings. The waxy red tips to the secondaries are most obvious on males.

DIPPER
Cinclus cinclus

18cm. A small bird completely confined to areas with swift-flowing water. Usually seen on rocks among the rapids, where it will bob up and down. It also immerses itself in the water, swimming and diving.

Where found: An inhabitant of fast-flowing rivers and streams, and also some lakesides. The Continental race is a rare winter visitor to eastern Britain, sometimes to lowland weirs.

Adult (British race): It is shaped like a large, fat Wren. The plumage is dark, but for the bright white front. It is often seen to "blink", revealing white eyelids. British birds have chestnut coloration between the white breast and dark-brown belly.

Adult (Continental race): Lacks any chestnut on the underparts.

WREN
Troglodytes troglodytes

12cm. Britain's third smallest breeding bird after Goldcrest and Firecrest. Its brown coloration, cocked-up tail, long bill and questioning expression are all distinctive. It hardly ever leaves deep, low cover, but when perched, it can be seen to bob up and down like the Dipper. Very noisy.

Where found: Found everywhere all year round, particularly in woods, scrub and riversides. Several subspecies of Wren are found on cliffs on Scottish islands.

Adult: Mostly brown, darker above, with a network of bars and spots. The pale eyebrow is very obvious, making it look quizzical.

adult

DUNNOCK
Prunella modularis

14cm. A quiet, retiring species, nevertheless very common. It is usually seen on the ground near cover, progressing with a creeping, jerky gait, often with intermittent wing- and tail-flicks. It tends to be seen alone, and is easily overlooked. Intermediate between Robin and sparrow, it has the thin bill and movements of the former, but the streaky-brown plumage of the latter.

Where found: A very common resident in woodland, hedges, gardens and other bushy places. Usually seen at moderate heights only.

fresh adult

Adult: Look for extensive grey about the head and breast, which should eliminate similar birds. Seen well, the rich streaking on the mantle and flanks is attractive. The legs and eyes are reddish.

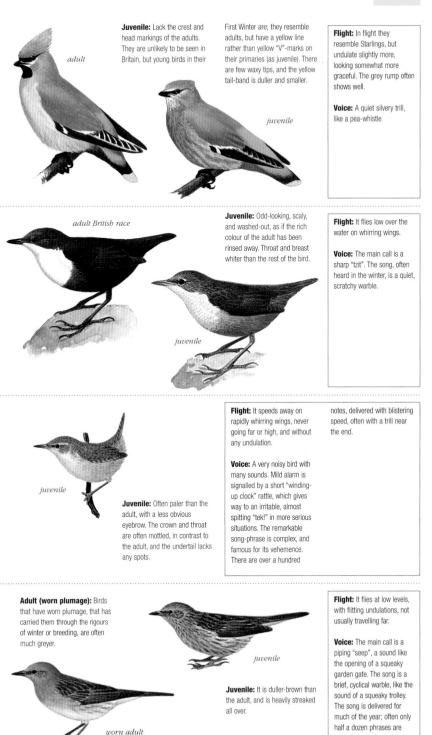

adult

juvenile

Juvenile: Lack the crest and head markings of the adults. They are unlikely to be seen in Britain, but young birds in their First Winter are; they resemble adults, but have a yellow line rather than yellow "V"-marks on their primaries (as juvenile). There are few waxy tips, and the yellow tail-band is duller and smaller.

Flight: In flight they resemble Starlings, but undulate slightly more, looking somewhat more graceful. The grey rump often shows well.

Voice: A quiet silvery trill, like a pea-whistle

adult British race

juvenile

Juvenile: Odd-looking, scaly, and washed-out, as if the rich colour of the adult has been rinsed away. Throat and breast whiter than the rest of the bird.

Flight: It flies low over the water on whirring wings.

Voice: The main call is a sharp "tzit". The song, often heard in the winter, is a quiet, scratchy warble.

juvenile

Juvenile: Often paler than the adult, with a less obvious eyebrow. The crown and throat are often mottled, in contrast to the adult, and the undertail lacks any spots.

Flight: It speeds away on rapidly whirring wings, never going far or high, and without any undulation.

Voice: A very noisy bird with many sounds. Mild alarm is signalled by a short "winding-up clock" rattle, which gives way to an irritable, almost spitting "tek!" in more serious situations. The remarkable song-phrase is complex, and famous for its vehemence. There are over a hundred notes, delivered with blistering speed, often with a trill near the end.

Adult (worn plumage): Birds that have worn plumage, that has carried them through the rigours of winter or breeding, are often much greyer.

juvenile

worn adult

Juvenile: It is duller-brown than the adult, and is heavily streaked all over.

Flight: It flies at low levels, with flitting undulations, not usually travelling far.

Voice: The main call is a piping "seep", a sound like the opening of a squeaky garden gate. The song is a brief, cyclical warble, like the sound of a squeaky trolley. The song is delivered for much of the year; often only half a dozen phrases are given from each perch.

Habitat, feeding and breeding behaviour

Waxwing

Waxwing

An unmistakable bird, the Waxwing is named after the strange, waxy-red tips to its secondary flight feathers. While most colourful birds are popularly expected to come from the Tropical regions, the Waxwing comes instead from the far north. The European breeding population mostly occurs above the 60°N line of latitude, and penetrates well above the Arctic Circle.

Only rarely do Waxwings visit us in any numbers. About once in a decade or so, high population levels in Scandinavia or Russia coincide with a poor rowan berry crop there, and many birds are forced south and west towards the British Isles in autumn and winter. These movements are called "irruptions".

As well as rowan berries, Waxwings also eat the berries of hawthorns together with the fruit of a wide variety of other trees. In summer they rely mainly on a diet of flies, in particular mosquitoes and midges, but also mayflies and stoneflies.

Dipper

Many small birds live by the water, but only the Dipper lives in it. It is the only truly aquatic song-bird in the world, obtaining its food by paddling, swimming and diving into the turbulent waters of fast-flowing streams.

The Dipper's most famous trick is to walk under water, apparently defying buoyancy. Dippers do this by walking into the current and arching their body slightly upwards at the back, so adopting a bowing posture. The flow of water over their back pushes them down, and they can pick for insect larvae from the bed of the river.

Dipper

Wren

Wren

Due to the fact that the Wren is small, secretive, and lives close to the ground, is can be difficult to appreciate that it is probably the most numerous bird in Britain. However, its song is extremely loud for such a small bird, and comprises a shouted phrase of over 100 hurried notes. Primarily territorial in function, this song is one of the few that can be heard in our woodlands and gardens all year round. It always seems overstated, too loud and too long.

Male Wrens defend a territory year-round, and when spring comes they begin to build nests, lots of them – up to 12 in each territory. When a female visits, the male performs excited nest-showing displays, and it seems that the female's judgment of him is greatly influenced by the number and quality of the nests he has built. If the female finds a nest to her liking she will line it with bits of grass, and breeding begins. The nest itself is domed, offering extra protection for the brood of 6–10 chicks.

Dunnock

This drab, unobtrusive bird is the only British member of the Accentor family (*Prunellidae*), named for the fact that they sing ("Cantor" is Latin for singer). Most of the family are found at high altitudes among mountains

The Dunnock has a distinctive way of crouching on the ground and moving along with a shuffle. It also flicks its wings and tail, and these habits alone make it rather easy to identify. It is seldom noisy, making only a pleasant warble and a squeaky call.

The Dunnock is famous for its unique pair-bonding systems. Although ordinary pairs are the norm, other arrangements may be followed – a female with two males (polyandry – quite common), a male with two females (polygyny – infrequent), and several females with several males (so-called "polygnandry" – occasional). The interrelationships involved are complex, with conflicts of interests, infidelity and deception each playing their part.

Dunnock

ROBIN *Erithacus rubecula*

14cm. Everyone knows this perky, tame garden bird, with its plump body and upright posture. Most gardens have one, adorning their bird table or idle spade. Their friendly song, their habit of bobbing up and down, their ruffling of feathers on a cold day: all these and more make the Robin one of our most popular birds.

Where found: An extremely common resident of gardens and woodlands, scrub and hedges. Many come from the Continent to spend the winter with us, arriving in October.

Adult: Unmistakable, with the orange-red breast and forehead brightening up a fairly plain-brown bird. Note that the red breast is bordered with grey on the sides, and belly is white.

adult

REDSTART
Phoenicurus phoenicurus

14cm. The main claim to fame of this slim, Robin-like bird is its fiery-orange tail, which quivers constantly. The quivering is diagnostic to both Redstart species, which do not flick their tails in the way that Robins do.

Where found: A summer visitor, April–September, to mature woodlands, parklands and a few gardens. Commonest in the north and west, often associated with sessile oakwoods.

male summmer

Male summer: Grey on crown and mantle, black on cheeks and throat, orange on breast, and white forehead. **Male winter (not illustrated):** From July colours become dull. More scaly.

BLACK REDSTART
Phoenicurus ochruros

14cm. A dark version of the Redstart, inhabiting buildings and cliffs rather than woodlands. It is larger and bulkier than its commoner relative, and feeds more on the ground. The name means "Black Red-tail", which is highly appropriate.

Where found: Cliffs, industrial and urban sites. A rare breeding bird in Britain, summer visitor at breeding areas April–September, also a passage migrant in spring and late autumn. Rare in winter.

male

Male: Distinctive, with mainly sooty-grey plumage, intensifying to jet black on the throat, head-sides and breast. There is a prominent whitish patch on the wing and an orange-red tail.

NIGHTINGALE
Luscinia megarhynchos

16cm. A rather disappointing bird to look at – and hard to see because of its skulking habits – but what a singer! In appearance it is like a large, heavy-tailed Robin, often holding its tail cocked, and perching with an upright stance.

Where found: An uncommon summer visitor to some woodlands and thickets in England; local. Birds arrive in April, and the last migrants are seen in September.

Adult: Brown above, pale below, but with a distinctive rich chestnut tail. The dark eye is obvious on the expressionless face.

adult

juvenile

Juvenile: Very different, being pale brown and copiously spotted and speckled. Reddish colour appears on the breast by late summer, and all juveniles resemble adults by September.

Flight: The Robin has elegant, flitting flight, usually low over the ground. Journeys are usually short.

Voice: The commonest call is a clean "tick", repeated constantly, reminiscent of the sound of a car engine cooling down. The song is complex: rising and falling, with accelerating and decelerating phrases that each have a shrill, wistful air. Every phrase is different, and there are good gaps between phrases. The Robin is one of the few British birds that sings all year round, except for a short period in late summer when the moult takes place.

Female: Dull grey-brown above, orange-buff below; the best clue to its identity is the orange-red tail. Note, however, that it has a pale, almost white throat, and a pale eyering.

juvenile

female

Juvenile: Juveniles are spotted like Robins, but have the ever-present Redstart tail. Later, they resemble females as they pass into First Winter plumage.

Flight: Like the Robin, it flits around elegantly, often high in trees. The tail flashes as it moves.

Voice: The call is a loud "hweet", often combined with lower notes to make a distinctive "hwee-tuk-tuk". Song-phrases always begin the same way, but end differently, often as an imitation of another bird, typically petering out.

Female: Basically sooty grey-brown all over, with the red tail. In contrast to female Redstart, the throat is dark (no different from, say, the crown colour), and the eyering is obscure.

juvenile

female

Juvenile: These are much browner and less grey than the adults, and look scaly. First Winter birds resemble the female.

Flight: It has broader wings than the Redstart, but flits in a similar way. However, it does seem to flaunt the tail less.

Voice: Its call is a "sweep", often accompanied by a mechanical ticking. The song is extraordinary: a brief warble is followed by a pause then a sound similar to the one produced by rubbing ball-bearings together.

juvenile

Juvenile: They are spotted like Robins, but watch for the heavy, rich chestnut tail.

Flight: The Nightingale's flight is Robin-like, but less flitting due to the overbearing tail.

Voice: The call is a remarkably unmusical, frog-like croak, often accompanied by a "hweet". The song is powerful and varied, rich and pure; the most distinctive sections are the sensational "Piu-piu-piu" crescendos, but most parts are memorable. Although these birds are famous for their night serenades, Nightingales sing at all times of day, and they are only heard in a short period between late April and June. The Nightingale is famous for its song but actually has two slightly different types of song: shorter phrases by day to proclaim its territory, and longer, richer phrases at night to attract females.

Display, feeding and nesting behaviour

Display

All the chats show off their colourful plumage to advantage when displaying:

• Rival *Robins* squaring up to each other fluff out their red breasts, and align themselves so that the red is always pointing towards their opponent.

• *Redstarts* spread their wings, and in particular their spectacular tail.

• *Whinchats* and *Stonechats* both spread their wings to show off their prominent white patches (see right).

• The *Wheatear* spreads its black-and-white tail, sometimes brushing it along the ground.

Habitats and feeding

The *Robin* is primarily an insect or invertebrate eater. When not hopping across the lawn in search of worms, it is most often seen using the "Watch and Pounce" technique. It sits on a low perch, such as a spade handle, watching the ground, then pounces when it detects the movement of prey.

The open-country *Stonechat* and *Whinchat* also use the "Watch and Pounce" method, the Stonechat mostly in gorsey heathland, the Whinchat in more grassy places. The Stonechat sits still on favourite perches, flying down intermittently. The Whinchat uses the ground more, and is less attached to its watching-posts. It takes a few seeds to supplement its diet.

The *Wheatear* forages mostly on the ground, running from place to place like a small thrush, but also dropping down from stones or rocks that give it a slightly elevated view (see right). Wheatears are found on mountains, pastures and by the sea. This is the only small British bird that breeds both at sea-level and on the highest mountain tops.

A far cry from the Wheatear, the *Nightingale* is a secretive feeder among the dense undergrowth of broad-leaved woodland and scrub, but it, too, forages mostly on the ground. It takes ants and beetles from the leaf-litter and bare soil.

Redstarts share the woodlands with Nightingales, but these are birds of the sunny tops rather than the shaded undergrowth. They pick food from trunks or leaves, and may even catch insects in flight (all chats sometimes do this, however). Occasionally they also forage on the ground, but do not shuffle through leaf-litter or probe for hidden prey.

The *Black Redstart* is a rare breeding bird in Britain, despite the abundance of its favoured habitat – industrial complexes, cities, ruins and docklands. It forages mostly on the ground, sometimes probing, but will also search around walls, masonry and even on machinery. Its diet, however, is conventional for a chat – invertebrates of various kinds.

Nest-sites

Most chats nest on or near the ground, but the Redstarts are an exception. *Common Redstarts* are usually found in holes in trees or buildings, and can be encouraged to use nest-boxes. *Black Redstarts* usually find a ledge high up in a building, although they will also use holes in walls or other man-made structures. *Stonechats* choose a site among thick vegetation, on or just above the ground. *Nightingales* and *Whinchats* follow this pattern, although the latter always nest on the ground itself. *Wheatears* often nest in rabbit burrows, although a hole in a wall or among rocks is more usual.

Wheatears looking
for food

Stonechat

*juvenile Robin
waiting to be fed*

adult male Robin

Whinchat

The *Robin* is famous for its unusual
nesting places, especially those in and
around the garden – old kettles are
often used where provided. More
unusual sites have included: coat
pockets, letter boxes, the skeletons of
animals (including cats and people),
items of machinery, filing cabinets,
old tins, old boots and even unmade
beds! A more usual site is in a hollow
or a bank on the woodland floor.

A Robin nesting in an old kettle

BLUETHROAT
Luscinia svecica

14cm. In many plumages this bird could be overlooked as a dark, skulking Robin. Although the blue throat is spectacular, the species' most consistent features are the whitish eyebrow and the rufous bases to the tail-sides.

Where found: Rare but regular passage migrant, mostly from late August–October, especially to the east coast. Found in coastal scrub and reedbeds, where it hides itself well.

Adult male summer (Northern and Russian race) (below left): Blue throat and breast are interrupted by a red-brown spot, and bordered by a black band. A red-brown band divides this from the pale belly.

adult male summer

WHINCHAT
Saxicola rubetra

12cm. Whinchat and Stonechat both sit on prominent perches, often for lengthy periods, allowing themselves to be studied. The Whinchat, a summer visitor, is the flatter-headed, longer-winged bird of the two, but both are compact, with short tails. The pale eyebrow and white tail-pattern are diagnostic of this species. Tends to favour uplands.

Where found: Summer visitor, April–September, to a range of grassy habitats. Migrants are widespread in grassy and scrubby areas in spring and autumn, as late as October.

Male: Streaky-brown above, marmalade-coloured below. White moustachial stripe, white eyebrow, white patch on wing, and white base to the tail-sides.

adult male

STONECHAT
Saxicola torquata

12cm. This is a close relative of the Whinchat, but has a rounder head and noticeably shorter wings. It perches in a more upright manner, sentry like, in contrast to the Whinchat's more horizontal posture; this accentuates the shortness of the tail. The Whinchat is a summer visitor only, the Stonechat is a resident. At all ages the tail is all black.

Where found: A common resident in many heathy areas, especially with gorse; obvious coastal bias. Most common to the west. Many move away from their breeding areas in winter.

Male summer: Blackish head contrasts with bright white half-collar, and a reddish-orange breast. The tail, unmarked in contrast to Whinchat's, is almost as dark as the head.

adult male

WHEATEAR
Oenanthe oenanthe

15cm. This bird has no association with wheat, but its name is derived from the white (= wheat) of its rump, a prominent field-mark. This is a handsome species, and knows it, often sitting proudly and upright on a rock or a wall. The tail is black-and-white, the black making the shape of an inverted "T". Wheatears from Greenland pass through on migration: they are larger than our Wheatears.

Where found: Summer visitor, March–September to treeless habitats such as mountains, moorland, coastal shingle and pasture, and is commonest in the north and west.

Male breeding: Smart grey back and crown, fine black mask, buffy breast, and black wings. White eyebrow between crown and mask. Breast becomes whiter over the summer.

adult male

adult female

juvenile

adult male non-breeding

Flight: This is flitting like a Robin's, but the bird lands with a characteristic sweep. Look out for the rufous on the tail.

Voice: Its calls include the usual chats' "hweet", together with a hard "tack". The song is unlikely to be heard in Britain or Ireland.

Adult male summer (Continental race) (see left): The red-brown spot is replaced by a smaller, white one.

Adult female: The upperparts resemble those of the male. The throat is buffy coloured, and bordered by dark, stubble-like

mottling that makes a rough necklace. Sometimes blue or reddish colouring appears among the stubble, or a reddish spot appears on the throat. **Adult male non-breeding:** The blue on the throat is diffused by pale edges to the feathers.

Juvenile: These look like juvenile Robins, but the tail, rufous at the base, gives them away. They moult in late summer into First Winter plumage, which resembles that of the female.

---

adult female

Juvenile: They are rather like spotty versions of the female, although the eyebrow is more difficult to see. They show the adults' tail-pattern.

juvenile

Female: Duller, with much less prominent head-markings: eyebrow is buffy, not white, there is no obvious moustachial streak because its buffy colour fades into the orange of the breast.

adult female

Flight: It moves jerkily from perch to perch, with low, whirring flight on its long wings.

Voice: When calling, it often combines a low whistle with a vowelless "tk" sound, to give "u-tik-tik." The song is tricky: it sings short, fast phrases which are prefaced by a brief introduction, but are highly varied, and include much mimicry.

Male winter (not illustrated): Altogether duller, with the blackish coloration sullied by pale edges to the feathers, and the breast less orange-red.

juvenile

Juvenile: Dark birds, especially above, where they are strongly streaked. Darker than young Whinchats, with more orange on the breast, and lack the latter's eyebrow and tail pattern.

adult female

Female: The female has a duller brown head than the male, and only has a hint of a white collar. She lacks the white rump, and has less white on the wings. In winter, the plumage is duller still.

adult female

Flight: It dashes from perch to perch in low flight, with whirring wings. Wings are shorter than Whinchat's.

Voice: The call is "tsak", said to be similar to two pebbles being tapped together. Often combined with a "swee" to make a rapid, distinctive "sweet-sack". The song is a series of squeaky phrases, which flow better than those of Whinchat.

Male non-breeding (not illustrated): After July, plumage becomes paler; back is grey-brown. All the wing feathers have buffy edges; black mask and white eyebrow are retained.

juvenile

Juvenile: A scaly, slightly spotted version of an adult female, with the tail-pattern typical of the species.

adult female

Female breeding: The female is darker on the back and crown, with a brownish-grey colour. The cheek mask is brown rather than black, and diffuse, while the eyebrow is buffy.

adult female

Flight: It has the statutory flitting flight of all the chats, and usually keeps low. The white rump is hard to miss.

Voice: The call is a hard "tak", sounding more like the sound of two pebbles being tapped together than the Stonechat's call; often combined into "tsi-tak-tak". The song has short, rapid phrases, always with a whistled "Heet", and often with crackling notes.

RING OUZEL
Turdus torquatus
24cm. This is the upland version of the Blackbird, seldom found below 250m in the breeding season. It has longer wings and a longer tail than a Blackbird, and adults have a white "ring" around the breast. Beware of some albino Blackbirds, which have white on the breast, but lack the Ring Ouzels pale wing-panels. A shy, wild species.

Where found: Uncommon summer visitor, April–September. It inhabits upland areas with moorland, rocky outcrops and small shrubs or trees, and can be very elusive.

Flight: Fast, swooping flight on long, pointed wings, necessary for dashing among rocks and crags. The pale wing-panels appear translucent.

Voice: The main call is a hard "tack", often elaborated into a chatter. The song consists of short phrases delivered slowly; often phrases are repeated two or more times. Song has the tuneful

BLACKBIRD
Turdus merula
25cm. One of our commonest and best known birds, celebrated for its marvellous song. Often seen on garden lawns looking for worms. It runs in short bursts, and also hops. It scratches around in leaf-litter, and forages among flower-beds.

Where found: An abundant resident in gardens, woodlands and areas of scrub. Often found in city centres. Many Continental birds visit us for the winter, arriving in October.

Flight: It has a hesitant, flicking flight, usually low between bushes. When landing, it raises its tail slowly. Birds burst away low, with loud alarm rattles.

Voice: A number of calls, including a soft "chook, chook", a louder, irritable "chink, chink" (often used at roost or when mobbing), and the alarm rattle. The song's complex phrases end with a squeak or chuckle.

REDWING
Turdus iliacus
21cm. The Redwing is our smallest thrush, and is in fact equal in size to Starling. It is smaller, darker, slimmer and shyer than the Song Thrush, and is almost exclusively a winter visitor to our shores. The prominent eyebrow is this species' giveaway field-mark, rather than the red colour under the wing.

Where found: A common winter visitor between September and April, frequenting fields and woods. A few pairs also breed in Scottish woodlands and plantations.

Adult: The head pattern shows a strong pale eyebrow and moustache, presenting a "well made-up" face. There are streaks rather than spots on the underparts, and the belly is snowy-white. These things, together with the darker upperparts, all help to distinguish Redwing from Song Thrush. Some of the red-brown coloration under the wing spills down on to the flanks.

Nests and nest-sites

Ring Ouzel
Nest:A cup of grass lined with finer blades of grass.
Nest-site: In vegetation, usually near the ground or under and overhanging bank or in heather.
Period: Eggs from mid-April–July. Bluish-green, speckled brown.

Blackbird
Nest: Grasses and roots, often with sticks and moss, solidified with mud. Lined with grass.
Nest-site: In trees or shrubs, average 1.9m above ground.
Period: Eggs often in mid-March. Pale green-blue, strongly speckled reddish-brown.

Redwing
Nest: twigs, grass and moss, lined with grass.
Nest-site: In trees or shrubs.
Period: Eggs laid May–July; greenish with reddish-brown markings.

Fieldfare
Nest: Made from grasses, twigs and mud, and lined with fine grass.
Nest-site: Mainly in trees, at the edge of woods and often near water; Fieldfares often nest in colonies.
Period: Eggs from late April–July; greenish-blue and speckled

Male summer: The sooty plumage is not as jet-black as male Blackbird's, and is broken by the white gorget, and pale edges to the wing-feathers. The bill is usually yellow with a black tip.

Female summer: The female is much browner than the male, and has a much more scaly pattern, especially on the breast (more scaled than winter male). The gorget may be hard to see.

First Winter: Both sexes can be almost unmarked where the gorget should be, but still have the typical scaly plumage and pale-edged wing-feathers. They usually have dark bills.

Juvenile: Distinctive: they are dark brown, and very heavily spotted, streaked and barred.

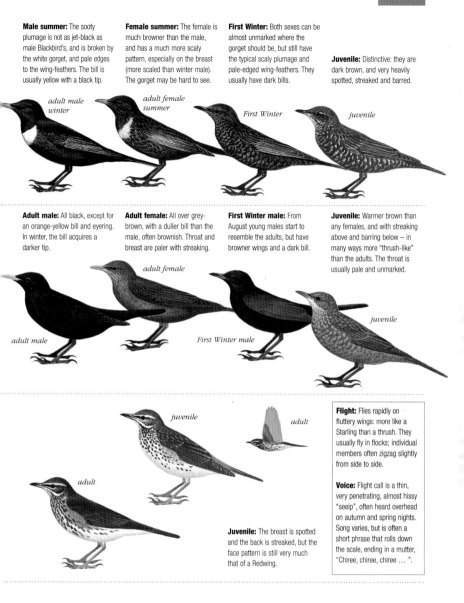

adult male winter

adult female summer

First Winter

juvenile

Adult male: All black, except for an orange-yellow bill and eyering. In winter, the bill acquires a darker tip.

Adult female: All over grey-brown, with a duller bill than the male, often brownish. Throat and breast are paler with streaking.

First Winter male: From August young males start to resemble the adults, but have browner wings and a dark bill.

Juvenile: Warmer brown than any females, and with streaking above and barring below – in many ways more "thrush-like" than the adults. The throat is usually pale and unmarked.

adult female

adult male

First Winter male

juvenile

juvenile

adult

adult

Juvenile: The breast is spotted and the back is streaked, but the face pattern is still very much that of a Redwing.

Flight: Flies rapidly on fluttery wings: more like a Starling than a thrush. They usually fly in flocks; individual members often zigzag slightly from side to side.

Voice: Flight call is a thin, very penetrating, almost hissy "seeip", often heard overhead on autumn and spring nights. Song varies, but is often a short phrase that rolls down the scale, ending in a mutter, "Chiree, chiree, chiree … ".

Song Thrush
Nest: Grasses, roots, sticks, solidified with mud. Lined with dung or rotten wood.
Nest-site: In shrubs or hedges, average 2.5m (8ft) above the ground.
Period: Eggs in late March. Bright pale blue with limited light brown speckling.

Mistle Thrush
Nest: Grasses, roots, moss, solidified with mud and often covered with lichens and other material on the outside. Lined with grass.
Nest-site: In fork of a tree, average 5m (16ft) above ground.

Period: Eggs in late February. Pale green-blue with red-brown spots, usually larger blotches than on Blackbird's egg.

Please note Blackbird, Song Thrush and Mistle Thrush are common and widespread; Ring Ouzel, Redwing and Fieldfare are uncommon to rare breeding birds in Britain.

Singing and feeding behaviour

Blackbird

Song and singing habits

*Our three common breeding thrushes
are all famous for their fine songs; it is
helpful to be able to distinguish them:*

Blackbird – phrases are long, mellow,
relaxed. They start tunefully, but most
tail off into squeak or chuckle. There
are good pauses between each
phrase. Sings best in early morning
and evening. Selects high perch such
as treetop or roof. Singing period:
February–July, rarely at other times.

Song Thrush – phrases are short,
penetrating, urgent. They are perfectly
enunciated, and most phrases are
repeated 2–5 times at a very regular
pace; this repetition is peculiar to the
Song Thrush, making the song easy to
learn. Usually sings in early morning
and evening. Sometimes sings from
within a tree, not clearly visible.
Singing period: November–July.

Mistle Thrush – phrases are shorter
than Blackbird's, longer than Song
Thrush's. They are near to Blackbird
pitch, but shorter, less relaxed; they
have a narrower range of pitch, and a
desolate ring. The Mistle Thrush often
sounds distant, even when quite close
at hand. It sings best in late morning
and during the afternoon, and
regularly during inclement weather
(rain, wind). Always selects high
(treetop) post. Singing period:
November–July.

Feeding

All our thrushes have a varied diet, including both animal and plant food. All our species hunt for worms and insects on the ground, and they all take fruit in the autumn and winter. At times, all six species may be seen feeding in one field, or on one berry-laden shrub.

There are differences, however. The Song Thrush is a specialised snail-hunter; alone among our thrushes, it has learnt the trick of hitting snail shells against a hard surface (an "anvil") to break them open. Unfortunately, the larger and less talented Blackbird is often on hand to steal the fruits of the thrush's labour.

Currently, the Song Thrush is in decline, and competition with the Blackbird has been put forward as one contributory factor. Other factors could include the use of molluscicides (that kill slugs and snails) and harsh winter weather, although no-one is certain exactly what is to blame.

When feeding on fields, Mistle Thrushes and Fieldfares prefer wide

Song Thrush feeding on a snail

open spaces, where they can see any danger approaching. Both these species adopt a very upright, droop-winged stance, keeping a careful look-out. Song Thrushes, Redwings and Blackbirds prefer to be in, or at least near cover, and so shun the centres of large, open fields. These three often feed in the litter of the woodland floor, which the larger species avoid.

Redwing and Fieldfares feeding on apples

FIELDFARE
Turdus pilaris

26cm. A big thrush that visits us for the winter. It is larger than Blackbird, but smaller than Mistle Thrush. In flight, the longish wings and tail show well. Flocks feed on fields, and harvest berries from hedgerows.

adult

Where found: A common winter visitor, September–April to farmland, hedgerows and woodland edges. Also breeds in very small numbers at a few scattered localities, mostly in Scotland.

Adult: When seen well, a fine sight, with its cold grey-blue head and rump, its chestnut mantle and wings, and its arrow-shaped marks on the breast and belly. The tail is black. At long distance,

SONG THRUSH
Turdus philomelos

23cm. This is usually the commonest of the spotted thrushes. It is smaller and more compact than the similar Mistle Thrush, and with darker brown plumage. A well-proportioned bird: the head is of the "right" size and the tail is of the "right" length.

adult

Where found: A very common resident of gardens, woodlands and bushy areas. Some Continental birds come to us in October to spend the winter, but in smaller numbers than Blackbirds.

Adult: The adult Song Thrush is brown above, with dark brown spots set against a buff-coloured breast. The spots often give the

MISTLE THRUSH
Turdus viscivorus

27cm. This is our largest thrush. It has a slightly disproportionate look: the head seems too small for the heavy, barrel-chested body, and the tail rather too long. It moves along the ground with heavy, powerful hops, and stands with a more upright, alert posture than Song Thrush.

adult

Where found: A common resident of open woodlands, parks, and wherever there are large trees and open ground.

Adult: It is much paler than the similar Song Thrush, more sandy-brown than earthy-brown. There are pale edgings to many of the wing feathers, forming panels.

Food and feeding techniques

Although all our thrushes eat similar types of food, their feeding techniques are often very different.

Ring Ouzel
Feeds on insects and their larvae and earthworms in spring and early summer. In autumn eats mainly berries and fruit.

Blackbird
Food comprises insects and earthworms, with fruit, berries, seeds and grains, from late summer to early winter. Forages on the ground, typically running or hopping in a straight line, and pauses before moving off again, perhaps in a different direction.

Fieldfare
The Fieldfare eats a varied diet consisting of fruits from late summer to early winter, and also worms, insects and their larva and spiders. Forages on the ground, turning over stones and pieces of earth, and scratching up snow, and will take insects in the air.

Song Thrush
Eats large quantities of fruit and berries from late summer to winter. Forages in ground litter sweeping bill from side-to-side. Pounces on earthworms and pulls them from the ground. Snails are held by the lip and beaten against a stone or other hard surface ("anvil") until the soft body of the snail

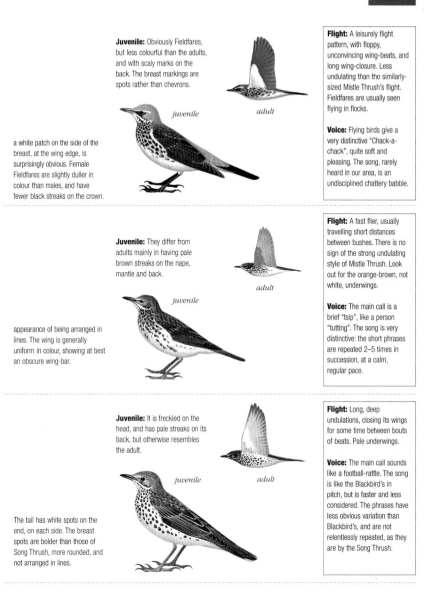

Juvenile: Obviously Fieldfares, but less colourful than the adults, and with scaly marks on the back. The breast markings are spots rather than chevrons.

juvenile

adult

Flight: A leisurely flight pattern, with floppy, unconvincing wing-beats, and long wing-closure. Less undulating than the similarly-sized Mistle Thrush's flight. Fieldfares are usually seen flying in flocks.

Voice: Flying birds give a very distinctive "Chack-a-chack", quite soft and pleasing. The song, rarely heard in our area, is an undisciplined chattery babble.

a white patch on the side of the breast, at the wing edge, is surprisingly obvious. Female Fieldfares are slightly duller in colour than males, and have fewer black streaks on the crown.

Juvenile: They differ from adults mainly in having pale brown streaks on the nape, mantle and back.

juvenile

adult

Flight: A fast flier, usually travelling short distances between bushes. There is no sign of the strong undulating style of Mistle Thrush. Look out for the orange-brown, not white, underwings.

Voice: The main call is a brief "tsip", like a person "tutting". The song is very distinctive: the short phrases are repeated 2–5 times in succession, at a calm, regular pace.

appearance of being arranged in lines. The wing is generally uniform in colour, showing at best an obscure wing-bar.

Juvenile: It is freckled on the head, and has pale streaks on its back, but otherwise resembles the adult.

juvenile

adult

Flight: Long, deep undulations, closing its wings for some time between bouts of beats. Pale underwings.

Voice: The main call sounds like a football-rattle. The song is like the Blackbird's in pitch, but is faster and less considered. The phrases have less obvious variation than Blackbird's, and are not relentlessly repeated, as they are by the Song Thrush.

The tail has white spots on the end, on each side. The breast spots are bolder than those of Song Thrush, more rounded, and not arranged in lines.

can be picked out of the shell (see pp.192–193). Most food is collected on the ground, but the Song Thrush will also take fruit and berries from trees and bushes.

Redwing

The diet of the Redwing consists of berries in autumn and winter, and insects and their larvae, worms, snails and slugs. It often feeds on the ground, running or hopping in short bursts and then stopping to look around, and also feeds in trees and bushes.

Mistle Thrush

Snails, worms, ants, insects and their larvae, also fruit and

berries, such as Yew and Holly in autumn and winter. Usually a ground feeder with an upright stance and strong, bounding hops, the Mistle Thrush will also take insects in flight. Often defends its "own" berry tree in winter.

CETTI'S WARBLER
Cettia cetti

14cm. The Cetti's (pronounced "Chetti's") Warbler is an elusive species which remains hidden in the waterside vegetation. It is stout-bodied, with strong legs, short wings and an oversized tail, with a rounded tip. The crown is also rounded.

Where found: The population is resident, unusually for a warbler (most are exclusively summer visitors). It occurs where scrub adjoins reedbeds, but is very local, occurring only in southern England and Wales.

GRASSHOPPER WARBLER
Locustella naevia

13cm. The Locustella warblers have long, broad, rounded tails, a feature shared with Cetti's, as is their habit of holding their tails up when alighting, feeding etc. The Grasshopper Warbler is a retiring, skulking species, hard to observe unless singing.

Where found: A summer visitor from April–October, inhabiting a variety of wet or dry habitats: marshes, moorland, tussocky places, scrub. Each habitat needs thick ground cover, small bushes or stems for song-posts, and plenty of insects. Recently, the Grasshopper Warbler has declined steeply.

SAVI'S WARBLER
Locustella luscinioides

14cm. This species shares the Grasshopper Warbler's shape and habits, although it is less secretive. In plumage it most resembles a Reed Warbler. Look out for the long, rounded, frequently-cocked tail, the rounder crown and the shorter bill.

Where found: A rare summer visitor, April–August, to a few large reedbeds in southern England and Ireland.

REED WARBLER
Acrocephalus scirpaceus

12cm. *Acrocephalus* warblers have long bills at the end of a sloping forehead. Usually the crown is peaked, giving a characteristic "sharp" profile. Their tails are less heavy-looking than those of *Locustella* warblers, sometimes appearing pointed.

Where found: Very much a reedbed warbler, and confined to low-lying country. A summer visitor from mid-April–September (late migrants in October).

MARSH WARBLER
Acrocephalus palustris

12cm. This species is rare in Britain, found in only a few places which are drier than the Reed Warbler's habitat. As it is almost identical to Reed Warbler, perhaps this is just as well! It is slightly plumper than the Reed Warbler, with a flatter crown.

Where found: A very rare summer visitor, arriving as late as June, to just a few sites in southern England. It needs tall vegetation with adjacent bushes.

SEDGE WARBLER
Acrocephalus schoenobaenus

13cm. The Sedge Warbler is usually easy to identify because of its stripy upperparts. It is a slighter bird than the Reed Warbler, with a flatter head and a broader tail.

Where found: Arriving in mid-April and departing by October, the Sedge Warbler is much more widespread than its close relative, the Reed Warbler. This is partly because it occurs in a variety of habitats with tangled vegetation, usually near water.

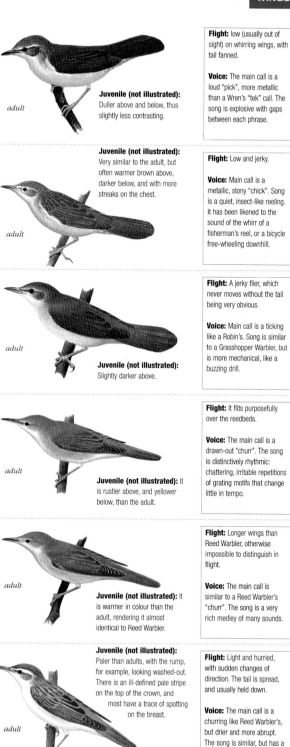

Adult: It is basically chestnut-brown above. The greyish tone on breast and neck-sides is distinctive. There is a narrow, but noticeable pale eyebrow. This species might be confused with a Nightingale, but is much smaller, has obviously mottled under tail coverts, and lacks the Nightingale's richly rufous tail.

adult

Juvenile (not illustrated): Duller above and below, thus slightly less contrasting.

Flight: low (usually out of sight) on whirring wings, with tail fanned.

Voice: The main call is a loud "pick", more metallic than a Wren's "tek" call. The song is explosive with gaps between each phrase.

Adult: Upperparts vary in colour, but are generally olive-brown, with unobtrusive dark-brown streaking; this streaking is also found on the rump. The underparts are paler, often yellowish-brown, with limited thin streaking on the breast and undertail coverts. There is only a faint supercilium.

adult

Juvenile (not illustrated): Very similar to the adult, but often warmer brown above, darker below, and with more streaks on the chest.

Flight: Low and jerky.

Voice: Main call is a metallic, stony "chick". Song is a quiet, insect-like reeling. It has been likened to the sound of the whirr of a fisherman's reel, or a bicycle free-wheeling downhill.

Adult: It completely lacks any streaks, being rather plain reddish-brown above and pale brown below. The paler underparts can appear blotchy. The long undertail coverts are mottled, unlike Reed Warbler's but less obviously than Grasshopper Warbler's. The legs are paler than those of Reed Warbler.

adult

Juvenile (not illustrated): Slightly darker above.

Flight: A jerky flier, which never moves without the tail being very obvious.

Voice: Main call is a ticking like a Robin's. Song is similar to a Grasshopper Warbler, but is more mechanical, like a buzzing drill.

Adult: Upperparts are warm brown, with a tinge of chestnut on the rump and base of tail. The underparts are mainly buffy-brown, but throat, upper breast and undertail coverts are white. Legs are a dark greyish-pink. Savi's Warbler is larger, has a different shape, has mottled undertail coverts, and lacks any contrasting colour on the rump.

adult

Juvenile (not illustrated): It is rustier above, and yellower below, than the adult.

Flight: It flits purposefully over the reedbeds.

Voice: The main call is a drawn-out "churr". The song is distinctively rhythmic: chattering, irritable repetitions of grating motifs that change little in tempo.

Adult: Colder, greyer-brown above than Reed Warbler (the rump shows no trace of chestnut), slightly paler below, especially on the flanks.Also has paler, almost yellowish legs. In Marsh Warbler, the fringes of the primaries are noticeably pale, contrasting with the dark brown of the rest of the wing-tip. This is not the case for Reed Warbler.

adult

Juvenile (not illustrated): It is warmer in colour than the adult, rendering it almost identical to Reed Warbler.

Flight: Longer wings than Reed Warbler, otherwise impossible to distinguish in flight.

Voice: The main call is similar to a Reed Warbler's "churr". The song is a very rich medley of many sounds.

Adult: It is brown like all the "Reedy" warblers, but has several prominent features: a very obvious creamy eyebrow, a black eyestripe, dark streaks on the crown and back, and a contrastingly chestnut rump. When the plumage is worn, in late summer, the back loses some or all of its streaking.

adult

Juvenile (not illustrated): Paler than adults, with the rump, for example, looking washed-out. There is an ill-defined pale stripe on the top of the crown, and most have a trace of spotting on the breast.

Flight: Light and hurried, with sudden changes of direction. The tail is spread, and usually held down.

Voice: The main call is a churring like Reed Warbler's, but drier and more abrupt. The song is similar, but has a less well defined rhythm.

How to identify warblers

The warbler family represents a challenge to birdwatchers, mostly because of the wealth of species (16 breed and nearly 30 others have been recorded). There are three stages to warbler identification.

1. Identifying the bird as a warbler.

2. Identifying which group of warblers the bird belongs to.

3. Identifying the particular species you are looking at.

Is it a warbler?
Warblers are small, usually no larger than a tit, they exhibit fidgety behaviour and generally have a weak, flitting flight. Feeding mainly on insects collected with their thin bills, they forage by picking from vegetation, either while perched or in flight, sometimes hovering. While foraging, most warblers are secretive, remaining deep in the vegetation, affording the birdwatcher only the occasional glimpse. Plumage is plain and drab: none of our species has more than a few streaks or a brightly-coloured breast. As a rule, males, females and juveniles all have very similar or identical plumage.

Almost all our species are summer visitors only, migrating here from tropical Africa. As soon as they arrive they sing, often incessantly. The song is often a very useful clue in identifying the main group to which the species belongs.

Which group does it belong to?

Grasshopper Warblers:
Genus *Locustella*
Colour is mostly brown. Very "tail-heavy", with long rounded tails and very long undertail coverts. Primaries are slightly curved. Long bill, rounded crown. Move jerkily, cock their tails. Walk along ground (all other warblers hop). Found in marshes or tangled vegetation. Songs are reeling and insect-like, continuous.

Reed Warblers:
Genus *Acrocephalus*
Colour is mostly brown. Fairly long, rounded tails; shorter undertail coverts than *Locustella*. Straight primaries. Long bill, sloping forehead, often peaked crown. Do not cock tails. Hops on ground. Has large feet for clambering on vertical stems. Found in marshes or tangled vegetation. Songs are chattery and continuous. (*Cettia* has rounded crown, huge tail, short wings, cocks its tail and has simple song.)

Hippolais or "Tree Warblers":
Genus *Hippolais*
Also called "Hippos", they are quite large warblers. Yellow or greyish, without any streaks or other markings. Fairly long, square tails. Long bills, orange at base. Foreheads often sloping. Usually eyestripe begins behind eye (if any), so "lores" plain. Mainly in trees and bushes (nest usually well above ground). Fast, complex songs, fairly continuous. Sung in upright posture. Note: birds belonging to this genus are rare.

Sylvia or "Scrub Warblers":
Genus *Sylvia*
The most colourful warblers, showing black and reddish and white. Males often brighter than females. Short to very long tails. Short, thickish bill, usually rounded head (sometimes peaked crown). Short scrub to woodland edge. Songs in phrases, with pauses in between; usually dry and scratchy.

Grasshopper Warbler,
Locustella naevia

Chiffchaff,
Phylloscopus
collybita

Whitethroat,
Sylvia communis

Marsh Warbler,
Acrocephalus palustris

Icterine Warbler,
Hippolais icterina

Leaf Warblers:
Genus *Phylloscopus*
Also called "Phylloscs", these birds are small to tiny. The most active warblers. Olive-green to yellowish plumage, unstreaked. Medium-length tails. Flitting flight. Short, thin bills. Head markings, especially supercilia, a feature: usually have a stripe through or above the eye. Rounded crowns. Favoured habitats include woodland, particularly with mature broad-leaved trees, bushy habitats or scrub. Songs are delivered in phrases, with pauses; they are sweet and highly distinctive.

DARTFORD WARBLER
Sylvia undata
12cm. This is probably the easiest warbler to identify, since its shape and colour are unique. The wings are extremely short, the tail extremely long, and the body extremely dark.

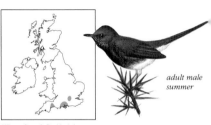

adult male summer

Where found: Resident; lowland with heather and gorse.

LESSER WHITETHROAT
Sylvia curruca
13cm. The two Whitethroats are grey, brown and whitish warblers that live up to their name by having prominent white throats. The Lesser Whitethroat is the smaller, darker, more compact bird of the two, with a much shorter tail. It has black, not reddish legs.

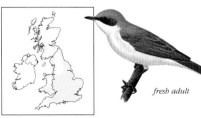

fresh adult

Where found: A summer visitor, late April–September.

WHITETHROAT
Sylvia communis
14cm. This Whitethroat is longer-tailed than its relative, and has a more peaked crown. Its legs are reddish coloured. A demonstrative species, often performing a dancing song-flight.

adult male summer

Male: Wing colour is the best way to distinguish this species from Lesser Whitethroat: most feathers are broadly fringed with

Where found: Common summer visitor to scrubby areas.

GARDEN WARBLER
Sylvia borin
14cm. This bird is famous for having absolutely no distinguishing features. Note, however, that it is thickset, with a rounded head and a short, thick bill. The wings are quite long, but the tail is rather short. The dark eye on the unmarked face gives it a gentle expression.

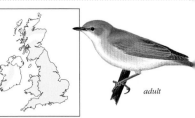

adult

Where found: Summer visitor to woodland and dense scrub.

BLACKCAP
Sylvia atricapilla
14cm. For a warbler, this is a pushover to identify, because all plumages have a distinctively coloured cap. It is a slimmer bird than Garden Warbler, but is otherwise similar in shape and size.

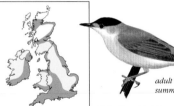

adult male summer

Male: It is mainly drab grey-brown, paler below, and with an unmistakable black skull-cap.

Where found: Mainly a summer visitor to broad-leaved woodland.

Male: It is all slate-grey above, but with a fiery red eyering. The throat and breast are pink-brown, broken by a sharply defined white belly and vent. There are usually a few white flecks within the red of the throat. Note that the legs are yellow.

adult female summer

juvenile

Female: It is less grey above, and slightly paler, almost plum-coloured below. The white of the belly is less sharply demarcated.

Juvenile: Young birds have a shorter tail, and their plumage is duller than that of either parent, especially below.

Flight: Low on whirring wings; undulating flight. The shape should render it unmistakable.

Voice: The main call is a strange, harsh grating which falls slightly in pitch. The song is scratchy and metallic, with short, breathlessly fast phrases. It gives the impression of jabbered verse.

Adult (fresh plumage): The crown and nape are grey, with the colour intensifying around the lores and ear coverts to give a black mask (although this is not always obvious). The rest of the upperparts are a uniform greyish-brown, contrasting with clean, cream-washed underparts.

worn adult

Adult (worn plumage): If a dark mask has been present, it becomes much less well-defined, and the underparts become whiter.

Juvenile (not illustrated): The crown is darker, a more brownish-grey, and the underparts are duskier.

Flight: It has direct, uncluttered flight, appropriately for a compact bird. Most movements are low and quick.

Voice: The call is a "tuc" sound, like two pound-coins being knocked together. The song begins with a quiet mumble, but develops into a loud, quite tuneful rattle.

---

a rich, warm chestnut-brown. Head is more extensively ash-grey, there is a white eyering, and the underparts are usually duller. Many, but not all, male Whitethroats, have a rose-pink wash to the breast.

adult female summer

Female: The head tends to be browner than on most males.

juvenile

Juvenile: Warmer brown above, with no grey on the head, and often with a brighter brown wing-patch than the adult. It is duller below, never pink. The tail-sides are pale brown, those of the adults are white.

Flight: Jerky and erratic, usually with obvious undulation.

Voice: The main call is a harsh, grating sound with a slight downwards inflection. The main song is a very short, scratchy warble with most impetus at the beginning. It is often delivered in a song-flight.

Adult: It is soft-brown above, slightly paler below, and a good view will show up a greyish wash to the neck. The legs are dark.

juvenile

Juvenile: There are traces of rusty coloration.

Flight: It flies more determinedly than a Whitethroat, and quite fast. It is heavy-looking for a warbler.

Voice: The call is a harsh, grating sound: "tshurr". The song is a high-spirited, sustained bubbling, which has some of the shrillness of a Skylark, but is uttered from deep in the vegetation.

Female: The cap is red-brown, not black, and much of the plumage is browner, especially on the underparts.

juvenile

adult female summer

Juvenile: All-over brown; no grey. The cap of the juvenile male is darker brown than that of the female (juvenile female's is paler however). This is retained into the first winter.

Flight: It has a similar flight to Garden Warbler, but is perhaps less heavy-looking.

Voice: The call is a hard "tack", much sharper and less grating than Garden Warbler's. Song is similar to that species in many ways. However, the mumbly notes break out suddenly into a sweet, loud, whistling refrain.

How to identify warblers (continued)

Which warbler am I looking at?

Cetti's Warbler – difficult to see, easy to hear. Our only warbler that can be heard regularly singing all year round (most warblers are summer migrants anyway). Characteristic delivery: sings loud phrase from concealed position, then moves some distance to next song-post and sings there. Therefore, long pauses between phrases. The nest is in thick vegetation on the edge of a marsh. Our only warbler in which most males are polygynous (have two or more mates).

Grasshopper Warbler – widespread summer migrant. Nests in marshy or dry places, placing its nest on the ground, usually in a tussock. Sings from low perch, often concealed, and often at night.

Savi's Warbler – summer migrant. Very rare. Nests in marshes, building its nest at some height over wet ground. Sings from less concealed perches than Grasshopper Warbler and sings less at night.

Reed Warbler – summer migrant to lowlands of England and Wales. Breeds mostly in reedbeds. Usually builds a nest above the water, entwined between four or five reed stems. Sings from the tops of reeds, but is often difficult to see.

Marsh Warbler – very rare summer migrant. Not usually a marsh dweller, favours tall vegetation such as osiers, nettles, meadowsweet and cow-parsley. Nests in thick, often woody vegetation. Often sings from the tops of bushes or shrubs.

Sedge Warbler – widespread summer migrant, usually found in waterside scrub. Nests in similar sites to Marsh Warbler. When singing prefers exposed perches on bushes, but also has a special song-flight, rising a couple of metres above the reeds and spiralling down.

Dartford Warbler – our only species confined to heathland, where it is a resident. While most *Sylvia* warblers take berries in the autumn, this tiny bird relies almost exclusively on invertebrates year-round. It hunts mostly on gorse bushes within its habitat, because heather yields less food. The nest, however, is usually built in heather. The scratchy song is sometimes delivered in a dancing song-flight.

Whitethroat – widespread summer migrant, favours open land. Showy singer, often from exposed perches. Also performs a song-flight in which it rises with heavy wing-beats, then "dances" jerkily up and down.

Lesser Whitethroat – summer migrant found mostly in England. Prefers tall scrubby vegetation. Remains hidden when singing. Sings for a while in one place, then moves some distance to sing again (in a similar way to Cetti's Warbler).

Blackcap – summer migrant although some do winter, probably German or Scandinavian birds. Inhabits woodland or tall scrubby areas. High, prominent song-posts. Song similar to Garden Warbler, and they are known to mimic each other which often causes confusion. Nests low down in bushes, especially brambles and nettles.

Garden Warbler – summer migrant. Similar habitat to Blackcap but is associated with less tall vegetation.

Reed Warbler

Sedge Warbler

Savi's Warbler

Dartford Warbler

Cetti's Warbler

Song and nest-sites similar to Blackcap (see above).

Wood Warbler – summer visitor, mainly found in the west and north, but not Ireland. Found in mature deciduous forest with minimum understorey. Prefers sessile oakwoods and beechwoods, but also likes chestnuts and mixed woods with a few conifers. Although it feeds high in the canopy, it builds its nest on the ground, often against a fallen tree. When singing the Wood Warbler will either swivel its body, or perform a special song-flight, progressing horizontally through the branches with fast, shallow wing-beats.

Chiffchaff – summer visitor but is also seen in winter, although these are probably not British breeding birds. More common in south. Mainly a woodland bird that forages in the treetops, but it prefers to have some understorey, where it can hide its nest in tall vegetation, usually just above the ground. Fidgety singer, that wags its tail strongly in time with the "Chiffs" and "Chaffs".

Willow Warbler – our commonest summer visitor of any species, with nearly two million pairs. A familiar bird in most parts of the British Isles, but more common in north. Prefers very open woodland, woodland edge and scrub, especially birch. It builds its nest on the ground, among thick vegetation. Stays relatively still when singing, although it will turn its body and wag its tail somewhat.

BARRED WARBLER
Sylvia nisoria

15cm. This is the largest, most heavily-built of our regular warblers. It moves sluggishly. It is big-headed, relatively long-tailed and has sturdy legs and feet. The forehead is steeper than that of the similar Garden Warbler. Most Barred Warblers visiting Britain are first winters.

adult summer

Where found: Rare migrant to east coast, August–September.

Adult breeding: Grey-brown above, whitish below; barring on the underparts can be difficult to see. Note the staring yellow eye,

ICTERINE WARBLER
Hippolais icterina

13cm. The Icterine Warbler belongs to the *Hippolais* group of warblers, of which there are several species in Europe. They have the head shape of a Reed Warbler: long, spiky bill, sloping forehead. Bills are mostly orange. More tree-loving than the "Reedy" warblers, they have distinct songs.

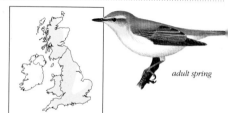

adult spring

Where found: As above, but more frequent in spring.

WOOD WARBLER
Phylloscopus sibilatrix

12cm. The Leaf warblers *Phylloscopus* are small, very active green or yellowish birds, with rounded heads, thin bills, usually with a stripe through or above the eye. The Wood Warbler is the largest, smartest and yellowest, with long wings and a relatively short tail, giving a tapered profile.

adult spring

Where found: April–August in mature woodlands.

CHIFFCHAFF
Phylloscopus collybita

11cm. This and the next species are very difficult to tell apart unless they sing. The Chiffchaff is slightly more compact, with a more rounded crown and shorter wings. The tail is relatively long and is constantly wagged. Look also for quite a prominent white eyering.

adult spring

Adult spring: Messier and dingier than the Willow Warbler in all plumages. In spring, the Chiffchaff is olive-green above and greenish-yellow below.

Where found: Mature, broad-leaved woodland; a few winter.

WILLOW WARBLER
Phylloscopus trochilus

11cm. A long-distance migrant, the Willow Warbler has longer wings than Chiffchaff; it is also flatter-crowned and slimmer, giving it an overall "longer" profile. The tail is wagged much less. The Willow Warbler has a strong face pattern, with a well-defined eyebrow, but the eyering is less obvious.

adult spring

Adult spring: Pale olive-green upperparts and clean yellowish and whitish underparts. The contrast is quite strong (less so in Chiffchaff).

Where found: Arrives in April from sub-Saharan Africa.

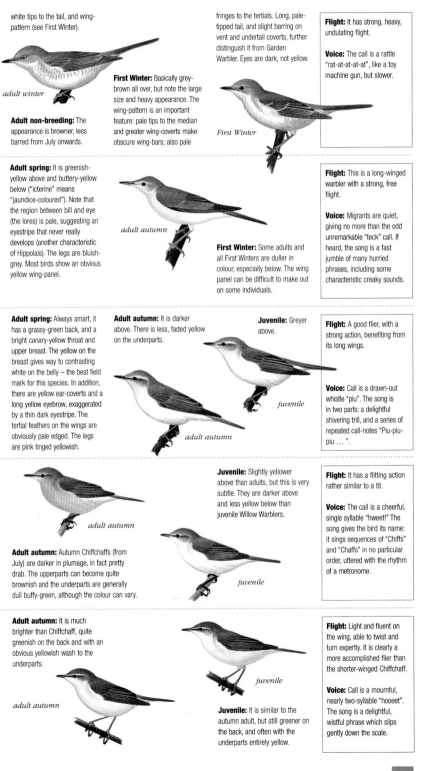

white tips to the tail, and wing-pattern (see First Winter).

adult winter

Adult non-breeding: The appearance is browner, less barred from July onwards.

First Winter: Basically grey-brown all over, but note the large size and heavy appearance. The wing-pattern is an important feature: pale tips to the median and greater wing-coverts make obscure wing-bars; also pale

fringes to the tertials. Long, pale-tipped tail, and slight barring on vent and undertail coverts, further distinguish it from Garden Warbler. Eyes are dark, not yellow.

First Winter

Flight: It has strong, heavy, undulating flight.

Voice: The call is a rattle "rat-at-at-at-at", like a toy machine gun, but slower.

Adult spring: It is greenish-yellow above and buttery-yellow below ("icterine" means "jaundice-coloured"). Note that the region between bill and eye (the lores) is pale, suggesting an eyestripe that never really develops (another characteristic of Hippolais). The legs are bluish-grey. Most birds show an obvious yellow wing-panel.

adult autumn

First Winter: Some adults and all First Winters are duller in colour, especially below. The wing panel can be difficult to make out on some individuals.

Flight: This is a long-winged warbler with a strong, free flight.

Voice: Migrants are quiet, giving no more than the odd unremarkable "teck" call. If heard, the song is a fast jumble of many hurried phrases, including some characteristic creaky sounds.

Adult spring: Always smart, it has a grassy-green back, and a bright canary-yellow throat and upper breast. The yellow on the breast gives way to contrasting white on the belly – the best field mark for this species. In addition, there are yellow ear-coverts and a long yellow eyebrow, exaggerated by a thin dark eyestripe. The tertial feathers on the wings are obviously pale edged. The legs are pink tinged yellowish.

Adult autumn: It is darker above. There is less, faded yellow on the underparts.

Juvenile: Greyer above.

juvenile

adult autumn

Flight: A good flier, with a strong action, benefiting from its long wings.

Voice: Call is a drawn-out whistle "piu". The song is in two parts: a delightful shivering trill, and a series of repeated call-notes "Piu-piu-piu … ".

---

adult autumn

Adult autumn: Autumn Chiffchaffs (from July) are darker in plumage, in fact pretty drab. The upperparts can become quite brownish and the underparts are generally dull buffy-green, although the colour can vary.

Juvenile: Slightly yellower above than adults, but this is very subtle. They are darker above and less yellow below than juvenile Willow Warblers.

juvenile

Flight: It has a flitting action rather similar to a tit.

Voice: The call is a cheerful, single syllable "hweet!" The song gives the bird its name: it sings sequences of "Chiffs" and "Chaffs" in no particular order, uttered with the rhythm of a metronome.

Adult autumn: It is much brighter than Chiffchaff, quite greenish on the back and with an obvious yellowish wash to the underparts.

adult autumn

juvenile

Juvenile: It is similar to the autumn adult, but still greener on the back, and often with the underparts entirely yellow.

Flight: Light and fluent on the wing, able to twist and turn expertly. It is clearly a more accomplished flier than the shorter-winged Chiffchaff.

Voice: Call is a mournful, nearly two-syllable "hooeet". The song is a delightful, wistful phrase which slips gently down the scale.

GOLDCREST
Regulus regulus

9cm. Goldcrest and Firecrest are referred to collectively as Kinglets, because of the golden "crowns" on their heads (often hard to see). These two are the smallest British birds, looking simply tiny, with minute thin bills, short wings and short tails. They are tame, inquisitive, and never stop moving. The Goldcrest is by far the commoner of the two.

adult male

Where found: Coniferous woods and scrub all year-round. More varied habitats in winter: deciduous woods, gardens and scrub. Many Continental birds winter, arriving in October.

Male: The black-edged crown is mostly yellow, but shows some orange colour, especially towards the rear. Both sexes are dull green above and washed-out green below. The eye is set in an otherwise unmarked face, giving

FIRECREST
Regulus ignicapillus

9cm. The rare Firecrest is slightly heavier and more bulky than the Goldcrest, and has a tendency to be less exhaustingly fidgety. Otherwise the species are much alike in character.

adult male

Where found: It breeds in a few southern woodlands, especially spruce, but mostly an uncommon passage migrant. A few over-winter, mostly on the coast of south-west England.

Male: The male has a quite strongly orange crown, the colour being much more noticeable than on any Goldcrest. The Firecrest is a class above the Goldcrest in smartness and colour: the upperparts are greener, with a striking bronzy patch on the

SPOTTED FLYCATCHER
Muscicapa striata

14cm. Flycatchers sit upright and motionless on bare perches, then make rapid flycatching aerial sallies, twisting and turning until they make a capture. Spotted Flycatchers tend to return to the perch they originally left, or one nearby. Both our species of flycatchers have flattened bills with a large gape, long wings, large heads and small black legs.

adult

Where found: A summer visitor from late April–October, inhabiting a variety of insect-rich wooded habitats, including gardens.

PIED FLYCATCHER
Ficedula hypoleuca

13cm. This is a smaller, more compact, neater bird than the Spotted Flycatcher. It is plumper, shorter tailed, rounder-crowned and has a smaller, thicker bill. When flycatching, it changes perch between sallies. It has more of a tendency to flick its wings and tail than the Spotted Flycatcher.

adult male

Where found: A summer visitor, mid-April–October. Breeds mostly in sessile oakwoods, but also in other types of mature woodland in hill country.

Male: Smart, with black-and-white (pied) plumage. Basically bold black above and white below. Small white blob on the forehead, large white wing-patch. Tail is white-edged (same in all

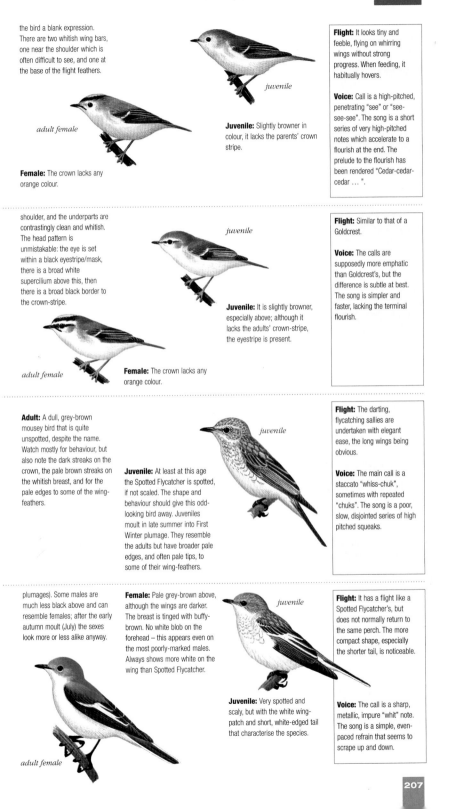

the bird a blank expression. There are two whitish wing bars, one near the shoulder which is often difficult to see, and one at the base of the flight feathers.

adult female

juvenile

Juvenile: Slightly browner in colour, it lacks the parents' crown stripe.

Female: The crown lacks any orange colour.

Flight: It looks tiny and feeble, flying on whirring wings without strong progress. When feeding, it habitually hovers.

Voice: Call is a high-pitched, penetrating "see" or "see-see-see". The song is a short series of very high-pitched notes which accelerate to a flourish at the end. The prelude to the flourish has been rendered "Cedar-cedar-cedar … ".

---

shoulder, and the underparts are contrastingly clean and whitish. The head pattern is unmistakable: the eye is set within a black eyestripe/mask, there is a broad white supercilium above this, then there is a broad black border to the crown-stripe.

juvenile

adult female

Juvenile: It is slightly browner, especially above; although it lacks the adults' crown-stripe, the eyestripe is present.

Female: The crown lacks any orange colour.

Flight: Similar to that of a Goldcrest.

Voice: The calls are supposedly more emphatic than Goldcrest's, but the difference is subtle at best. The song is simpler and faster, lacking the terminal flourish.

Adult: A dull, grey-brown mousey bird that is quite unspotted, despite the name. Watch mostly for behaviour, but also note the dark streaks on the crown, the pale brown streaks on the whitish breast, and for the pale edges to some of the wing-feathers.

Juvenile: At least at this age the Spotted Flycatcher is spotted, if not scaled. The shape and behaviour should give this odd-looking bird away. Juveniles moult in late summer into First Winter plumage. They resemble the adults but have broader pale edges, and often pale tips, to some of their wing-feathers.

juvenile

Flight: The darting, flycatching sallies are undertaken with elegant ease, the long wings being obvious.

Voice: The main call is a staccato "whiss-chuk", sometimes with repeated "chuks". The song is a poor, slow, disjointed series of high pitched squeaks.

---

plumages). Some males are much less black above and can resemble females; after the early autumn moult (July) the sexes look more or less alike anyway.

Female: Pale grey-brown above, although the wings are darker. The breast is tinged with buffy-brown. No white blob on the forehead – this appears even on the most poorly-marked males. Always shows more white on the wing than Spotted Flycatcher.

juvenile

adult female

Juvenile: Very spotted and scaly, but with the white wing-patch and short, white-edged tail that characterise the species.

Flight: It has a flight like a Spotted Flycatcher's, but does not normally return to the same perch. The more compact shape, especially the shorter tail, is noticeable.

Voice: The call is a sharp, metallic, impure "whit" note. The song is a simple, even-paced refrain that seems to scrape up and down.

Habitat, feeding and breeding behaviour

Kinglets

The Goldcrest and Firecrest are the smallest birds in the British Isles, even tinier than the Wren. Technically they belong to the warbler family, but are treated separately here. Their behaviour is quite tit-like, with perky movements and weak flight, and they will often join roving tit flocks outside the breeding season. In winter, because of their small size, they must spend over 90% of the day feeding in order to survive.

Habitat

The Firecrest is the slightly bulkier bird, but, strangely, the Goldcrest seems to be better able to survive our climate: while the Goldcrest is a common resident, even in Scotland, the Firecrest is mainly a rare breeding bird and passage migrant, mostly in southern England. Both inhabit conifer woods, although both will stray outside, especially when not breeding.

Feeding

The two species differ in their feeding behaviour. Goldcrests are more single-minded about hunting in conifer trees, Firecrests are less fussy. Goldcrests take smaller-sized prey than Firecrests, although both go for the same general menu of insects and spiders. Goldcrests opt mostly for foraging up and down twigs, whereas Firecrests are more likely to fly from perch to perch, and pick food from a standing position. Firecrests also hover slightly more often.

Display

The head pattern distinguishes the two species for the birdwatcher and is also of significance to the birds themselves. Most Goldcrest displays, both territorial and sexual, involve bowing the head to show off the crown. Most corresponding Firecrest displays involve looking straight at the rival or partner, to show off the stripy head.

Here the Goldcrest and Firecrest are shown in proportion to the Robin to demonstrate just how small they really are.

Goldcrest

Robin

Firecrest

Flycatchers

Both our flycatchers are birds of high summer. The Pied Flycatcher arrives in late April, and mainly inhabits the woods of Sessile Oak to be found in the north and west of Britain. The Spotted Flycatcher arrives late in May, and spreads over the whole of Britain and Ireland, inhabiting a variety of wooded habitats.

Feeding

When catching food flycatchers wait for a short moment, sitting still on a perch, before making a dart into the air, twisting and turning until the snapping sound of the bill confirms a capture. The two species have slightly different food requirements. The Spotted Flycatcher is a specialist in catching flying insects. Flies, bees, wasps and butterflies often find a place on the menu. Such large items become available in profusion only towards summertime, which is why this species is such a late migrant. It uses standard flycatching as its main method, feeds in quite open areas, and usually returns to the same, favoured perch after a sally. Berries are occasionally taken during the breeding season. The Pied Flycatcher relies much less on standard flycatching, and takes a higher proportion of static (ie. non-flying) prey. It changes perch much more regularly in between sallies, and commonly forages among the foliage of trees and on the ground. Small quantities of fruit and seeds are taken when feeding conditions are poor.

Breeding

The two species also show marked differences in their breeding behaviour. The Spotted Flycatcher is usually monogamous, is double-brooded, and selects a flat but

Spotted Flycatcher nesting in an old kettle

sheltered surface for nesting – eg. in an open-fronted nest-box, old nest of other bird, or in a creeper. The nest itself is loosely-built from twigs, grass, moss and lichens and is lined with softer material, eg. feathers and hair. The Pied Flycatcher is frequently polygamous (polygynous – one male can have more than one mate), the female brings up only one brood, and the nest-site is in a hole – a tree-hole or an enclosed nest-box. Once again the nest is a loose construction of roots, bark and grass, and is lined with finer material.

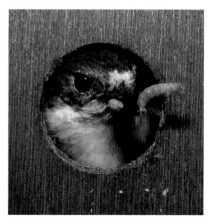

Pied Flycatcher in a nest-box

BEARDED TIT
Panurus biarmicus

16cm. A unique bird of the reedbeds, with its tiny body, whirring wings and long, graduated tail. Characteristic and unmistakable.

Where found: A scarce resident of extensive reedbeds.

Male: It is mostly a rusty, chestnut-brown in colour, but has a grey head, bold black moustache (not beard), and black undertail coverts. The bill is orange.

LONG-TAILED TIT
Aegithalos caudatus

14cm. Flocks of this tiny-bodied, long-tailed bird are a common sight in our woodlands. No other tree-haunting species has a shape like it. Unmistakable.

Where found: A common resident in woodland, woodland edge and scrub throughout Britain. It regularly enters gardens. The Northern race is a very rare winter visitor.

Adult: It is an unusual mixture of black, white and pink. The underparts are mostly white, the upperparts mostly black. Pink is found on the back (the scapulars), and more subtly on the rump and flanks. On the head, a black stripe begins just in

adult

BLUE TIT
Parus caeruleus

11cm. A tiny, stubby-billed mite, overflowing with effervescence. It is noisy and colourful, and exceedingly common.

Where found: An abundant resident in most wooded habitats throughout Britain and Ireland. A familiar user of bird tables in gardens.

adult

GREAT TIT
Parus major

14cm. This is much the largest true tit, and one of the most boldly patterned. It is also the longest-tailed. Aggressive, it uses its bulk to dominate the other species in competition for food and nest-sites. Otherwise, it is just as perky and active as the other tits.

Where found: An abundant resident in wooded areas and gardens, with more inclination towards conifers than Blue Tit.

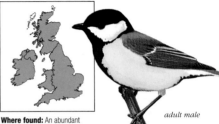

adult male

adult female summer

juvenile male

adult male summer

Flight: It flies with whirring wing-beats low over reedbeds. Its progress seems to be impeded by the twisting tail.

Female: Similar in colour to the male, but it has a plain, pinkish-brown head and lacks the black undertail. The bill is browner.

Juvenile: Both sexes differ from adults by having extensive black on the tail-sides and back. Head pattern similar to female, but

young males have a small black patch between the eye and bill, and the females have an obscure greyish patch in the same place.

Voice: The call is most distinctive, a lively, twanging, metallic "pching" or "ping".

juvenile

Juvenile: The tail is shorter, and the plumage lacks any pink. Although the tail is white, most of the side of the head, including the cheeks, is sooty-black, so there is not much of a stripe. Juveniles resemble adults by September at the latest.

Adult (northern race): It has much less pink than a British bird, but is entirely white on the head, and shows more white on the wing.

Flight: It has a weak, bouncing flight, impeded by the tail.

front of the red eye, and runs back, broadening, to meet the black nape and mantle, leaving the crown white. The tail is black, bordered white.

adult northern Europe

Voice: There are three main calls, which are uttered constantly by flocks: a quiet, clicking "tupp", a louder spluttering call, and a penetrating "see-see-see" or "see-see-see-see".

Adult: It is the only tit with a sky-blue crown (bordered by white). The tail is also entirely blue. The white cheeks are bordered with black, above by a thin black eyestripe. The underparts are yellow, sometimes showing a weak, thin belly stripe. There is a single white wing-bar on the blue wings, and the back is greenish.

juvenile

Juvenile: It is a yellowish, insipid version of the adult, suggesting that the yellow has run and washed through the whole plumage. On the head, only the dark eyestripe of the adults' bold markings has developed.

Flight: It flies quickly from tree to tree on whirring wings. On longer trips, progress looks weak and erratic, with feeble undulations. It also has a display-flight, with ultra-fast, shallow wing-beats, or with glides.

Voice: It has a wide vocabulary, including many petulant scolds. The full song is a clear, lively trill, preceded by drawn-out introductory notes.

Adult male: The best distinction from Blue Tit, apart from size, is the pattern of the underparts. Great Tit has a yellow breast like Blue Tit, but it is split by a broad, bold black stripe, much more obvious than the very weak dark mark on the Blue Tit's breast. In addition, the crown is black, forming the upper border of a white cheek-patch. The back is greenish, and this colour extends up the nape. The wing is bluish, with a white wing-bar, and the tail is white-sided.

juvenile

Adult female (not illustrated): The breast-stripe is much thinner, and often broken, especially on the belly (broad all the way down on male).

Juvenile: It is sooty where the adult is jet black; the black lower border to the cheeks (which are yellowish, not white), is often broken or missing altogether. The whole bird is duller, particularly below.

Flight: Stronger, heavier flight than the other tits, with more even undulations.

Voice: It utters a very cheerful "pink-pink", almost identical to Chaffinch's call, and a number of scolds (of fewer syllables than those of Blue Tit). The main song is a cheerful, chiming, upbeat "Teacher, teacher, teacher", with many variations. It is harsher than the comparable song of Coal Tit.

Ecology and behaviour

Apart from the Bearded Tit, which actually belongs to the Asiatic Babbler family (see below), all our tits are woodland birds, but the type of woodland they favour varies. They feed on invertebrates (especially caterpillars) in spring and summer, and seeds and nuts in autumn and winter. Apart from Long-tailed Tit, they roost alone, spending the night in a variety of secret places, such as holes in trees, and all tits, again except the Long-tailed Tit, nest in holes.

Bearded Tit – also known as the Bearded Reedling since it is not a close relative of the other tits. Its unusual "parrot-like" bill structure, loose plumage and various other anatomical features are distinct from those of tits. Confined to large reedbeds, this bird is rare in Britain. Populations periodically "erupt", a process in which pioneers, usually juveniles, are sent off in search of new reedbeds to colonise. In the summer they eat invertebrates such as moths and beetles, and in winter the diet changes to seeds. In order to accommodate this change, the stomach doubles in size, and the bird takes in vast numbers of tiny stones to aid digestion.

Bearded Tit

Long-tailed Tit

Long-tailed Tit – found on the thinner branches in broad-leaved woodlands. It is almost entirely insectivorous, since its bill is not very strong and is therefore ill-equipped to deal with nuts (however some Long-tailed Tits have recently taken to feeding from garden peanut-bags). When roosting groups of birds huddle together as they perch on a sheltered branch; their combined body-heat serves to keep them warm. They spend every day of the non-breeding season in small flocks, which are based around a family unit of parents and offspring. These flocks stay together as they forage, and the group possesses a territory that is defended against other flocks. These flocks may be joined by a loose grouping of Blue, Great and Coal Tits. The Long-tailed Tit creates a marvellous, domed nest of intricate design, and places it in a thorny bush or in the fork of a tree. The main structure is of moss, bound together with cobwebs; lichen and other materials are placed outside for camouflage, and the interior is lined with hundreds, if not thousands, of feathers.

Blue Tit

Great Tit

Blue Tit – is also largely restricted to broad-leaved woodlands. Takes small prey and feeds high up in the canopy, has a stubby bill and is able to search among the flat surfaces of the leaves of oak and other broad-leaved trees. Forms flocks in winter with a looser composition than the Long-tailed Tit, and may join up in with Great and Coal Tits. These flocks may in turn join with Long-tailed Tits. Nests in natural holes in trees and walls, and also in nest-boxes. The nest is made from moss, often mixed with other plant material, and is lined with softer materials, eg. hair, wool and dry grass.

Great Tit – mostly an inhabitant of broad-leaved woodland where it forages over the trunks and larger branches for food. Populations overflow into coniferous woodland, although its preference is always for the former. Because of its size it takes the largest food items of the all the tits. Only this species, along with the Crested Tit and Marsh Tit, spends a substantial amount of time on the ground. The Great Tit forms loose flocks in winter that may associate with Blue and Coal Tits (see above). Makes its nest in natural holes and will readily use nest-boxes. .

MARSH TIT
Parus palustris

11cm. This and the Willow Tit are almost identical, and are tricky to separate. The best clue is voice. Marsh, however, is the neater, better proportioned bird, with a head that seems about the right size. It has a fractionally longer tail than Willow, square or notched at the end rather than rounded.

adult

Where found: A fairly common resident in deciduous woodland with a scrubby understorey, especially if oak or beech is present.

Adult: This and the Willow are brown tits with black caps and bibs; they have no wing-bars. The Marsh Tit, in contrast to Willow, has a glossy, not matt-black cap. It has a smaller, neater bib, and overall a cleaner look.

WILLOW TIT
Parus montanus

11cm. The Willow Tit is distinctly larger-headed than Willow, with a thick bull-necked appearance. The bird seems to have looser plumage and can look rather dowdy. It is much less perky and noisy than other tits, including Marsh. It is more likely to be found in damp woodlands on the edge of marshes than is the Marsh Tit!

adult

Where found: A fairly common resident in three habitats: coniferous woodland, hedgerows/scrub (including elder), and damp woodland of birch or alder.

Adult: It has a matt-black cap which extends further down than the Marsh Tit's – onto the mantle, in fact. The white of the cheeks also extends further back. The bib is larger and more diffuse, and the flanks are often

CRESTED TIT
Parus cristatus

11cm. This is the only small bird in Britain to have a crest, rendering it unmistakable. Otherwise a small, brown tit without any wing-bars.

adult

Where found: Fairly common in its restricted range and habitat, the Caledonian Pine Woods of north-central Scotland.

Adult: Brown above and warmly buff below. Throat is black, slight black collar. A black stripe begins behind the eye and curves back to make a "C"-shape. The crest is black with scaly white edges.

COAL TIT
Parus ater

11cm. The smallest of our tits, with a comparatively large head and short tail. It is a frequent visitor to garden bird tables, but is shyer than Blue or Great Tits. Note the two white wing-bars.

adult

Where found: A common resident of many woodlands and gardens, but a particular fan of coniferous woodland.

Adult: The Coal Tit has its own special colour on the upperparts – a slaty grey-brown. The lower underparts are buffy, especially towards the flanks. The head and wing-patterns are important in

Flight: A typical tit-like flitting, undulating over longer distances.

Voice: Peculiar to the Marsh Tit, the call is a sneezing "pitchou!", elaborated into a quick "pitch-a-bee-bee". The song has a Great Tit-like pattern, double notes repeated several times, but with a definite bubbling quality, and the first note almost lost eg. "Chiup-chiup-chiup."

juvenile

Juvenile: The cap is sooty, thus removing an important distinction from Willow Tit. The upperparts have a greyer wash, and the underparts are whiter than those of the adult.

---

quite darkly shaded buff (paler in Marsh Tit). One of the most reliable features to look for is the pale wing-panel made by the secondary and tertial feathers, which contrasts with the outer wing. (Occasionally, freshly plumaged Marsh Tits may hint of this, but it is only a hint.) Willow Tits also have a pale edge to their tails.

juvenile

Juvenile: Not separable from Marsh Tit juvenile.

Flight: Flitting, like a Marsh Tit, but said to be less fluent.

Voice: A quiet bird whose main call is a drawn-out, buzzy "tchay-tchay-tchay", with an emphatic, scolding quality. It never gives a "pitchou" call like Marsh Tit's. The song is a high-pitched, sweet "Tsui-tsiu-tsiu", more mournful than the other tits' songs.

Flight: It has a flitting flight, quite undulating, making this large-headed bird look slightly top-heavy.

Voice: A very distinctive bubbly trill "prululull" constitutes the main call. In song, this alternates with high-pitched "Zee-zee" notes.

juvenile

Juvenile: The crest is shorter and less spiky. All the black markings are duller except the collar, which is missing.

Adult Irish race (not illustrated): The cheeks and nape are tinged yellowish.

juvenile

Flight: It has the usual weak, flitting, undulating flight of all the small tits. The tail looks especially small.

Voice: The main call is a sighing, piping "seeuu" or "suee", but the vocabulary is wide. Most songs are higher-pitched and faster than Great Tit's, with a weaker quality, but they have the same repetition of a double note eg "Swee-choo, swee-choo, swee-choo".

recognition: the head is black-capped and white-cheeked, but with a broad white nape that is not found in other tits. The wing has two clear wing-bars, made up from white dots.

Juvenile: It is browner above and yellowish below. The cheeks and nape are also yellowish.

Ecology and behaviour (continued)

Marsh Tit

Marsh Tit – is confined to England, Wales and extreme south-east Scotland, and has quite a restricted habitat in dry deciduous woodland with a good understorey – but definitely not marshes. Its favourite trees are oak and beech, and it avoids conifers altogether. Feeds on the lower branches, and also in the herb layer searching for beechmast. Stores food amongst the leaf litter during the winter. Remains throughout the year as a pair in a territory. If a roving flock of Blue, Coal and Great Tits should pass through the pair's territorial boundaries, they will happily join in the communal foraging for a while, but will stay behind when the flock moves on. Only nests in natural sites.

Willow Tit – is a conifer bird in many parts of its range but occurs in smaller numbers in broad-leaved woodland, mainly in birch, alder and elder. On conifers, the Willow Tit takes to the trunks and branches,

rather than the leaves. On broad-leaved trees feeds on the lower branches, and also in the herb layer. Stores food in winter. Probably remains in pairs in a territory, too, but the general evidence suggests that this species seldom tags on to a mixed-species flock. Excavates its own holes but can be tempted to nest in boxes containing wood-chippings or even polythene chippings, so that they can be "excavated" first!

Willow Tit

Crested Tit – a rare bird, unlike the other tits that are common and widespread. Restricted to the Caledonian Pine forest of north-central Scotland. The Crested Tit forages on the branches themselves, and their most adjacent foliage. Also spends time on the ground. Stores food in winter. Remains throughout the year as pairs in a territory. Like the Marsh Tit it may forage with a flock passing through its territory but will not stray beyond its boundaries. Excavates its own holes but like Willow Tit can be encouraged to nest in boxes.

Coal Tit – favours coniferous woodland but occurs in smaller numbers in broad-leaved woodland. Feeds in the topmost branches of trees taking smaller prey than the other tits. Obtains its food items from among the needles of conifers and has a thinner bill for this purpose. Stores food among pine needles during the winter. Forms loose flocks, sometimes with Blue and Great Tit (see pp.212–213). Nests in natural holes and boxes but its small size is a disdvantage when competing for nesting sites, and means it often have to use holes on the ground.

Crested Tit

Coal Tit

NUTHATCH
Sitta europaea

14cm. This and the Treecreeper are two birds which cling to the trunks and branches of trees, searching the surfaces. They have very different shapes. The Nuthatch has a powerful, straight bill, a compact body and a short, stubby tail. It moves briskly up and down trunks, also sideways, with a jerky, hopping motion.

adult male

Where found: A woodland species which requires mature trees. It also occurs in parks and gardens, readily using bird tables and nest-boxes. Birds remain on their territory all year round.

Adult male: It is blue-grey above, and sandy-brown below. A black stripe runs through the eye, separating the blue-grey crown from the white throat. The tail has two white spots, one on each corner, and the undertail coverts have whitish fringes. Males have chestnut flanks, which contrast noticeably with the paler breast/belly.

TREECREEPER
Certhia familiaris

12cm. This bird creeps up (and only up, not down) trees, progressing in short hops and appearing mouse-like against the trunk. When it reaches the top of a tree, it flies down to the next. In contrast to Nuthatch, it has a thin, curved bill, and a long, straight tail which is used as a prop.

adult

Where found: A common resident in all kinds of woodland. Like the Nuthatch it visits gardens, but it rarely uses bird tables and only occasionally settles in specially designed nest-boxes.

Adult: The upperparts are intricately patterned with browns and blacks, with lots of streaks, bars etc. In complete contrast, the underparts are dazzling white. The rump is rufous in colour.

RED-BACKED SHRIKE
Lanius collurio

17cm. The shrikes are predatory birds with powerful, hook-tipped bills. They perch, sentinel-like, on the tops of bushes or on wires, scanning for prey. The long tail is often waved or flicked or fanned. The Red-backed Shrike is the smaller of our two regular species.

adult male

Where found: Now mainly a migrant, found in coastal scrub in spring and autumn. It once bred on heathland and commons over much of Britain, but now only one or two pairs nest annually.

Adult male: A handsome combination of grey, brown, black and white. The head and rump are blue-grey, and the back and wings are a rich rufous brown. The tail is black, with broad white

GREAT GREY SHRIKE
Lanius excubitor

24cm. A much larger species and more fearsome predator than the Red-backed Shrike. It has shorter, more rounded wings, which have a white wing-bar.

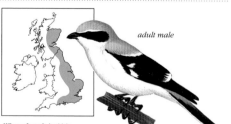

adult male

Where found: A widely scattered, rare winter visitor to open areas with scattered trees and bushes, notably heathland. October–April. They winter singly. Also a rare passage migrant.

*adult male
Northern Europe*

adult female

juvenile

Juvenile: The mask is much less obvious, being greyish rather than neatly black. The upperparts are slightly browner.

Adult female: Its flanks are paler, shading into the buffy breast/belly rather than forming a contrast.

Flight: It appears portly and short-tailed as it undulates strongly from tree to tree, like a small woodpecker.

Voice: Cheerful whistles at different tempos; the commonest being "chwit, chwit". The song is a fast whistling trill on the same pitch, but there are slower versions of drawn-out, insistent notes, like an unimaginative Song Thrush.

---

juvenile

Juvenile: The upperparts are a frosted, colder brown, with more spots. The underparts are stained buff, and the rump is less reddish-brown. At least at first, the bill is shorter.

Flight: Most flights begin in the treetops and end at the foot of a treetrunk. The action is light and undulating. The long tail is obvious, and sometimes the wing-bars show, too.

Voice: It has a gentle, soft voice. It often utters a series of evenly spaced, rhythmic, sibilant whistles, sounding like a squeaky tap being slowly rotated. The song-phrase drops down the scale and rises at the end, much as a Treecreeper

drops from the treetops and then tilts upwards at the last moment on to a trunk. It is a high-pitched phrase, easy to miss.

---

sides, but there is no white on the wings. The underparts are whitish, tinged pink. A bold, black "highwayman's mask" accentuates the predatory look.

adult female

Juvenile: It is similar to the female, but is scaled on the upperparts. In early autumn, they moult (into First Winter plumage) and lose most but not all of this scaling, so resembling the female more closely.

Adult female: Largely brown above, redder on the back and mantle and greyer on the crown and nape. The head mask is poorly defined.

juvenile

Curiously, the tail has a different pattern to the male's, being only thinly white-sided. The whitish breast and belly are adorned with crescent-shaped bars.

Flight: It darts down from its lookout perches, with fast wing-beats. Over longer distances, the flight is strong and undulating, interspersed with glides. It lands, as a woodpecker does, with an upward flourish.

Voice: The most distinctive call is sore-throated "chev"; also calls "shack, shack" like a warbler or chat. The song is an introverted, scratchy warble, with much mimicry.

Adult male: It has a black face-mask like a Red-backed Shrike, also largely black wings and tail. There is a narrow white supercilium, the tail is white-sided, and there are several white patches on the wings. The crown and back are grey, whitening where the back meets the wings. The underparts are greyish-white, like dirty snow.

Juvenile: It is browner grey than the adults, with more barring on the underparts. First Winters retain some barring, and have less obvious pale markings on the wings.

juvenile

adult female

Adult female: Some, but not all females have a few crescent-like bars on the breast.

Flight: It resembles that of the Red-backed Shrike, but the wings appear broader and more rounded.

Voice: Calls include a very grating sound, almost a screech like that of a Jay.

Climbing, feeding and hunting behaviour

Nuthatch and Treecreeper

These small birds hug the trunks and branches of trees, and both can be said to creep, but they hunt in subtly different ways in their search for slightly different food.

Treecreeper – has a well defined creeping system: it works its way up trees, searching the nooks and crannies during its steady progress from base to top, sometimes in a spiral pattern. Although it will cling to the underside of a branch, its movement is always upward, for it is unable to cling on to trees with its head pointing downwards. Part of the reason for this is the tail, which acts as a steadying prop when the bird goes up, but is of no use to any downward climb. The bill, furthermore, is long and curved, ideal for reaching into small crevices, but equally a hindrance when pointing down. The diet of the Treecreeper is exclusively invertebrates. When breeding, Treecreepers select a cavity for their nest, especially that made by a piece of flaking bark.

Nuthatch – climbs up, down, and also to the side. It often ascends with bill pointing skywards, but if anything, is more inclined to perch with its head below the body and one foot above the other. The short tail is useless as a prop. When the Nuthatch hunts, there is no regimented upward climb and downward flight, the pattern is more haphazard. Although the Nuthatch takes many insects, it also feeds on plant material, including nuts. To obtain these, it often forages on the ground, something a Treecreeper would never do. Nuthatches select a hole for their nest, usually an old woodpecker hole in a tree. Both birds plaster the entrance with mud, making sure that the hole is just the right size for themselves, and not for competitors.

Shrikes

Shrikes are fascinating birds that, regrettably, are rare in Britain. The Red-backed Shrike was once a fairly common summer visitor, but is now mostly a scarce passage migrant. Great Grey Shrikes are, and always have been, rare winter visitors and passage migrants. Less than 100 birds occupy our heathlands and open country each winter.

Feeding

Both shrikes are highly predatory, taking large insects, small mammals, birds and a few reptiles. To obtain insect or mammal prey, they drop down straight from the perch, or hover first. Flying insects or birds are captured in pursuit-flights, which are often prolonged. Both shrikes regularly store food, impaling it on thorns or barbed wire. Sometimes these caches are scattered, but often stored together forming a grisly "larder". This behaviour has earned shrikes the colloquial name of "Butcher Birds".

Great Grey Shrike – watches from high perches, often treetops, and takes a higher proportion of mammals (up to the size of a stoat). The Great Grey Shrike has to live with frequent inclement weather, being a winter visitor, so the habit of food-caching is a vital part of its system of survival.

Red-backed Shrike – is less of a butcher then the Great Grey Shrike as it stores only for short-term emergency rations in poor summer weather, or when feeding young. It hunts from lower perches and takes smaller prey.

Treecreeper

Treecreeper

Nuthatch

Nuthatch

Red-backed
Shrike

Great Grey Shrike

Red-backed Shrike

JAY
Garrulus glandarius

34cm. A woodland species, the only common British bird that is pink, black, white and blue. It is usually seen flying unsteadily between trees, but also feeds on the ground, progressing with bounding hops.

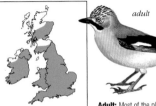

adult

Where found: A common resident in many parts of our area, but much less so in Scotland and Ireland. All kinds of woodland, but especially favours oak. Regular visitor to gardens.

Adult: Most of the plumage is brownish-pink, but the head, wings and tail have black-and-white markings. The primary covert feathers are coloured Kingfisher-blue. The crown is white, streaked with black, and

MAGPIE
Pica pica

46cm. This is another unmistakable bird, boldly black-and-white and with a long tail. On the ground it walks or hops, holding its tail up. The length of the tail varies, in accordance with the owner's standing in the community.

adult

Where found: Common to abundant in most of Britain and Ireland, but missing from large parts of Scotland. A resident of gardens, woodland edge, hedges and scrub.

Adult: Sparkling white on the scapular feathers of the back, and on the belly. Otherwise, it is black with various sheens: turquoise on the wings, bronzy-green and purplish on the tail.

CHOUGH
Pyrrhocorax pyrrhocorax

40cm. This bird could be difficult to identify, were it not for its curved red bill and red legs. A perky, noisy character, which loves to perform aerobatics around the cliffs and mountains where it lives.

adult

Where found: A uncommon and local inhabitant of coastal cliffs and a few inland quarries. Resident where it is found.

Adult: The plumage is all-black, but more glossy than that of any other black crow species. The wings and tail are green-glossed, and the rest of the plumage is glossed purplish or bluish.

Feeding and nesting behaviour

Jay
In the autumn, Jays collect large numbers of acorns and nuts as a winter/spring food-store. Several thousand are collected by each bird, hidden in a number of caches placed among leaf-litter, among plant roots, and other such places. Jays keep their nests well hidden amongst the foliage of a leafy bough.

Magpie
Magpies usually feed on the ground, as do all crows. Sometimes, however, they will rob the nests of other birds, particularly thrushes and finches, taking eggs and young. Although other crows, especially the Carrion Crow, also do

this, the Magpie is popularly considered to be the main villain. The Magpie builds a large, domed nest of sticks. No attempt is made to hide it, so it is obvious and distinctive. The roof protects the eggs and young from predation.

Chough
Feeds largely on insects and worms, which it takes by probing in the cliff-top soil. Its diet is therefore much more restricted than that of other crows, which are omnivores. Part of its rarity can be explained by its need for close-cropped turf, and part by its need for sheltered, rocky sites for nesting. In Britain, at least, it favours places with an Atlantic-dominated climate. Choughs often build their nests in caves.

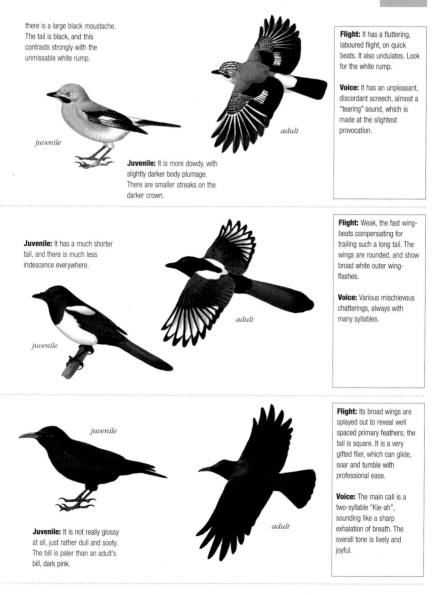

there is a large black moustache. The tail is black, and this contrasts strongly with the unmissable white rump.

juvenile

Juvenile: It is more dowdy, with slightly darker body plumage. There are smaller streaks on the darker crown.

adult

Flight: It has a fluttering, laboured flight, on quick beats. It also undulates. Look for the white rump.

Voice: It has an unpleasant, discordant screech, almost a "tearing" sound, which is made at the slightest provocation.

Juvenile: It has a much shorter tail, and there is much less iridescence everywhere.

juvenile

adult

Flight: Weak, the fast wing-beats compensating for trailing such a long tail. The wings are rounded, and show broad white outer wing-flashes.

Voice: Various mischievous chatterings, always with many syllables.

juvenile

adult

Juvenile: It is not really glossy at all, just rather dull and sooty. The bill is paler than an adult's bill, dark pink.

Flight: Its broad wings are splayed out to reveal well spaced primary feathers; the tail is square. It is a very gifted flier, which can glide, soar and tumble with professional ease.

Voice: The main call is a two-syllable "Kie-ah", sounding like a sharp exhalation of breath. The overall tone is lively and joyful.

Jackdaw

Jackdaws nest in colonies where there are enough holes. The holes may be in trees, cliffs, or even chimney-pots in built-up areas. When nest-building, sticks are thrown at random down the chimney. Jackdaws and Rooks often nest together, almost always in trees.

Rook

Rooks prefer to feed in fields, especially when just ploughed. The recent switch from spring sowing to autumn sowing on farms makes finding food especially difficult during the early breeding season. Rooks build open nests in colonies. Refurbishment begins very early in the year, often January.

Crows

The Carrion Crow pair builds at the top of a tree, always on their own. Normally, the nests are more concealed than those of Rooks. Sometimes a Crow territory is occupied by three birds, including one mated pair and a "Third Bird", usually a male interloper.

Raven

Ravens, together with all the larger crows, are enthusiastic scavengers; they may often fight with other species of crow over carrion for example. The nest is built on a cliff ledge or in a large tree.

Flight and social interaction

Jay – distinctive flight and plumage. Wings rounded, fully spread in flight. Progress weak and fluttery, at treetop height at most. Could almost be described as butterfly-like, but undulating. Usually seen alone or in pairs, but in autumn is regularly seen in small groups, commuting between woods in search of acorns. Nests well dispersed. Roosts in pairs or small groups of same species. Noisy spring gatherings (up to 20) also occur, which have a display function.

Magpie – distinctive flight and plumage. Wings short and rounded, tail trails behind in flight. Weak, fluttery progress like Jay, fast wing-beats alternating with glides. Sometimes flies high. Birds live as pairs, or as non-breeding flocks of usually less than ten birds. Nests well dispersed. Roosts in pairs or groups, sometimes with other crow species.

Chough – one of five "black crow" species, has distinctive red bill and legs. Wings are broad, ragged and obviously "fingered", slightly backswept; tail fairly square-ended. Expert flier, enjoys acrobatic manoeuvres that are indulged in at any time. Flight is effortless. Sociable. Spends much of its time in flocks, usually small; pairs join and leave them as a pair. Nests well dispersed. Roosts in groups outside breeding season, not usually with other crow species.

Jackdaw – smallest black crow, pigeon-sized. Has narrow wings, relatively blunt and unfingered, hardly backswept; tail slightly rounded. Has flight with quick beats ("Flap-Jack"), but can glide. Over breeding colony and at roost, indulges in aerial manoeuvres, but is not as expert as Chough. Very sociable. Usually nests in colonies, often with Rooks. Pairs stick together for most activities, even within feeding or flying flocks. Often roosts in large flocks, typically with other crows.

Rook – larger than Jackdaw, similar in size to Carrion/Hooded Crow. Has narrower and longer, more backswept wings, and a clearly round-ended tail. Flight with quicker wing-beats, more "flexible" action. Very sociable. Nests in colonies, sometimes with Jackdaws. Pairs stay together, but almost all activities, including roosting, are flock oriented.

Magpie at nest

Jay

Chough

Raven

Carrion/Hooded Crow – straighter wings than Rook, with relatively shorter "hands" and longer "arms"; tail is square-ended. Flight is slow and methodical ("Slow-Crow"), with slower wing-beats than Rook or Jackdaw. Often not sociable, but some birds live in small non-breeding flocks. Pairs always nest well apart, never in colonies. Aggregations occur at good feeding sites, and at roosts, which can also contain Rooks and Jackdaws.

Raven – by far the largest crow. The head projects further forward than on the Crow or Rook, and both the wings and tail are long. The wings are narrow-ended and often backswept; the tail is obviously wedge-shaped. The beats are slow, but the bird is adept at aerial manoeuvres such as rolls and tumbles (unlike Crow). Often flies very high and will soar, which Crows and Rook tend not to do. Mostly in pairs, or small flocks. Pairs nest well apart, not in colonies. The nest comprises a number of layers, that include woven twigs on the outside, and a soft inner layer. Often roosts in flocks with other black crows.

JACKDAW
Corvus monedula

33cm. The Jackdaw is our smallest crow, and the only black species with a pale eye. It has a compact appearance, with a short bill, short tail and somewhat chunky body. It walks with jaunty confidence, and flies with great skill.

Where found: A common resident in parkland, towns and cliffs – anywhere there are holes for nesting (it can use chimney pots), and where there is grassland over which to forage.

Adult: It hardly deserves to be called a black crow, because its nape and head-sides are most definitely grey. The underparts are also grey, although much darker. The black on the wings and tail is slightly purple-glossed. Look out for the neat contrast between the black throat and skull-cap and the grey on the rest of the head.

ROOK
Corvus frugilegus

46cm. There are many subtle differences between the Rook and the very similar Crow. This species, mainly a bird of agricultural land, has a steeper forehead, a more pointed bill, and a more ragged look because of the loose feathers on the thighs forming "baggy shorts". It is more sociable than the Crow, especially when nesting, and it walks on the ground with a sedate action, looking quite friendly.

adult

Where found: A very common resident, mainly in farming areas, since it needs fields over which to forage, and tall trees for nesting.

Adult: The bill is dirty-white, and so is the face. With the steep forehead, it looks as though the bill has been stuck on from another bird, and does not seem to fit properly. The plumage is all-black, with a definite purple gloss.

CARRION/HOODED CROW
Corvus corone

47cm. The Crow is a more fearsome prospect than a Rook, with an angry, menacing air. It always nests singly, but will happily socialise at food sources and at roosts. When distinguishing Carrion Crow from Rook, look for the thicker, slightly more downcurved bill of this species, which fits properly into the flatter head. It looks leaner, and wears leggings, not baggy shorts.

Carrion

Hooded

Where found: The species as a whole is an abundant resident almost everywhere, including the deepest woods, the most lonely moors and the busiest cities. The Carrion Crow is found in

England, Wales, and south and east Scotland. The Hooded Crow replaces it in northern and western Scotland, and Ireland. There is a narrow zone of overlap between the two.

RAVEN
Corvus corax

64cm. A huge member of the crow family, as big as a Buzzard, and found in appropriately impressive places such as mountains and cliffs. It has a heavy, dangerous-looking bill, a shaggy throat, and a long, wedge-shaped tail, all of which distinguish it from the other black crows. It is usually seen in pairs.

adult

Where found: This is mostly a northern and western bird, found all year in hilly and mountainous country, and also on cliffs. It is rarely as numerous as the other widespread black crows.

Adult: It is all-black, with something of a purplish/green gloss.

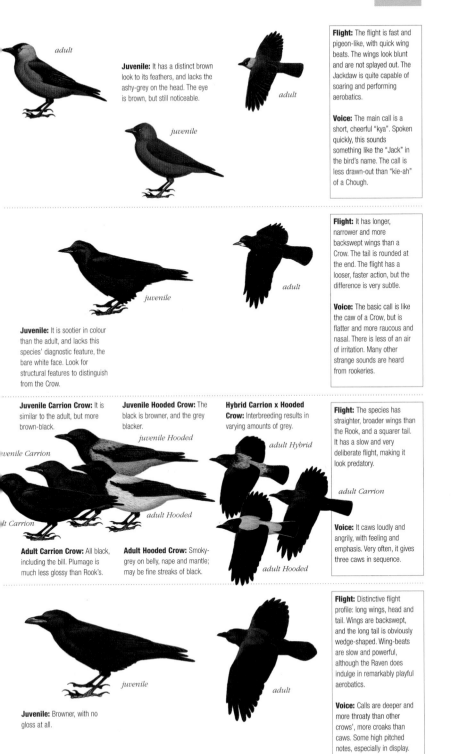

adult

Juvenile: It has a distinct brown look to its feathers, and lacks the ashy-grey on the head. The eye is brown, but still noticeable.

juvenile

adult

Flight: The flight is fast and pigeon-like, with quick wing beats. The wings look blunt and are not splayed out. The Jackdaw is quite capable of soaring and performing aerobatics.

Voice: The main call is a short, cheerful "kya". Spoken quickly, this sounds something like the "Jack" in the bird's name. The call is less drawn-out than "kie-ah" of a Chough.

juvenile

adult

Juvenile: It is sootier in colour than the adult, and lacks this species' diagnostic feature, the bare white face. Look for structural features to distinguish from the Crow.

Flight: It has longer, narrower and more backswept wings than a Crow. The tail is rounded at the end. The flight has a looser, faster action, but the difference is very subtle.

Voice: The basic call is like the caw of a Crow, but is flatter and more raucous and nasal. There is less of an air of irritation. Many other strange sounds are heard from rookeries.

Juvenile Carrion Crow: It is similar to the adult, but more brown-black.

Juvenile Hooded Crow: The black is browner, and the grey blacker.

juvenile Hooded

Hybrid Carrion x Hooded Crow: Interbreeding results in varying amounts of grey.

adult Hybrid

venile Carrion

lt Carrion

adult Hooded

Adult Carrion Crow: All black, including the bill. Plumage is much less glossy than Rook's.

Adult Hooded Crow: Smoky-grey on belly, nape and mantle; may be fine streaks of black.

adult Carrion

adult Hooded

Flight: The species has straighter, broader wings than the Rook, and a squarer tail. It has a slow and very deliberate flight, making it look predatory.

Voice: It caws loudly and angrily, with feeling and emphasis. Very often, it gives three caws in sequence.

juvenile

adult

Juvenile: Browner, with no gloss at all.

Flight: Distinctive flight profile: long wings, head and tail. Wings are backswept, and the long tail is obviously wedge-shaped. Wing-beats are slow and powerful, although the Raven does indulge in remarkably playful aerobatics.

Voice: Calls are deeper and more throaty than other crows', more croaks than caws. Some high pitched notes, especially in display.

GOLDEN ORIOLE
Oriolus oriolus

24cm. A secretive summer apparition, as rare and elusive as it is beautiful. The size of a thrush, it stays hidden in the tops of trees, giving away its presence mainly by sound.

Where found: Rare summer visitor and passage migrant, usually seen in spring and early summer. Breeds mainly in East Anglia, nesting in poplars and other deciduous trees.

Flight (not illustrated): Loose, thrush-like flight, with long undulations. Upward swoop when coming in to land, like a woodpecker. Could be confused with Green Woodpecker, which also has long undulations and upward swoops, but latter has a yellow rump.

Voice: It has a variety of calls, including one like a cat's miaow. The song is fluty, liquid and tropical.

STARLING
Sturnus vulgaris

21cm. Well-known to all, the Starling is one of our commonest birds. Its shape is distinctive – longish, spiky bill, short tail, squat body – and its character unique. It bustles over the lawn, walking with a swagger, bickering with its neighbours and other birds, and bolting its food impolitely. Usually seen in groups or enormous flocks.

adult male summer

Where found: Abundant in all sorts of places, including cities and farmland. A resident, but enormous numbers of Continental birds arrive in October to boost the wintering population.

Adult (male) summer: Superficially similar to a Blackbird, but tail is shorter, and black plumage is iridescent. Speckles on belly and undertail. Bill base blue (male), pink (female).

HOUSE SPARROW
Passer domesticus

14cm. There can be few more familiar birds than the boisterous, cheeky House Sparrow. Much regarded as a "small brown bird", it is actually quite intricately coloured. A species found mostly in association with human activity, but still wary.

Where found: An abundant species, very much associated with people and their dwellings. Resident around cities, towns, farmland.

Adult male summer: Grey crown and rump, dirty grey breast. Small black face-mask and large, quite diffuse black bib, which reaches on to the breast. A chestnut band runs from behind the eye on to the nape, forming the rear border of the dirty-grey cheek. Chestnut and black wings, short white wing-bar, black bill.

Adult female: A much duller bird, mostly muddy-brown, and without most of the male's contrast. There is, however a large buffy stripe that works back from the eye, forming a useful

TREE SPARROW
Passer montanus

14cm. It is smaller, more compact, shyer, and much less common than its overbearing relative. Overall, it is cleaner in appearance. In contrast to House Sparrow, the sexes look alike.

Where found: It is far less common than the House Sparrow, and much more local. Generally associated with farmland, gardens, outbuildings, cliffs and watercourses. Resident.

Adult: It differs from male House Sparrow in its complete chestnut-brown cap, its white neck-collar and its clear black cheek-spot on the clean white cheek. In addition, the bib is smaller and much neater than that of House Sparrow, and the rump and underparts are pale sandy-brown, not grey. There are two white wing-bars, one obvious, one less so. The bill is all-black in summer, yellow-based in winter.

juvenile

adult male

adult female

Juvenile: It differs from the female in having streaking on the upperparts, and a brown bill.

Adult male: It is unmistakable, a combination of deep yellow and pitch black. Black is on the lores (between bill and eye), on the wings and on the tail. The bill is red, as it is in most plumages.

Adult female: Most are bright apple-green above, except for the brownish-black wings and tail. The underparts are pale grey-green, with faint streaks. The lores are grey, not black. A few older females resemble the males, except for their grey lores.

adult winter

juvenile

two immature stages (not to scale)

Adult winter: After moulting birds are more spotted. The bill becomes black. The spots are buff on the upperparts, and white on the underparts. The female has more and larger spots.

Immatures: The period between June and September throws up some interesting plumages on youngsters; the ratio of adult feathers to juvenile feathers varies.

Juvenile: Other than in shape, it could hardly look more different from its parents, being mostly muddy-brown, with a whitish throat and some whitish shading on the breast and belly.

Flight: Distinctive flight profile, with triangular wings, pointed at the tip. It flies straight, with only very slight undulations (if any). Wing-beats are fast, will glide to the ground when landing, and also at other times.

Voice: It has many calls, including a grating "tschurr", and a whistling sound. The song is a rambling, gurgling, dotty babble, with lots of whistles, clicks and rattles.

field-mark. Where the male is grey, the female is brown. The female has a buffy, not white, wing-bar. The bill is brownish-yellow.

Adult male winter: In contrast to summer plumage, the bib is smaller, and all grey plumage, is variably stained brownish. The bill is brownish-yellow.

Juvenile: It resembles the female closely, but looks washed-out, and the edges of the yellow gape are visible at the bill-base.

Flight: It has surprisingly direct flight for a small bird, without bounding undulations. The wing-beats are hurried and lack fluency. Flocks are densely packed and well-drilled.

Voice: It makes a variety of cheeps, chirps and chirrups, often in chorus.

...ult male ...brid with ...ee Sparrow

adult male winter

adult female

juvenile

adult male summer

Flight: It resembles that of House Sparrow, but is faster, with even more whirring wing-beats.

Voice: The chirps are generally sharper and harder than the House Sparrow's, especially a unique "teck" flight-call.

juvenile

adult

Juvenile: The bib and cheek-spot are grey-brown and mottled, and the cap is also peppered with grey. The wing-bars are buffy, not white, and the bill resembles that of an adult in winter.

Habitat, feeding and breeding behaviour

Starling

The Starling has black plumage and a squat, spiky-billed shape. It waddles across the lawn with jaunty, busy steps. The Starling's eyes are set well forward so that it can see easily into the holes that it makes with its long bill when looking for invertebrates and their larvae. It also takes a variety of other animal and vegetable food, including scraps from gardens.

Flight

In flight the profile is distinctive: short tail, triangular wings. Thrushes have longer tails and wings.

Roosting

The Starling is famous for its enormous communal roosts. In the breeding season, most pairs roost at or near the nest, but at other times they join up in groups to spend the night, in reedbeds, trees, bushes or buildings. In winter, Britain's residents are joined by Continental immigrants creating roosts of 100,000 or more. At the end of the day, groups of birds coalesce into larger and larger aggregations, eventually joining up in a pre-roost gathering where they sing and preen. Then they fly to the roost itself, either going straight in or performing the most amazing aerial manoeuvres above it, swarming like bees and resembling great swirling columns of smoke. The following morning they leave the roost in well-ordered flocks, the departure staggered, apparently by prearrangement.

Song

Starlings nest in holes, usually in trees, but also in the eaves of houses. Outside the nests, males sing their rambling songs. Often they perform from TV aerials, their strange clicks and whistles sounding remarkably like the output from a receiver. Many imitations are incorporated into the song, including neighbourhood sounds such as sirens, cats, crying babies and telephones.

Starlings in pre-roost aerial manoeuvres

Tree Sparrow

House Sparrow

Sparrows

There are two species of sparrow in the British Isles. The House Sparrow is abundant and familiar, with a population of several millions of pairs; the Tree Sparrow is much less numerous, the population not exceeding 120,000 pairs. The House Sparrow inhabits man-made terrain, including farms, suburbs and city centres (especially if there are parks), whereas the Tree Sparrow is more of a rural bird, occurring in woodland edge, avoiding built-up areas, but often mixing with House Sparrows in farmland. House Sparrows will follow human settlements up to quite high elevations, but the Tree Sparrow is strictly confined to lowlands.

The two species often roost together, and will even form mixed colonies. They are obviously closely related, but rarely hybridise because the two sexes of Tree Sparrow look alike, and the sexes of House Sparrow look very different, preventing confusion.

House Sparrows nest mainly in crevices in buildings, utilising any nook and cranny, including eaves in the roof. Tree Sparrows are happier in more enclosed holes, especially tree-holes and holes in cliffs or ruins. For their diet, both species are seed-eaters, but the Tree Sparrow specialises in the smaller seeds of annual weeds such as chickweed. The House Sparrow is adaptable, and can subsist on the thrown-out scraps provided in gardens and urban areas.

Starlings at roost

CHAFFINCH
Fringilla coelebs

15cm. This is one of our commonest birds. At all times, look for the white shoulders diagnostic of this species. It has a fairly slender body and a longish, white-sided tail. The bill is short and thick, and the crown often appears peaked. It has a more horizontal posture than most finches when perched, and, when on the ground, it walks and hops with a jerky action.

Where found: Abundant in woodland (any kind), farmland and suburbia. When breeding it concentrates in wooded and bushy areas. Large numbers of Continental visitors winter.

Adult male summer: Colourful, with a blue-grey crown and nape, rich chestnut back, and pink breast. The bill is blue-grey.

Adult male winter: The features noted above are all less bright; the bill turns yellowish. Winter plumage is acquired by September, and as winter progresses, the colours become brighter by the wearing away of dull feather tips.

BRAMBLING
Fringilla montifringilla

14cm. The northern equivalent of Chaffinch, visiting us for the winter only. It is similar in shape to Chaffinch, but has a slightly shorter tail. Look for the orange shoulders and white rump.

Where found: Largely a winter visitor, October–April or May. Well distributed in Britain, scarcer in Ireland, but numbers vary from year to year. Occasionally breeds in Scotland.

Adult male summer: This plumage is most likely to be seen in Britain in spring, before the birds disappear north. An unmistakable mixture of black, white and orange. The bill is black.

Adult male winter: The head and mantle are black mottled with orange-brown, while the breast, shoulders and inner wing-bar are all the colour of autumn beech-leaves (no coincidence). Spots on the flanks are visible against the whitish belly. The bill is yellow with a black tip.

BULLFINCH
Pyrrhula pyrrhula

15cm. Although gaudy in plumage, the Bullfinch is a shy and secretive species, difficult to see. Note that the thick bill is deeply set into the head, not interrupting the curve of the crown. In flight it shows a prominent white rump.

adult male

Where found: A common resident of woodland and scrubland, and an unwelcome visitor to gardens and orchards with fruit buds.

Male: Black chin and thick, black cap; also black on wings and tail. Back is smoky grey; neck-sides, breast and upper belly are all deep strawberry-red. White wing-bar and rump.

HAWFINCH
Coccothraustes coccothraustes

18cm. It is heavily built, has bold markings, and should be easy to see, but the Hawfinch is incredibly shy and hard to find, hiding in the treetops. The massive bill can crush the hardest of nuts and stones. If it is seen, the Hawfinch's top-heavy shape makes identification easy.

adult male

Where found: A very local resident in mature deciduous woodland, especially with hornbeam, beech or wild cherry. Hard to find.

Adult male: The face and underparts are pink-brown, dominating first impressions. On the face there is black at the base of the bill, and a neat black chin. The hindneck is ash-grey

Adult female: Upperparts are greenish-brown. The centre of the crown is greyish up to the nape. Subtle pale eyebrow. Underparts grey-brown, tinged light pink. Bill is light brown.

juvenile

adult female summer

adult male winter

adult male summer

adult female summer

Juvenile: It resembles female plumage, but is paler, especially on the underparts. There is often a whitish patch on the nape.

Flight: Strongly undulating flight, wings are closed every few beats. Undulations are long and shallow compared to most other finches. Look for the white shoulders, white wing-bar, white-sided tail and green rump.

Voice: There are many calls, including a very cheerful "pink-pink!", and a quiet "chup" flight-note. The song is an accelerating rattle ending with a flourish.

Adult female winter: Mottled-brown on crown and mantle; nape and sides of the head are distinctly greyish. Females always lack flank spots, and always have black-tipped yellow bills. Less orange in summer.

juvenile

adult female summer

adult male winter

adult male summer

adult female winter

Juvenile: It resembles the female in summer, but the breast is even paler, almost yellowish, and the head pattern is ill-formed.

Flight: Shorter tail than Chaffinch, giving it a slightly more up-and-down flight. Look for orange shoulders, white rump and black tail.

Voice: Flight call is sharper than Chaffinch, more of a "jep" than "chup". Another important sound is a wheezy "zweep". The song, seldom heard here, is a harsh "Dzwee … ", a flatter and less emphatic sound than the wheeze of the Greenfinch.

Female: It has the same crown, wings and tail as the male, but the back is browner and the underparts are a plum-coloured pink-brown. The nape has a greyer wash.

adult female

juvenile

adult female

Juvenile: It lacks the adults' black cap, giving it a slightly gormless expression. The wing-bar is tinged pinkish.

Flight: If flying some distance, it has a strong, bouncing flight at quite a height. Usually flights are low, short, and close to cover. White rump is obvious.

Voice: Call is distinctive, a soft, melancholy, single-syllabled whistle. The very quiet song is a mixture of calls and remarkable creaking, broken notes, sounding like a pub-sign creaking in the wind.

---

and the back is mahogany-brown. A huge white-and-rusty-brown bar runs across the wing, while the main flight-feathers are black, glossed purple; they are curiously swollen and blunted at the tips. The tail is brown, with a white tip.

adult female

juvenile

Adult female: It differs by being generally paler, and has fractionally less black on the face. The outer fringes of the secondary flight feathers are grey, forming a clear panel. In both sexes, the bill is blue-grey in summer, yellowish in winter.

adult female

Juvenile: Although the wings are recognisably Hawfinch-like, the head is only a blotchy brownish-green, and the buffy breast has well spaced spots, like those of a thrush.

Flight: It has fast, deeply undulating flight, usually at a considerable height. The wing-beats have to hurry to keep this top-heavy bird airborne. Look out for the heavy head, short tail and broad white wing-bar.

Voice: It has a far-carrying, explosive "tick" or slightly strained "tseep". The weak song is a restrained, faltering series of call-like notes, rarely heard.

Food and feeding behaviour

All finches are seed-eaters, and their various different bills are adapted to extracting the seeds of various different kinds of plants. Here we look at the birds' specialist bills and look at the different foods they eat.

Chaffinch – a generalist, eating a wide variety of seeds, with no particular favourite. Its bill is short, only relatively thick, so it tends to take smaller grains. Mainly on the ground.

Brambling – preferentially takes the nuts of the Beech tree, which are called beechmast. The plumage is adapted to the colour of their fallen leaves. Mainly on the ground.

Bullfinches – are much attracted to the keys of the Ash tree, and also Dock and Bramble. In spring, they take the buds of Fruit Trees such as pears, cherries and plums. Feeds directly from trees and plants.

Hawfinch – an elusive bird found in woods with Hornbeam, and also Beech and Wild Cherry, the stones or nuts of which it can crush with its huge bill. Searches both the ground and trees.

Greenfinch – another generalist, but its heavy bill can tackle such large seeds as Sunflowers. Also takes Rose hips and Yew berries. On ground and on plants.

Goldfinch – a thin-billed specialist, with a particular taste for Thistle seeds. In the same family, it also takes Teasel and Groundsel. Mostly on the plant, less often on the ground.

Redpolls – strongly associated with the seeds of Birch, which they extract with their short, broad bills. Also feed in Alders with Siskins.

Linnets – feed on the very small seeds of agricultural weeds, taking many different types. They feed regularly on the ground, also on low plants (not trees).

Twite – takes small seeds from the open country where it lives, so it often feeds from coastal plants. These include weeds in the Goosefoot family, for example. On the ground and low plants, occasionally trees.

Siskins – also thin-billed, and mostly feed on Spruce in the summer. In winter they feed mainly in Alder, but also on Larches and Birches. They feed mainly in trees, less often on the ground.

Crossbill (not illustrated) – has a bill that is adept at taking conifer seeds from cones, which it extracts with a tweezer-like action. The common Crossbill prefers Spruce, but will also use Pine and Larch. The Scottish Crossbill only feeds on the seeds on Caledonian Scots Pine.

GOLDFINCH
Carduelis carduelis

12cm. A flock of Goldfinches is called a charm, a word that sums up this species well. Its bright colours, neat but delicate form, and joyful song are all a delight.

adult

Where found: Common in woodland edge and open country with a good growth of weeds, especially thistles. Although resident, many winter in southern Europe or North Africa.

Adult: The head has a unique pattern of red, white and black bands. The wing is black, with a broad and stunning yellow wing-bar which makes a slight S-shape when the wing is closed. The forked tail is black,

GREENFINCH
Carduelis chloris

14cm. The largest of three finches that are predominantly green and yellow (the others being Siskin and Serin). It is a large-billed, heavy-headed finch, with a muscular appearance and quite a fierce, frowning expression. When the bird is perched, the yellow wing-bar is seen to follow the edge of the wing, not go across it.

adult male summer

Where found: Very common by woodland edge and in various bushy places. A resident, which often visits gardens in winter.

Adult male summer: A pleasing apple-green all over, except for the yellow wing-bar, yellow tail-sides and dark flight feathers. There is a hint of darker shading over the eye, causing a frown. The wing-coverts and secondaries are washed grey.

SISKIN
Carduelis spinus

12cm. Smaller than the Greenfinch, with a less bulky head and short, sharp bill. The short, forked tail adds to a compact impression. Note that there are two wing-bars (only one of which is really obvious), and that they go across the wing when the wing is closed, not along the edge (see Greenfinch). All ages show streaks on the belly and flanks.

adult male

Where found: Breeds in coniferous woodland, most common in Scotland. Some breeding birds and many Continental immigrants winter further south.

Adult male: Distinguished by having a black crown and chin. The back is faintly streaked, as is the rump; the flanks are well streaked. In winter, the black chin and crown are scaled with grey.

SERIN
Serinus serinus

11cm. A tiny, almost bill-less, yellow-green finch that is rare in Britain. It is distinguished by its shape, its bright yellow rump and its dingy, less than striking wing-bars.

adult male summer

Where found: A rare but annual passage migrant (mainly in spring) and occasional breeding visitor, to a few southern parks and gardens.

Adult male summer: Heavily streaked on the back and flanks, lightly streaked on the crown. Lemon yellow colour is most evident on the head and breast. The wings and tail are greenish and black, with two very faint yellowish wing-bars.

contrasting with the white rump. The main body colour is a warm fawny-brown, fading to white on the belly. In winter, the main flight feathers and tail are tipped with white dots. The thin bill is a pale yellowish-brown.

Juvenile: The wing-pattern resembles that of the adult, but otherwise it is generally pale-brown, with streaks. All the adults' head coloration is lacking, and it will continue to lack until the moult is completed in late September.

adult

juvenile

Flight: Light and very bouncy, often with an erratic dancing action. This is the only finch with both a white rump and yellow wing-bar.

Voice: The call is a cheery, trickling "tickelit". The song is on the same theme, a sweet, effortless medley of liquid twitters.

Adult male winter (not illustrated): Greyer on the belly and side of the head than in summer, but the difference is subtle, and some birds are browner than others.

adult female summer

Adult female: It is darker green than the male, with a hint of streaking on the back. There is less yellow on the wings and tail-sides. Winter and summer plumage are similar.

Juvenile: Browner than the adults, especially on the upperparts, and much more streaky. Wings as adult.

juvenile

adult female summer

Flight: Look for a heavy-headed, fairly short-tailed finch with a strong, undulating flight. The single yellow wing-bar and yellow tail-sides are useful features. Look out for the elegant, swallow-like song-flight.

Voice: The main call is an abrupt but quiet "chichichit". The song is based on dry, rattling trills on various pitches, often with a drawn-out, strained wheeze.

Adult female: It lacks the male's black head markings, and is more heavily streaked above and below. Otherwise it is similar.

Juvenile: Young birds resemble the female, but are browner above and paler, almost white below. Everywhere the streaking is denser.

adult female

juvenile

adult female

Flight: Fast and free, with strong undulations. Look for the double yellow wing-bar, and green rump.

Voice: Its main call is a creaky, "tseu", but it also has a sparrow-like chatter. The song is continuous creaky twitter, often interspersed with absurd, wheezy, drawn-out buzzes.

Adult male winter: The plumage is duller and less contrasting. The summer yellow on the forehead and neck-sides is obscured by green streaks. The flank streaks, however, are less obvious.

Adult female: It is much duller than the male, being basically greenish-brown, but with the same bright yellow rump. It is far more heavily streaked than the male on the crown and breast.

 *adult male winter*

juvenile

adult female summer

Juvenile: The youngster hardly has any yellow at all, just the slightest wash on the breast. It is streaky brown, with obscure brown wing-bars. Identify by shape.

adult female summer

Flight: It has an easy, bouncy flight. The strong yellow rump, and also unmarked tail and wings, are good field marks.

Voice: The main call is a rippling "tirrilit", easy to recognise when learnt. The song is a very fast, hurried twitter, sounding a little like the jangling of very small keys.

Flight identification of finches and buntings

Here we compare flying birds of some of our small seed-eating species. For this section, primary feathers fringed with bright edges is a "wing-flash".

Colourful features shown by the coverts are called "wing-bars". The birds illustrated here are female unless otherwise indicated.

Chaffinch (female summer)

Brambling (female summer)

Bullfinch (female)

Hawfinch (female)

Greenfinch (female summer)

Goldfinch (adult)

Siskin (female)

Linnet (female summer)

Chaffinch: white shoulders, long white wing-bar. Greenish rump (brighter on male). White tail-sides.

Brambling: orange shoulders usually, or brownish. One long wing-bar, sometimes orange on inner wing. White rump. Unmarked black tail.

Bullfinch: grey shoulders and wing-bar. White rump. Unmarked black tail.

Hawfinch: male and female have a large white/fawn panel on inner wing, white outer wing-flashes, and pink-brown rump and tail, latter with white tips. Female has greyish secondaries (inner trailing edge).

Greenfinch: yellow wing-flashes. Yellow-green rump. White-sided tail. (Latter two features less obvious on male.)

Goldfinch: broad, bright yellow wing-bar on black wings. White rump. Black tail, with white terminal spots in winter.

Siskin: one small yellow-green and one obvious yellow wing-bar. Lemon-yellow rump. Yellow tail-sides.

Linnet: prominent white wing-flashes, no obvious bar. Brown or grey-brown (male). White tail-sides.

Twite: Reddish-buff wing-bar on inner wing. Female has a brown rump; male's rump is pink or brown-pink. White tail-sides are less extensive than Linnet's. The male has less prominent white wing-flashes than the female.

Redpoll: two buff-coloured wing-bars on inner wing. Rump is brown, or pink in male, No tail marks.

Crossbill: plain blackish wing. No tail marks. Female has a grass-green rump; male's rump is crimson-red.

Lapland Bunting: two narrow wing-bars with chestnut in between. Rump brown/chestnut. White tail-sides.

Reed Bunting: no obvious wing-bars. Rump brown, greyish-brown in male. Prominent white tail-sides.

Yellowhammer: no obvious wing bars. Prominent chestnut rump. White tail-sides.

Cirl Bunting: no obvious wing-bars. Olive-brown/greyish rump. White tail-sides.

Corn Bunting: No obvious wing-bars. Brown rump. Unmarked tail.

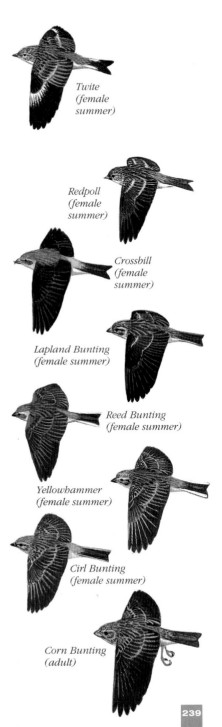

Twite (female summer)

Redpoll (female summer)

Crossbill (female summer)

Lapland Bunting (female summer)

Reed Bunting (female summer)

Yellowhammer (female summer)

Cirl Bunting (female summer)

Corn Bunting (adult)

LINNET
Carduelis cannabina

13cm. A small, slim finch of open country, which has long wings, a fairly long tail and a short bill. At all ages, it shows a silvery-white wing-bar running along the edge of the wing. Subtle shadings around the eye and just below give a distinctive facial expression.

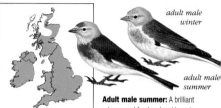

adult male winter

adult male summer

Where found: Common resident in scrubby country.

Adult male summer: A brilliant crimson-red forehead and breast, is set against a greyish head and a white, black-speckled throat.

TWITE
Carduelis flavirostris

13cm. The upland equivalent of the Linnet, also found by the coast. Very similar to the Linnet, but is more straw-coloured (winter) and streaky (summer). Most of the time the throat is clear and buffy, not white and streaked. Has a buffy wing-bar that the Linnet lacks, and less white on the wing.

adult male winter

Where found: Breeds on Scottish coasts and moors.

Adult male summer: In general plumage it is quite dark brown, with very strong streaking on the underparts. There is a characteristic pink rump.

REDPOLL
Carduelis flammea

13cm. This bird shares brownish coloration with Linnet and Twite, but unlike them, it feeds in the treetops, frequently with the Siskin in alders and birches. All adult Redpolls have a red forehead, black chin and two buffy wing-bars (the inner one quite hard to see).

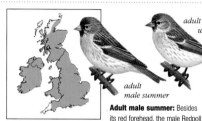

adult male winter

adult male summer

Where found: Fairly common resident in woods, mainly birch.

Adult male summer: Besides its red forehead, the male Redpoll shows a delightful raspberry-pink wash on the breast.

CROSSBILL
Loxia curvirostra

16cm. Crossbills are the only birds in the British Isles to have crossed mandibles, so, given a good view, identification is easy. A large, thickset, big-headed finch with a short tail, so it often looks top heavy. When clambering about in conifer branches, it is reminiscent of a small parrot.

Where found: Found all year in coniferous trees, but locally.

Flight: A powerful flier, with a considerably undulating flight. It looks big and heavy for a finch.

Voice: The main call, easy to recognise once learnt, is a loud, metallic "jip-jip". The song is based on this call, but interspersed with some quite musical twitters.

SCOTTISH CROSSBILL
Loxia scotica

16cm. In most respects, this bird is identical to the common Crossbill, but it has a larger head and a deeper (ie. thicker at the base) bill. The bill is also blunter. On such tenuous evidence, Scottish birds are considered to be a unique species.

Where found: Caledonian pine forests of north-central Scotland.

Flight: As Crossbill.

Voice: The main call is said to be stronger than that of Crossbill, more of a "jup" than a "jip".

Adult female: A browner, more streaky bird than the male, lacking the crimson coloration. The head is greyish-brown like a winter male's; facial pattern is clear.

Adult male winter: By late September the red disappears, and the grey on the head has turned to greyish-brown. The mantle is streaked, and the bill is pale brown (as female winter).

Juvenile: It resembles the female, but is slightly more reddish-brown on the upperparts. The streaking on the underparts is more spot-like. It also lacks much of a facial expression.

Flight: It has light, very undulating flight, almost bounding. Notice the white wing-flashes and white tail-sides.

Voice: The flight call is a hurried "chop-chop" or "chit-chit", with 2–5 notes. The song is a cheery twitter including both sweet and harsh notes.

Adult female: The plumage is similar to that of the male summer/winter, except that the pink on the rump is lacking at all times.

Adult male winter: Plumage acquires a warmer, buffy tone, contrasting with the whitish belly. Look for the consistently straw-coloured face and throat, and also the yellow bill, which both sexes have.

Juvenile: It shows the heavy streaks of a summer adult, but is distinctly rusty-coloured above.

Flight: Similar flight to Linnet, although the slightly longer tail may be noticeable.

Voice: Main call is similar to the Linnet, but slightly harder, usually with more syllables eg. "chululut". Another call heard from flocks is a harsh, nasal sound "twae-it", which gives the bird its name. Song is similar to Linnet.

Adult female: No pink on the breast, but still a red forehead.

Adult male winter: Less pink, pink is less bright. General plumage tone is warmer-brown.

Juvenile: The plumage resembles that of the adult female, but there is no red on the forehead. In addition, the underparts are more heavily streaked (mostly on the flanks in adults), and there is often something of a dark patch on the chin. By autumn, the red on the forehead will begin to appear, and the black chin will be well-formed.

Flight: Bouncy flight, like a Siskin, with long, sweeping undulations. Note the two buffy, not yellow, wing-bars; lacks the yellow tail-flashes.

Voice: The main call is a distinctive dry rattle "chuch-uch-uch", often alternated with buzzes. The song is similar, but more varied; it is usually delivered in flight.

Adult male: In all plumages, has dark brown, unmarked wings and tail. Otherwise unmistakably brick-red all over.

Male (variations): in their first year males show a variety of plumages. Some have streaks on underparts, some have mottling.

Adult female: Mainly green, slightly paler below, often with some subtle mottling on the head and breast.

Juvenile: Plumage is very different from adults: basically brown with heavy streaking above and below (not on wings).

Plumages: Colours and plumage sequence do not differ from Crossbill.

LAPLAND BUNTING
Calcarius lapponicus

15cm. The buntings are very finch-like, but as a rule they have smaller heads and bills, and longer tails. Their songs are less rambling. The Lapland Bunting is an uncommon coastal winter visitor. It is most similar to Reed Bunting, but is broader-bodied and much longer winged, giving quite a lark-like impression.

Where found: Scarce winter visitor and passage migrant. In winter, it occurs in saltmarshes, dunes and other coastal ground, mostly on the east coast of England.

adult male summer

Adult male summer: A very handsome bird, with a black breast and crown, a rich chestnut nape, and a creamy stripe between the two.

Adult male winter: Features shown by all winter Lapland Buntings, distinguishing them from Reed Buntings, are:

SNOW BUNTING
Plectrophenax nivalis

16cm. This appropriately named bird always shows plenty of white on its wings and tail, and usually on the body as well, so it is easily identified. Flocks moving in flight look like snowflakes. It is large and well-built for a bunting, with long wings.

Where found: Mostly a winter visitor, September–April, to coastal areas, and the mountains and moorland of Scotland. Also a scarce breeding bird on Scottish mountaintops.

adult male summer

Adult male summer: Head is all-white, showing up the black bill and eye.

Adult male winter: Underparts are white, except for the breast sides, crown and cheeks which are yellowish-brown. A similar colour (but greyer) going down the streaked back. A large white wing-panel is visible on the

REED BUNTING
Emberiza schoeniclus

15cm. A sparrow-like bird, but it has a longer, blackish tail that it jerks frequently, revealing the bright white outer tail-feathers. Although typically a species of waterside, it is found in some dry habitats, too.

Where found: A common and widespread resident in marshland and some drier areas, including heaths and hedgerows.

Adult male summer: The inky-black head and white collar makes it most striking and distinctive. A white stripe runs down from the bill to the collar, splitting the black in two. The breast and belly are whitish, with a few flank-streaks.

Adult male winter: From about September, the bold black "ink" is diluted by pale mottling.

Buntings in summer and winter

Summer

Five species of buntings breed in Britain and Ireland, of which three are widespread and two are rare. One rarity, the Snow Bunting, is found in the far north; the other, the Cirl Bunting, is found in the far south.

Snow Buntings breed in Britain only on certain mountaintops in Scotland, for example in the Cairngorm range. The population is low, for Britain is at the very south of the species' range; Snow Buntings are far more at home in Iceland or Greenland, and venture farther north than any other small bird in the world. The nest is made among rocks and scree, and it is sometimes lined with the feathers of another hardy bird, the Ptarmigan.

The Cirl Bunting is really a Mediterranean species, so Britain is at the very north of its range. It occurs in the agricultural fields and scrub of south Devon. Besides open ground, it also needs tall bushes and trees to be present if it is to breed.

The Yellowhammer is hardier, and occurs all over Britain and some of Ireland. It is much associated with farmland hedgerows, and also inhabits other scrubby places, even woodland edge.

The Corn Bunting is another bird typical of arable farming areas, but it only lives in districts with less than 1000mm (39in) of rainfall a year. There are two sub-populations, one on inland cultivation, and another living on grassland by the

1. yellow bill, 2. ear-coverts with rather obvious thick black corners, 3. a chestnut wing-band sandwiched between two white wing-bars (the easiest to see), and 4. less stripy face. Winter males also tend to show some black mottling on the breast, flowing down on to the flanks

adult male winter

adult female summer

Adult female winter (not illustrated): The plumage resembles winter male, but the nape is not chestnut-stained, and there is no black mottling on the breast or flanks (there are streaks, however).

Adult female summer: The male's summer black coloration is replaced by streaky brown.

Juvenile (not illustrated): Shares the adult's wing-pattern, otherwise browner and more streaked, with little distinctive plumage. By September most have moulted into First Winter plumage, which resembles that of winter adults. However, males lack chestnut on the nape, and the females are more strongly streaked below than the adults.

juvenile

Flight: It has rapid, high, undulating flight, the long wings being apparent.

Voice: The main call is a rippling or rattling "prrt", usually followed by a clear "chu". The song is unlikely to be heard in the British Isles.

---

perched bird. In flight that the whole inner wing is white, with the tips black. Winter males and females have yellow bills.

Adult female winter (not illustrated): Similar but with more brown on head and rustier underparts. Less white on wing.

adult male winter

adult female summer

Adult female summer: The head is not clean white but dull white, peppered black on crown and nape. The back is not plainly black, but has earthy-brown fringes to the feathers, producing scaling. There is much less white on the wing. Underparts still mainly white.

Juvenile: Mostly brownish-grey, with broad streaks above and below. Wing has only a narrow white band. Acquires First Winter plumage by mid-autumn, closely resembling respective adult winter plumage.

adult female summer

juvenile

Flight: It has strong, undulating flight when going some distance. Feeding flocks march over the ground, the birds at the back continually leap-frogging the others to get a front position.

Voice: The main call is a pleasant trilling "prillillit" (remarkably like call of Crested Tit). The song is a short, slightly creaky ditty with a tone very similar to the Skylark's song.

Adult female: Lacks the male's impressive attire. Note the stripy head, however: a whitish stripe runs down from the bill base to the ill-defined collar, and there is a black, slightly broadening stripe below this, separating it from the throat. This arrangement

distinguishes it from all other small brown birds.

Juvenile: It looks like the female, but is paler and rather more streaky, especially below. First Winter birds are similar to the adult female.

juvenile

adult male summer

adult male winter

adult female summer

adult female summer

Flight: It has a jerky, hesitant flight, produced by the irregular closure of the short, slightly rounded wings.

Voice: The main call is a "tseu", like taking a breath between clenched teeth. The song consists of 3–5 abrupt, rough notes uttered with short pauses in between eg. "Three ... blind ... mice". The effect is like a young child trying to count but forgetting what comes next.

---

coast. Corn Buntings, Yellowhammers and Cirl Buntings all nest low down in bushes, or less often among crops.

In former times, the Reed Bunting was ecologically separated from its relatives by requiring damp places, such as reedbeds and marshes, in which to feed and nest. Since the late 1960s, however, it has spread into dryer habitats such as hedgerows and heathland, often overlapping with the Yellowhammer. If given the choice, though, it still tends to prefer damp habitats in winter.

Many people who associate the dry songs of Yellowhammers and Corn Buntings with hot summer days would be surprised to know that, on the whole, there are more buntings to be found in Britain and Ireland during the

winter than in the summer. However, they are less colourful, quieter and less widely distributed at this time, being found mostly in flocks at favoured feeding sites. They also roost communally, Snow and Lapland Buntings on the ground, the others in thick scrub or reedbeds.

All buntings feed on seeds in the winter, which they hunt for on the ground.

Bunting identification

Lapland Bunting
(female summer)

Reed Bunting
(female summer)

Lapland Bunting
(male winter)

Reed Bunting
(male summer)

Linnet
(female summer)

Twite
(female summer)

Corn Bunting

Skylark

The first step in bunting identification is the ability to distinguish them from the wealth of seed-eating and ground-feeding birds in Britain. Look (and listen) for:

1. Head and bill shape – head is smaller and more "sunken" than a finch, bill is relatively small and conical, with an S-shaped cutting edge. Larks have longer, more pointed bills.

2. Tail shape – buntings have noticeably longer tails than finches or sparrows. They are only slightly forked at best in contrast to most finches.

3. Habitat – buntings are found in open country and scrubby hedgerows. They seldom feed in trees like some finches and are less inclined to visit gardens than either finches or sparrows.

4. Song – they have dry-sounding

songs that are delivered in brief phrases. The song of the Reed Bunting, for example, could be represented as "Tsweek, tswirrel, sizzit!......Tsweek, tswirrel, sizzit!.....Tsweek, tswirrel..s-sizzit!" That of the Goldfinch, a typical finch song, could not be represented in words; it is a rambling trickle of oft-repeated notes and short phrases.

Lapland Bunting (female): large, broad. Long wings. Yellow bill. Two white wing-bars, chestnut between. Black corners to ear coverts. Runs along ground quickly (highly characteristic). Mainly east coast of England; about 500 individuals winter.

Reed Bunting (female): smaller than Lapland Bunting. Face with obvious moustachial stripes. No wing-bars. Hops, does not run. Common and widespread.

Lapland Bunting (male): chestnut nape. Patchy black down to flanks.

House Sparrow
(female)

House Sparrow
(male) summer

Yellowhammer
(female summer)

Yellowhammer
(male summer)

Cirl Bunting (female
summer)

Snow Bunting
(male summer)

Snow Bunting
(female summer)

Reed Bunting (male): black face mask mottled paler.

Linnet (female): small. Silvery wing-bar. Head marked with pale washes.

Twite (female): warm buff all over, including head. Silvery wing-bar. Yellow bill.

Corn Bunting: plump. Speckles sometimes make a smudge on breast. Short, thick bill. No wing-bars or tail marks. Hops.

Skylark: plump. Usually with crest showing. Finer streaks on breast. Longer bill. Walks, does not hop. In flight, wings are slightly angled-back, and there is a white trailing edge to wing and white outer tail feathers. Flocks disperse in flight. Fluttery flight.

House Sparrow (female): unmarked breast. Obvious pale eyebrow. Colourful wings. Short bill. Hops.

House Sparrow (male): shorter tail than male Reed Bunting, unmarked with white. Cheeks pale.

Yellowhammer (female): yellowish wash, including on head. Somewhat coarse breast-streaks. Top of crown often has yellow, and is pale. Chestnut rump. White outer tail feathers.

Yellowhammer (male): very yellow.

Cirl Bunting (female): less yellow. Finer breast streaks. Top of crown relatively dark. Stripy face. Olive-grey rump. Slighter and more compact. Retiring.

Snow Bunting (male): large, long-winged. Always lots of white. Flocks look like snowflakes. Leap-frogging movement of flocks.

Snow Bunting (female): more rusty-coloured than male, and less white on wing.

YELLOWHAMMER
Emberiza citrinella

16cm. A long-tailed, slim bunting, and one of the yellowest birds of the countryside. It has a warm, chestnut coloured rump, narrow white tail sides, and no wing-bar. The male has yellow underparts with some chestnut streaking on breast sides and flanks.

adult male summer

Where found: A common resident in arable land with hedgerows over much of Britain and (more locally) Ireland. It also occurs in various types of scrubland.

Adult male summer: Often stunningly yellow on the head; face markings around the cheek are variable (often there are more than shown here). Usually, there is a dash of olive-green around the back of the neck (beware of confusion with Cirl Bunting).

CIRL BUNTING
Emberiza cirlus

16cm. A similar species to the Yellowhammer, but it is rare, and will only cause confusion in its restricted range. It has a more compact look than Yellowhammer, and can always be distinguished by its rump colour, which is greyish, not chestnut. A more elusive, secretive bird than Yellowhammer.

adult male summer

Where found: A very rare resident in agricultural and scrubby areas in coastal south Devon.

Adult male summer: The striking head-pattern is quite different from the Yellow-hammer's, being boldly yellow and black-striped. The olive-green crown is black-streaked, and the same olive-green colour surrounds the neck.

CORN BUNTING
Miliaria calandra

18cm. A large, plump bunting that is streaky but remarkably featureless. It has a large head and upper body, but a rather short tail. It is very much given to sitting on low wires and other prominent perches.

adult

Where found: As its name suggests, it is a bird of arable farmland, mostly in the drier, lowland areas in the east of Britain. Also found in coastal grassland. A resident.

Adult: Dull brown with much streaking above and below. On the breast, the streaks are at their strongest, sometimes becoming a smudge, especially in winter. The belly is whitish, bill is corn-coloured, and there are no white marks on the wings or tail.

The decline of buntings

All the breeding buntings of Britain, with the exception of the Snow Bunting, have recently been declining in population. Yellowhammers and Corn Buntings that once abounded in the fields of Britain, have fallen by up to a third, while the Cirl Bunting, which once occurred throughout the south of England, is on the verge of extinction. The reasons for these declines are mostly associated with what is happening on our farmland and other open country, and these also affect other birds as well as buntings. Some examples of cause and effect are given here.

The Reed Bunting's decline has been linked particularly to the use of herbicides. Most buntings rely on the presence of grass and weed seeds in the soil for their winter survival,

and the persistent use of herbicides on farmland, especially in the last 30 years, has adversely affected the abundance of soil seeds.

The Yellowhammer's breeding habitat has been reduced by the destruction of many miles of hedgerows. In addition, as farming has become more efficient and specialised, there has been an overall reduction in the amount of land under cultivation for crops, as opposed to being managed for livestock, which is also to this bird's detriment.

The Cirl Bunting relies for its winter survival on grass and weed seeds, the availability of which is affected by other factors beside herbicides (see above). In recent years, there has been a widespread switch towards the tilling of fields in

Adult male winter: The yellow is much less dominant, especially on the head, where the crown and cheeks are olive-green. There is more of a greenish hue to the chest, too.

Female: The yellow is duller, particularly on the head; more streaking on the underparts. Although the rump is chestnut in colour (as in male), there is none of this colour on the breast.

Juvenile: Duller still; brownish-yellow rather than yellow. Breast-streaks are finer than those of the female.

Flight: It usually flies with deep undulations, the long, thin shape being obvious.

Voice: Main call is a sharp "dzit". The song is a short series of high tinkling notes ending in a wheeze. At the end it sounds as if the bird has been holding its breath before exhaling heavily. The song is often rendered "A little bit of bread and no cheese" but sometimes the "cheese" is lacking.

adult male winter

adult female summer

adult female summer

juvenile

Adult male winter: The head pattern remains, but is duller and more clouded. There is always enough black on the throat to distinguish it from Yellowhammer.

Female: Very similar to female Yellowhammer, but less yellow below, finer streaking on breast and belly, stripier head pattern, more obvious yellow-buff supercilium, darker crown. The grey or olive-brown rump is diagnostic.

Juvenile: Similar to the Yellow-hammer juvenile, but more stripy on the head, and with a dull-coloured, not chestnut rump.

Flight: A little bit more undulating than that of Yellowhammer, and less sweeping.

Voice: The main call is a short "tsip", often thin-sounding, but it can go right through your head when the bird is close. The song is a very dry rattle on one note, similar to the rattle of the Lesser Whitethroat's song, but more insect-like.

adult male winter

adult female summer

adult female summer

juvenile

juvenile

Flight: Strong, purposeful flight, often high and undulating when travelling some distance. Uniquely, on some short flights between nearby perches, the legs are left dangling; it is a form of display.

Voice: The main call is a rough, almost clicking "tick", often with a rasping sound. The song is unmistakable: a series of ticks accelerates into a discordant jangle.

Juvenile: It is slightly paler than the adult, and with slightly paler fringes to the wing-feathers.

adult

autumn rather than spring, which has adversely affected the amount of winter stubble available to birds. The process of harvesting itself, has also become cleaner and more efficient, and once again this means that less food is available.

Less barley has been grown in Britain and Ireland in recent years (wheat has often replaced it), and this is to the detriment of the Corn Bunting, although other factors have contributed too. Like most buntings, the Corn Bunting is perfectly able to raise two or even three broods, but earlier harvesting has cut out this option. A third threat has been the reduced tendency to practise crop rotation, with the result that fewer root crops or clover, which the birds like,

are grown. Yet another reason is that, on modern farmland, there are increasing fewer roosting sites for birds, such as marshy ditches and patches of scrubland.

Glossary

Arboreal: Lives in trees.

Arm: The inner part of a bird's wing (nearest the body).

Bowed: Bending downwards, or arched down.

Brood: A cluster of chicks representing a breeding attempt. Many birds have several in a season and are called double-brooded or triple-brooded.

Call: A sound made by a bird in response to a situation (eg. alarm, contact). Usually brief.

Carpals: The area where the front edge of the wing kinks (the "wrist"). Sometimes there are marks here called "carpal patches".

Carrion: The flesh of dead animals.

Chick: General term for a young bird, but usually refers to an active, fluffy one than can run or swim around, but is unable to fly (see fledgling, nestling).

Covey: A collective noun for partridges.

Crest: An adornment of the head which juts out from the crown.

Cryptic: Hidden. Used as a term for camouflaged.

Dabbling: Moving the bill around on the surface of the water in order to find food.

Display: A posture or series of ritualised postures used to convey a message eg. threat, appeasement, courtship.

Disyllabic: A word, and therefore a bird sound, that has two syllables eg. "Cuck-oo".

Diurnal: Active by day.

Drumming: The tapping of woodpeckers to make a series of beats, or the throbbing sound of a Snipe's tail. Both are displays.

Eclipse: A female-like plumage adopted by some birds when moulting, which has a camouflage purpose.

Eyebrow: A stripe over the eye, often curved.

Eyestripe: A stripe through the eye.

Feral: Refers to a species that has escaped from captivity and has established itself in the "wild".

Field-mark: A mark which is of use in field identification.

Fingered: Refers to the feathers of the wing-tip being spread out to give an effect like fingers.

First Winter: A bird living its first winter of life, having hatched a few months before. Also refers to the plumage thereof. Its next plumage is called First Summer.

First Year: A bird living its first year of life (a First Winter or First Summer).

Fledgling: A young bird that has just left the nest.

Flushed: A bird that has been scared away.

Foraging: Looking for food, as opposed actually to eating it.

Forewing: The front part of the wing (leads in flight).

Generalist: A species that is good at lots of things, as opposed to being very good at one thing (eg. eats many different foodstuffs, or has many methods of feeding).

Gleaning: Picking from a surface, usually for items that are well dispersed.

Gliding: Forward propulsion without wing-flaps.

Graduated: Gets narrower, or broader, towards the tip.

Ground colour: Refers to the basic colour of the bird, upon which there can be various markings.

Ground predator: Refers to a predator that is unable to fly, although it might climb well.

Habitat: The place where the bird lives (eg. heathland, sea-cliff).

Hand: The outer part of the wing (away from the body).

Hindwing: The back part of the wing (trails in flight).

Hover: Flying on the spot, with wings flapping in order to maintain position.

Immature: Refers to any bird (and any plumage adopted) which is not yet adult. (But normally excludes juveniles).

Introduced: A bird that has been imported.

Invertebrates: A term referring to a vast array of small creatures (eg. insects, spiders, worms, crustaceans, molluscs) with no backbone.

Juvenile: A young bird with its first set of feathers, having left the nest. Also refers to that plumage.

Leading edge: The front edge of the wing, which leads in flight.

Lek: A communal display (ground) used by certain bird species.

Local: Only found in a few scattered places.

Mandibles: The two parts of the bill which open.

Migration: Refers to any movement of a substantial or complete part of a bird's population.

Mobbing: A general word for bird harassing a potential predator.

Monogamous: The pair-bond is between one male and one female.

Morph: A section of a population with a different plumage pattern to the rest.

Motif: A part of a bird's song, rather like a word in a sentence.

Moult: The process of replacing one set of feathers with another (either all the feathers or some of them).

Nestling: A young bird confined to the nest.

Nocturnal: Active mostly at night.

Omnivorous: Will eat anything.

Passage migrant: A bird passing through an area during its migration. The area concerned is not its destination.

Phase: Much the same as "morph". Certain sections of a population have a certain plumage pattern or colour.

Phrase: For our purposes here, a part of a song separated by pauses.

Polygamous: Having a pair-bond with two or more members of the opposite sex. This can be polygyny (one male, several females) or polyandry (one female, several males).

Predator: An animal that may eat the bird, its eggs or its young.

Preening: Feather care, undertaken by the bill.

Promiscuous: For our purposes, refers to birds which do not have a pair-bond beyond a strictly sexual one, and in which each sex will mate with several "partners".

Quartering: Refers to a slow, forward movement in flight low over the ground.

Race: See subspecies.

Raptor: A term for birds of prey, excluding owls.

Resident: Is found in an area all year long.

Roosting: Refers to activities associated with sleep and/or rest.

Scavenger: Eats the meat of dead animals (and also various items of rubbish).

Sedentary: Remains in the same place all the time, usually the territory.

Soaring: The process of rising high into the air, often on a thermal, and typically with a spiralling motion.

Song: A complex vocalisation, usually given by the male bird, to claim ownership of a territory and/or to attract a mate.

Specialist: A bird that is very good at one thing, to the exclusion of other things (may refer to procurement of certain specific food items, for example).

Species: A type of bird. Usually breeds among its own kind and does not interbreed with other types.

Speculum: The colourful bar(s) on the secondaries of ducks, best seen in flight.

Subspecies: A population of a bird that might look slightly different from other populations of the same species, but can interbreed with them to produce fertile young.

Subterminal: Just before the end.

Supercilium: The eyebrow of a bird ie. a stripe over, as opposed to through, the eye.

Terrestrial: Lives mainly on the ground.

Territory: A bird's defended space, either for breeding, feeding or both.

Towering: Flying very rapidly upwards, often to fall down gain just as quickly.

Trailing edge: The back edge of the wing, that trails in flight.

Trill: Refers to a number of the same or similar notes strung together in a series, usually a fast one.

Underwing: Shorthand for the underside of the wing.

Undulating: Referring to flight, a rhythmic up and down movement, like a rollercoaster.

Wader: A specific term referring to the families of Stone Curlew, Oystercatcher, Avocets and Stilts, Plovers, and Sandpipers etc. (*Scolopacidae*), all of which wade in the mud or water.

Index

WAXWING Associates

Little Okeford
Christchurch Road
Tring
Hertfordshire
HP23 4EF
Tel: 01442 823 356

TEACH YOURSELF BIRDSOUNDS

The innovative cassette series to help you learn birdsounds.

Each cassette in this ten-tape series concentrates on a particular habitat and covers the common song(s) and/or call(s) of each of the 20–30 species included each time. A spoken commentary, which stresses which aspects of each song or call make it individually identifiable, is backed up by brief printed notes. Comparisons of similar sounds of the different utterances of similar-looking species are usually included even if made by birds from a different family or habitat. Special tips on how many sounds can be remembered are also give. Each rape ends with a medley of unannounced sounds to enable listeners to check their learning progress.

The habitats covered in this series are: Gardens; Broad-leaved Woodland; Farmland and Scrub; Reedbeds and Open Water; Rivers and Wet Meadows; Heaths and Moors; Sea Cliffs and Islands; Coniferous and Mixed Woodlands; Estuaries and Coasts (from 1/3/97); Mountains and Upland Lochs (from 1/6/97).

Recordings:	From the Wildlife Sounds Section of the British Library, National Sound Archive, London
Compiled and written by:	Dominic Couzens, John Wyatt, Nigel Bewley
Narration:	Penny Gore
Consultants:	Anthony Chapman, Ian Dawson, John Kemp, Paul Duck, Ron Kettle, Philip Rudkin, Richard Ranft, Patrick Sellar, Bill Sinclair

SPECIAL OFFER: £6.00 PER CASSETTE INCLUSIVE OF POSTAGE AND PACKING AND VAT; USUAL PRICE £6.99

Enjoy a great day out at an RSPB nature reserve

There are over 100 superb RSPB
nature reserves open to the public
and they all provide a wonderful
opportunity to see a whole range of
birds and other wildlife.

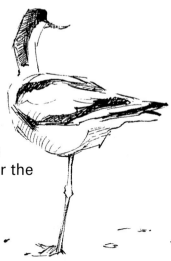

See some of the most stunning
wildlife in Britain – from red kites
flying over the valleys of Wales, to the
spectacular flocks of wading birds over the
Norfolk coast.

The RSPB has been managing land
as nature reserves for over 50 years,
as one of the most effective ways of
conserving wild birds and the places in which they live.

Now you can enjoy nature for yourself.

Simply complete the coupon below and you will be entitled
to a FREE one day visitor pass for one adult with one full
paying adult to any RSPB Nature Reserve.

Just fill in the details and hand the coupon to a member of
staff at any RSPB nature reserve.

Mr/Mrs/Ms Initials. _____ Surname. _____

Address. _____

_____ Postcode _____

I am an RSPB Member Yes/No ☐

Tick box if under 16. ☐

The RSPB may contact you with further details of its work.

Code. N3415 Registered charity no 207076.

Join the RSPB today

to help protect the UK's beautiful birds and claim your FREE BIRDTABLE to help the visitors to your garden survive the rigours of winter.

All members receive:

★ **A great welcome pack telling you all you need to know about the RSPB**

★ ***Birds* magazine four times a year**

★ **Plus free entry to over 100 nature reserves**

- -

Please enrol me as a member of the RSPB.

I enclose cheque/PO or debit my Access/Visa card number for:

☐ £22 for a year's single membership

☐ £28 for a year's membership for two people at the same address

☐ £34 for family membership (please attach name and date of all the children in the family)

Card expiry date

Cardholder's signature _____

(Please attach address of cardholder if different from below)

Mr/Mrs/Ms Initials_____ Surname_____

Address_____

Second member's name _____

Send to: **The RSPB, FREEPOST, The Lodge, Sandy, Bedfordshire SG19 2BR**

Registered charity no 207076   41/647/96   **AB6683**